Leek Wootton and its Hamlets

A history of

The Parish of Leek Wootton & Guy's Cliffe

Written to commemorate the advent of the Third Millennium

Published by The Leek Wootton History Group

© The Leek Wootton History Group

British Library Cataloguing in Publication Data
A catalogue record for this book is available from
The British Library

ISBN 0 9541 1490 6

Made and Printed in Great Britain by
Warwick Printing Company Ltd.
Theatre Street, Warwick CV34 4DR

Contents

	Foreword					v
	Preface					vii
1	The Story Begins	...	...	...	...	1
2	The Parish Church of All Saints		...	...	...	13
3	Alice, Duchess Dudley	...	...	...	...	25
4	Guy's Cliffe	...	...	...	...	27
5	Hill Wootton	...	...	...	...	34
6	The Wise Family at Woodcote 1832-1888			...	...	43
7	The Waller Family at Woodcote 1888-1947			...	...	51
8	The Farms of Woodloes, Middle Woodloes and North Woodloes				...	61
9	Wootton Grange and Broad Lane Caravans			...	...	67
10	Wootton Paddox	...	...	...	...	72
11	The School	...	...	...	...	75
12	Wootton Court	...	...	...	...	88
13	Elms Farm	...	...	...	...	103
14	Village Houses	...	...	...	...	107
15	From the Stable to the Bakehouse		...	...	...	121
16	Chesford Grange	...	...	...	...	125
17	The Anchor	...	...	...	...	128
18	Goodrest and Wedgnock Park		...	...	...	133
19	The Mothers' Union	...	...	...	...	137
20	Leek Wootton War Memorial Recreation Ground			...	...	139
21	Villagers Born and Bred	...	...	...	...	144
22	Reminiscences of the Wartime Years 1939-1945			...	...	149
23	Roll of Honour	...	...	...	...	156
24	The Women's Institute	...	...	...	...	161
25	Post War Developments	...	...	...	...	168
	Millennium Residents	...	...	...	...	181
	Acknowledgements	...	...	...	...	189
	Bibliography	...	...	...	...	191

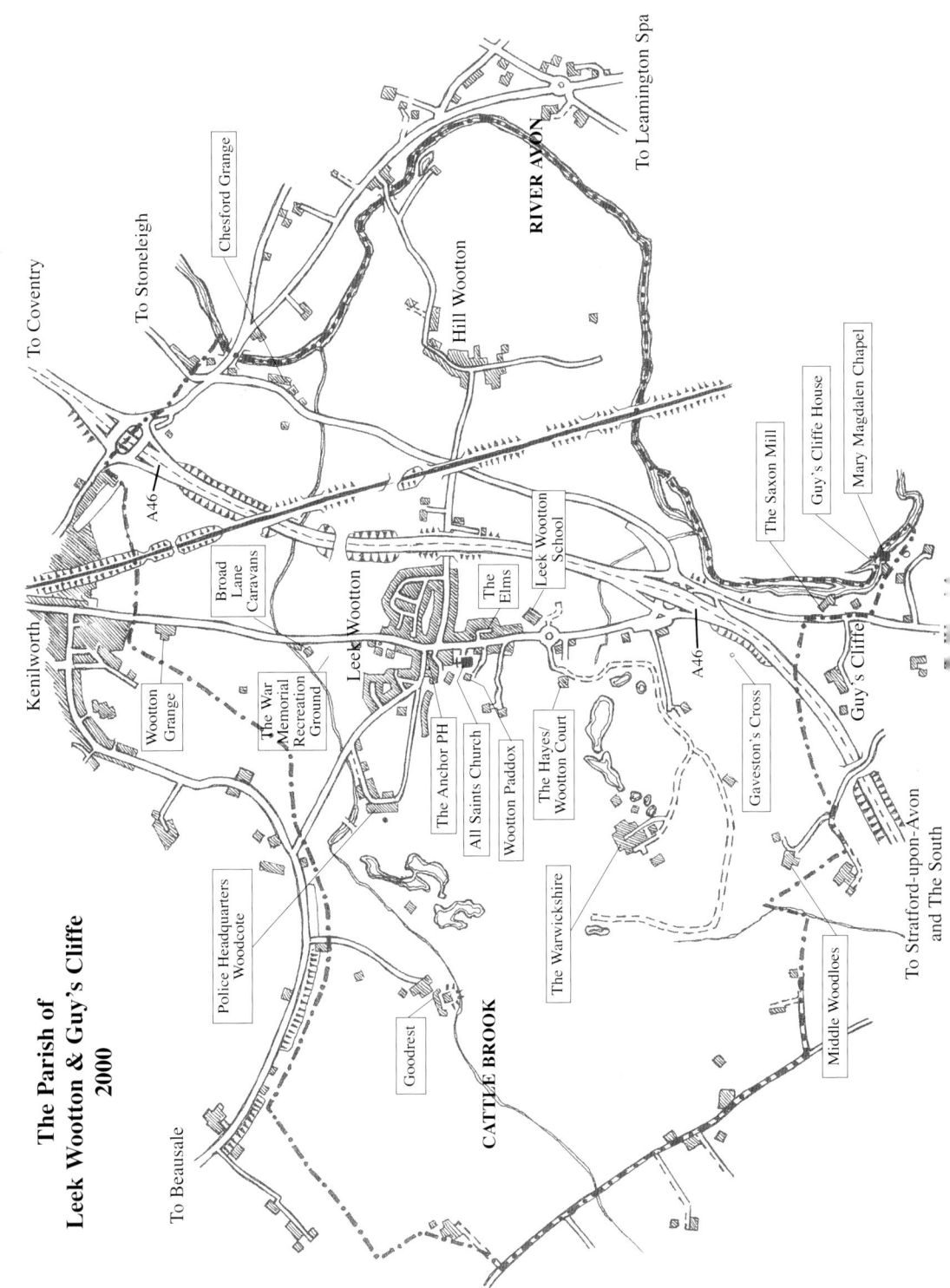

Foreword

Assembling a history is at one and the same time a deeply fulfilling and enormously frustrating task. There is the sense of excitement as each avenue of research yields surprise discoveries and new insights. But these taunt the researcher to delve still further into a complex web of events, achievements and, most fascinating of all, lives.

Readers of these pages will be able to enjoy the fruits of the labours of an enthusiastic and diligent team who, while gaining obvious satisfaction from their mammoth task, has presented us with a most valuable asset: a window into the history of our community which thereby becomes a window into our present.

As we read this collection of contributions we can receive it in many ways. It may satisfy curiosity, it may inform and entertain but it has 'added value' when we are stirred by the images of those who gave much and often risked much to improve the lot of their fellows. Even though we cannot be sure that all their intentions were entirely self-less, we can be thankful for their endeavours and for their examples of generosity and courage.

History at its best challenges and provokes because it has the potential to shape the future. If we have the desire and the will the history we have inherited can inform and motivate us to make our contributions to benefit the community of our day and the next.

Brian W Pearson, Vicar

Main Road, Leek Wootton
Helen Scott Collection

Main Road, Leek Wootton

Preface

It was in the spring of 1999 that a group of interested parishioners first met together to discuss the idea of updating a history of the village prepared by The Reverend Charles Nettleship in 1977, which in its turn was a revision of notes on the history of the parish compiled by The Reverend Sydney Longland in 1935. Many meetings and much researching later we present our Millennium History to you. We are very grateful for the generous financial sponsorship of Broad Lane Leisure, Castle Hotels & Taverns, Clubhaus plc, Leek Wootton & Guy's Cliffe Parish Council and Principal Hotels.

There will be many things that have been omitted and inevitably there will be statements that might not, in the opinion of some, be correct. We apologise for any inaccuracy, but sincerely hope that in general the compilation of this book will find favour.

Those who have taken part include Gillian Bailey, Peter Butler, Jean Chamberlain, Roselyn Commander, Jill Corbishley, Hilary David, Bernard Dee, Lesley and Paul Eldridge, Helen Eldridge, Caroline Gath, Christina Jackson, Audrey Jones, Robin Lawrence, Ian McAllester, Joy Maisey, Mary Murdoch, Jane Pain, Alan Richardson, Catherine Sandwell, Brenda Semple, and Jean Singleton. There are acknowledgements to the invaluable help and assistance of many other villagers and friends at the end of the book.

We have had much fun putting the book together and hope you will enjoy reading it.

The Team, 2001

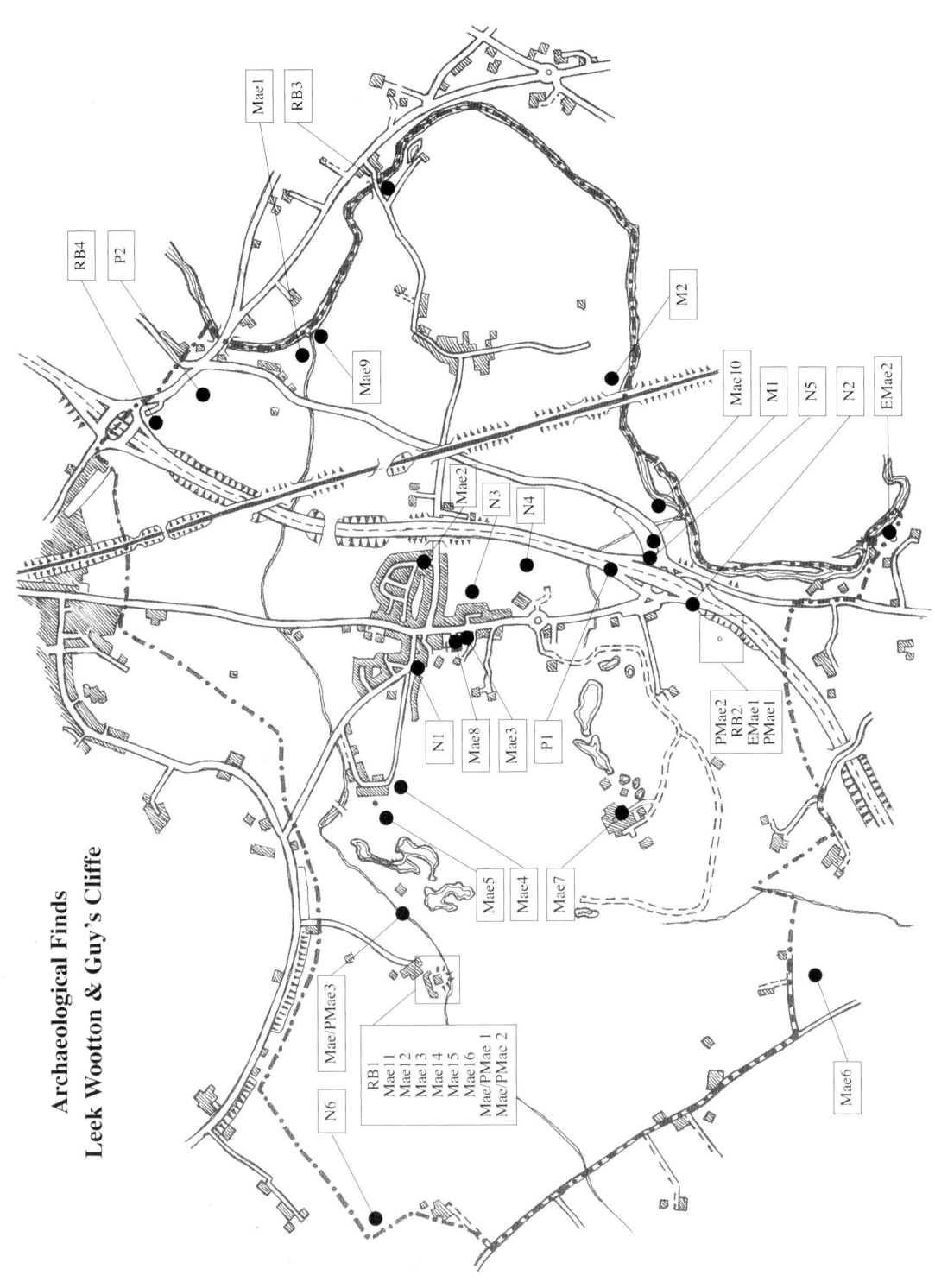

1

The Story Begins

"About a mile below Aſhow, there falls into Avon a torrent called Holbroke, which hath its head from the great Pool in Wedgnock park. On the top of the Hill, ſouthwards of this brook, ſtands Wotton, that antiently included Milverton, Leminton, Aſho, Lillinton, and Cobinton within its pariſh, which now are all distinct Mother Churches: but for the preſent containeth only Heathe, Woodcote, Hill (vulgarly called Hill Wotton) and Wedgnock Park..."

So wrote the eminent 17th Century historian Sir William Dugdale in 'The Antiquities of Warwickshire' when he opened the section on 'Wotton, Vulgo Leek Wotton'.

Our present day community, the civil Parish of Leek Wootton & Guy's Cliffe, contains the village of Leek Wootton, the hamlet of Hill Wootton, the settlement at Guy's Cliffe, numerous old farmsteads, some still working and some converted, and Woodcote. There are, however, indications of much earlier settlement within the parish boundary, and it is known that the agricultural potential of the Avon Valley and its environs attracted settlers from the Early Stone Age, around 3000 BC.

The construction of the A46 dual-carriageway bypass in the early 1970s, housing development also in the 1970s, and the change of use of some 450 acres of farmland to a major golf complex in the 1990s, have all afforded unique opportunities for archaeological investigation and so, together with some earlier discoveries, many facts about our parish are now recorded at the Warwickshire Museum. Maps, early returns of inhabitants (usually compiled for taxation or military purposes), church records and some private papers are lodged at the County Record Office in Warwick and at the Shakespeare Birthplace Trust Record Office. The writings of earlier historians, both professional and amateur also help to provide a picture of how our forefathers might have lived out their lives in this corner of Warwickshire.

Prehistoric flint objects have been found north-east of the Blacklow roundabout (P1*) (the roundabout south of the village, beneath the A46) and in the field to the west of Chesford crossroads (P2); Mesolithic flint objects at the Blacklow roundabout (M1) and near to the railway bridge over the Avon (M2); Neolithic flints on Woodcote Lane at the end of the Tinker-Tank path (N1), on Blacklow Hill (N2), in the paddocks area of the properties on The Elms (N3), in the field east of the school (N4), and in the Blacklow roundabout area (N5), together with a Neolithic stone object in the Deer Park Farm area (N6).

The next period of occupation recorded from finds is the Romano British period with coins at the site of Goodrest Lodge (RB1) and on Blacklow Hill (RB2), pottery to the west of Blackdown bridge (RB3) and the remains of a villa at Bullimore Lodge (RB4).

---

* See Archaeological Finds Map

Studies have shown that possible Prehistoric routes for travellers passed along the line of what is now the B4115 from Warwick to Coventry; also in a north-north-west to south-south-east direction from Leamington through Kenilworth and onwards, approximately parallel to but south-west of the railway line; along the line of the Warwick Road (which is recorded as a road in 1603); and along Hill Wootton Road, Woodcote Lane and the line of the old road through what is now Warwickshire Police Headquarters.

The latter part of the village name, 'Wootton', is Saxon, from 'wudu' or wood, with the addition of 'tun' (enclosure or homestead), but there is no known explanation for the use of the word Leek which appears to have come into use in about the 13th Century.

The excavations on Blacklow Hill in 1972 revealed evidence to suggest that there had been a possible pagan Saxon 'grove' on the site (EMae1). A series of enigmatic circular pits had been cut into the sandstone bedrock at the east end of the hill, and there were two human burials within the arcs. One grave, that of a male, contained a scramaseax (single-edged sword) with a blade 30cm long. The same excavation provided the largest assemblage of Mesolithic flint implements ever collected in the Midlands.

A heavy scatter of Romano British pottery revealed by the plough on the north slope of Blacklow Hill in 1983, and other earlier Romano British finds, suggest it may also have been a site of Roman occupation. There are indications of a Post Mediaeval glassworks on the south slope of the Hill (PMae1) and, of course, there is a Post Mediaeval inscription to be found (with some difficulty now) recording the beheading of Piers Gaveston on the Hill in 1312 (PMae2) (see Chapter 4).

Excavations on Blacklow Hill

A Saxon origin is claimed for The Saxon Mill, the present day 'Harvester' restaurant at Guy's Cliffe, but there is no archaeological proof. However, Guy's Cave and other rock cut features in the vicinity of Guy's Cliffe are reasonably certain to date from Saxon/Early Mediaeval times (EMae2) (see also Chapter 4).

The Domesday Book records only Woodcote. Some have identified Leek Wootton with the 'Quatone' in Domesday, but this is disputed, and there is no reference to Heath, Hill (or Hulle) Wootton, Leek Wootton or other settlement names that are referred to elsewhere. However, archaeological evidence of other deserted Mediaeval settlements has been found. It is believed that the hamlet of Heath was probably in what is now called Hill Wootton, but that part of it stood on the other side of Holbroke, in the vicinity of the Chesford Bridge and the modern day hotel (Mae1). Holbroke is now Cattle Brook, and has been known as Cuttle Brook.

There is significant evidence, now re-buried, of a settlement in the vicinity of the entrance to The Hamlet and the junction with Tidmarsh Road (Mae2) which, together with a site to the south of the Parish Church (Mae3), suggests that Leek Wootton was

The Story Begins

Archaeological dig on site of Tidmarsh Road

a large settlement, or there was a group of settlements, in Mediaeval and Post Mediaeval times.

Mediaeval settlements are known to have existed at Lower Woodcote (Mae4), Upper Woodcote (Mae5), Middle Woodloes (Mae6), and North Woodloes (Mae7). The original Church was Mediaeval (Mae8) (see Chapter 2), and at least two Mediaeval mills are recorded in addition to Guy's Cliffe Mill or The Saxon Mill, one where Cattle Brook converges with the Avon (Mae9), and Yatford Mill on the Avon close to the Blacklow roundabout (Mae10). The settlement of Guy's Cliffe, including the well, chapel, house and mill, is steeped in history and has been inhabited throughout the Early Mediaeval, Mediaeval, Post Mediaeval, Imperial and Modern periods (see Chapter 4).

The location of Leek Wootton between Kenilworth Castle, a long time royal residence, and Warwick Castle, one of the most important strongholds in the kingdom, must always have been significant. There would have been much coming and going between the two places and, of course, the men of Leek Wootton would have had to obey the call to arms when it came. In the case of Warwick the great Castle Park known as Wedgnock contained some land now within our parish. The Wedgnock Rifle Range, part of The Warwickshire and farms (including Deer Park Farm) now occupy land which had been pasture, woodland and deer park. It was in the north eastern part of Wedgnock Park that Goodrest Lodge, a double-moated Mediaeval manor house, was constructed, and there is documentary and archaeological evidence of the house (Mae11), moats (Mae12), bridge (Mae13), fishpond (Mae14), well (Mae15) and an associated building (Mae16) (see Chapter 17).

There are further Mediaeval to Post Mediaeval sites in this western area of the parish, including a dam (Mae/PMae1), a single arch bridge (Mae/PMae2) and a section of the Wedgnock Park pale (Mae/PMae3), an earth mound which would have originally been surmounted by a wooden fence or a hedge, forming part of the boundary of the Park.

When Woodcote was recorded at the time of Domesday it was written as Widecote, a name which could possibly have been derived from the size of at least one of the holdings, and the two separate references may have related to Upper Woodcote and Lower Woodcote.

In 1086 Woodcote is recorded as:

"Land of the Count of Meulan:
1 hide Land for 2 ploughs. Kentwin and Thorburn held it; they were free.
4 villagers and 5 smallholders with 1 plough. Value before 1066 10s now 30s.

"1 hide Gilbert held from him Land for 1 plough. 1 man at arms with 2 villagers and 9 small holders have $1\frac{1}{2}$ ploughs. The woodland is 1 league long and $\frac{1}{2}$ league wide. The value was 10s, now 20s. Leofric held it freely before 1066."

Widecote or Wudechote (Woodcote) and part of Wudelaw or Woodlowe (Woodloes) formed more of the western portion of the parish. The antiquarian John Rous stated that the settlements of Lower Woodcote, Upper Woodcote, Middle Woodloes and North Woodloes were depopulated at the end of the 15th Century. The part of the Manor of Woodlowe within the parish is now the farmland around Middle Woodloes, and the site of the old manor house is probably Loes Grange (formerly Middle Woodloes Cottages).

Woodcote comprised two manors, Overwoodcote (Upper Woodcote) and Netherwoodcote (Lower Woodcote). They are, however, difficult to identify. It is thought that Overwoodcote was the area of North Woodloes Farm, which has now been amalgamated into the golf courses of The Warwickshire. The manor house became the farmhouse and is now incorporated within the clubhouse. The other manor, Netherwoodcote, included the old house of Woodcote with associated land. In the 12th Century Upper Woodcote appears to have been passed to the Earls of Warwick with various tenants. Lower Woodcote passed to the Earl of Leicester and subsequently to the Earl of Lancaster, again with various tenants. Both manors passed through many other hands in subsequent centuries.

The Anglo-Saxon settlements in our parish would have been the same as the tribal organisation of all such villages. The people of each settlement would clear for themselves an area for cultivation in the middle of the waste or forest and, as all shared in this work, so all shared in the fruits of it. These early farmers would have formed an open field system, cultivated in strips, and each man's holding would consist of a number of strips, one here and one there (never two strips together) scattered around the fields. The field system of this area was probably based on a three or more field system, using a three course rotation in which winter sown crops, e.g. wheat and rye were sown in one, spring sown barley, oats, peas and beans in another, whilst the third was left fallow. Stock would have grazed on the waste round the edge of the arable land and on the fallow. The meadows for grazing and making hay were the narrow strips along the banks of the streams and the Avon.

A tribal 'aristocracy' would have been established in the Anglo-Saxon settlements and there would have been a village 'lord'. The Norman invasion of England meant that a feudal aristocracy took the place of the Anglo-Saxon land-owners, who were probably reduced to the position of tenants, and Leek Wootton, like other villages, became what the Norman lawyers called a 'manor'. The ordinary villagers would not have found their lot much changed, and the open field system actually continued to be worked for another 750 years, but the tenants had to answer in different ways to many masters.

It is recorded that Henry I gave the Manor of Leek Wootton to Geoffrey de Clinton, the builder of Kenilworth Castle, in about 1120. Geoffrey de Clinton had also founded Kenilworth Priory, and he gave to his new Priory "the Church of Leek Wootton", meaning that the greater part of the income of the priest was taken by the Priory as part of its endowment. He also gave to the Priory some of the land in the parish; the forest area was incorporated into his own new park around Kenilworth Castle. The rest of the land went to Geoffrey Savage. In time part of Savage's portion of the Manor became a possession of the Cistercian Abbey of Stoneleigh, and the balance passed in the reign of Edward III, with the ownership of Kenilworth Castle, to the Duke of Lancaster. From then on the Manor of Leek Wootton belonged to the owner of the Castle, and when the son of the Duke became King of England (Henry IV) the Castle and lands and the Manor of Leek Wootton became the property of the Crown.

Ownership of land seemed to be constantly changing, and 'The Stoneleigh Leger Book' records:

> In 1203 Henry de Armentiers sued Geoffrey Savage, owner, for one knight's fee* in Leek Wootton. An armed duel was fought in the court. Savage granted to de Armentiers one-third of the knight's fee, in demesnes, rents, villenages and services of free men, in wood and plain, meadows, waters, mills and fisheries; saving the right of the prior and canons of Kenilworth in the church of the said vill of Wootton. To hold to him and his heirs by one-third of a knight's service. Savage retained the capital messuage, that is the house and outbuildings attached to the land.

> In 1212 John Belet sued Ralph Pincerna (or Butler) for the whole vill of Woodcote. Belet acknowledged Butler's right, and Butler, in return for 20 marks of silver, granted to him all the property to hold by the service of one-quarter of a knight's fee.

> In 1221 Alan de Morcote conveyed to the Earl of Warwick and the Prior of Kenilworth, after a duel fought in court, 3 virgates of land in Hull in return for 24 marks of silver.

---
* A knight's fee was the quantity of land held by a man in return for knight-service to an overlord.

Edward I commissioned a survey of the people in 1279, now known as the Hundred Rolls, and these record that in Wotton, Hulle and Cross Grange there were four Lords who held the village from the Earl of Warwick for which they jointly paid one knight's fee. Phillippa Savage had nineteen holdings of which twelve were held by serfs, four by cottagers and three by free tenants. Savage also held the assize of bread and ale, which meant that she issued the licences for baking and brewing, and had fishing rights on the Avon and the Holbrook. Robert Mortimer had ten tenants, eight were serfs and two were cottagers. He also owned one third of a water mill. The Abbot of Stoneleigh had eight tenants, three serfs and five free tenants. He owned two-thirds of a mill and had rights of the Avon and part of the Holbrook to Guy's Cliffe. The Prior of Kenilworth had fourteen tenants, two serfs, eight cottagers and four free tenants. He held a mill at Guy's Cliffe that had been given to the Priory in alms, and thirty acres of land given as alms by one Galfrid Glentone for the use of the church in Leek Wootton. All tenants had to attend the Manor Court of the appropriate Lord at which the procedures for working the open field system were laid down. The tenants paid rent partly in money and partly by undertaking work on the demesne land, i.e. the land farmed by the Lords in the village.

The Lay Subsidy Roll for Warwickshire, 1332, shows that taxes collected from Woodcote totalled 26s (£1.30), paid by thirteen people. These taxes were raised by Edward III to fight for the throne of Robert Bruce, and were raised on the value of moveable goods of all persons except clergy, but with no tax being raised on goods of less value than 10s (50p), thus excluding the poorest. Lec Wotton and Hull paid £1 13s 6d (£1.67) from sixteen persons.

By the reign of Henry VIII the Priory at Kenilworth had been raised to the dignity of an Abbey, the Abbey of St Mary the Virgin, but during the Dissolution of the Monasteries the Abbeys of both Kenilworth and Stoneleigh were destroyed. These two Abbeys had owned at least half of the land of Leek Wootton, and with their demise this also became the property of the Crown. The King gave to his cousin, Charles Brandon, Duke of Suffolk, the part owned by Stoneleigh Abbey, while the part formerly owned by Kenilworth Abbey was rented out.

In 1547, the year of Henry's death, a 'rental' was made of all the land in Warwickshire that had been monastic property but was now in the possession of the Crown, and there is a record of "... the farm of the whole manor of Leke Wotton, otherwise called Crosse Graunge, with all houses, buildings, lands, tenements, meadows, feeding grounds, pastures, tithes of sheaves and grain in the towns of Wootton and Wodecote, members to the same manor pertaining; the advowson of the vicarage of Leke Wotton; except all great trees and wood growing upon the premises and two groves of wood called Tyckethan (Thickthorn) and Grenegrove adjoining the Graunge aforesaid". This property had been "... granted by letters patent of our Lord King Henry VIII, under seal of the Court of Augmentation to Andrew Flamocke and Elizabeth his wife for a term of forty-three years without anything to be paid except one red rose at the feast of the Nativity of St John Baptist".

Mention is also made in the 'rental' of "... 10 shillings rent of tenements in Hill Wootton which had belonged to the Abbey of Stonley, of 3/7½d of annual tithe for land in Hill Wootton, and of 15 shillings for an annual and perpetual pension issuing from the churches of Asteley and Hill Wootton".

The Story Begins

The lands in Leek Wootton that were originally owned by the two Abbeys were eventually bought, in 1561, from the descendants of the Duke of Suffolk's cousin and the Crown respectively by Sir Rowland Hill (a rich merchant) and Sir Thomas Leigh his former clerk who had risen to be Lord Mayor of London in the year of Elizabeth I's accession (1558). Sir Thomas was the husband of Sir Rowland's niece and heiress, and the purchase of these lands also gave to him the patronage of the living of Leek Wootton.

Probably the most famous visit ever to both Warwick Castle and Kenilworth Castle was by Elizabeth I. It is recorded that, in 1572, Elizabeth was entertained at Warwick Castle for two nights by Ambrose Dudley, Earl of Warwick, and that she then journeyed to Kenilworth to be entertained for one night by his brother, Robert Dudley, Earl of Leicester (the Queen's long-time favourite). Apparently the Queen did not journey along the route of the present day Warwick Road and pass through the centre of our village; the track was deemed to be too muddy. She left Warwick by the North Gate, progressing along what is now simply a footpath past Woodloes, across the stream, and from the great park of Warwick straight into the great park of Kenilworth (north of Rouncil Lane).

Upon the death of Sir Thomas Leigh his estate was divided amongst his three sons, his second son Thomas was given Stoneleigh, and his grandson, another Sir Thomas, received Charles I at Stoneleigh at the beginning of the Civil War after the King was refused entry into Coventry on his way to Nottingham. For this act of loyalty Charles created Sir Thomas a peer.

Many of the battles of the Civil War took place in the fields of the Midlands, for example the Kineton Fight, below Edgehill in 1642. Stragglers from such battles wandered the area, and at least two arrived in Leek Wootton where, according to the Parish Register, they died and were buried in the church grounds, their identities and graves unknown.

October 24 1642 "A souldier that was a lieffetenante was buried in Wootton church."

November 3 1642 "A souldier, a poore fellow, died at Hill was buried in Wootton churchyard."

Much of the action of the Civil War would have taken place in this area. Warwick and Coventry were parliamentary strongholds and Robert Greville, 2nd Lord Brooke of Warwick, was appointed General of the Parliamentary Forces in Staffordshire and Warwickshire. Kenilworth Castle, by now far removed from its Elizabethan heyday, was claimed by the Royalists causing Brooke and his men to march on it in 1642. It changed hands a number of times during a succession of small battles, eventually being de-fortified by Cromwell's men to prevent it from harbouring Royalists again. Confusion reigned in the country for many years following the Civil War and, in common with many other communities, parish records are non-existent from 1642 to 1685.

Following the Restoration of the Monarchy Charles II gave the Castle of Kenilworth and its estates, including the Manor of Leek Wootton, to Earl Clarendon.

In the early part of the 20th Century his descendant sold to the 3rd Lord Leigh, of the 2nd creation, the Manor of Leek Wootton. The purchase of this land expanded upon the Leigh family's earlier purchase of the Abbey lands, and Lord Leigh of Stoneleigh became Lord of the Manor.

Henry Wise in 1709, together with other lands and The Priory at Warwick, purchased the manors of the Woodloes in the western part of the parish (see Chapter 6).

A manuscript history of the village records that "in the year 1769 a destructive fire took place in the village, by which the greater number, if not all, the cottages in the lower hamlet were destroyed. The following memorandum of the event is preserved in the Parish Chest:

> Account of goods burnt at the fire in the lower hamlet on Friday the 27th day of October 1769.

Elizabeth Hurdis	£19 6s 0d
William Lines	£4 13s 0d
Mary Lines	£8 5s 0d
John Hurdis	£5 11s 9d
Ann Newton	£4 10s 6d
Thos & Mary Russell	about £10 0s 0d
Total loss	£62 0s 0d "

The Enclosure Award of 1822 finally took away the long-held rights of villagers to farm under the 'strip' system. The open fields were pooled and re-divided by Commissioners, provided the new owners fenced the land and made new roads. Amongst others in Leek Wootton who gave up their rights and received fields as their own private property were Earl Clarendon, John Henry Leigh of Stoneley, The Reverend Thomas Cox, Bertie Greatheed of Guy's Cliffe, Ann and Thomas King of The Hays (later Wootton Court), Henry Mallory of Woodcote, and Joseph and James Perkins.

The Award was read in church on Sunday, 31st March 1822 and from this moment the parish began to take on the appearance we see today. A new road from Leek Wootton to Hill Wootton and beyond to Blackdown was eventually created. Some exchanges were negotiated between the new owners, and the present day field layout with hedges was created. The largest houses at this time were Woodcote, the original vicarage (Wootton Paddox), Leek Wootton House (then a farmhouse) and The Elms (a farmhouse long since demolished). The impact of the Enclosure Award on the general population of the village was enormous. Instead of working their own land they became employees of landlords, and in 1841 the Census refers to the majority of the village's men as agricultural labourers.

Fifty years after Enclosure the mood of the agricultural communities of England had become desperate, and farm workers throughout the country were protesting against low wages. On 7th February 1872 Joseph Arch held his famous first meeting of the incipient Agricultural Workers Trade Union under a chestnut tree on the green

The Story Begins

at Wellesbourne. Five days later the second meeting of disaffected farm workers was held at Leek Wootton.

The farming community, which has survived for centuries through wars and plague, has waned in the post-war years of the 20th Century. Crops are still grown and sheep and cattle still graze in fields around the village, but there are also equine establishments, recreational facilities, a children's playground and championship golf courses. The house at Woodcote became a convalescent home during World War II, and was taken over as the Headquarters of the Warwickshire Police in 1949.

Leek Wootton and its environs now provide a convenient rural home base for a large number of people who work in the nearby towns and cities, utilising its central location and proximity to the modern transport network of the Midlands.

The Lordship of the Manor of Leek Wootton was sold at auction by the 5th Lord Leigh in the early 1990s, and was purchased by The Warwickshire. This means it is the golf club that, in the 21st Century, has the power to convene a manorial court, to graze its cattle on the waste or common land and to shoot and take game. It owns the minerals and mines under the land, but has no right to hold a fair. However, the club co-operates with the village and the church to host an annual golf tournament for charitable causes which is known as the Manorial Golf Day.

Lesley and Paul Eldridge

<u>Minutes of The Parish Council</u>:

"In answer to a County Council enquiry asking for the Leek Wootton Inclosure Award with Map to be deposited in County Council chamber at Warwick, the following resolution was passed:-

'The Parish Council think the Leek Wootton Award is in safe keeping in the parish and they do not wish to deposit it at Warwick …'"

Tuesday, 24th October 1933

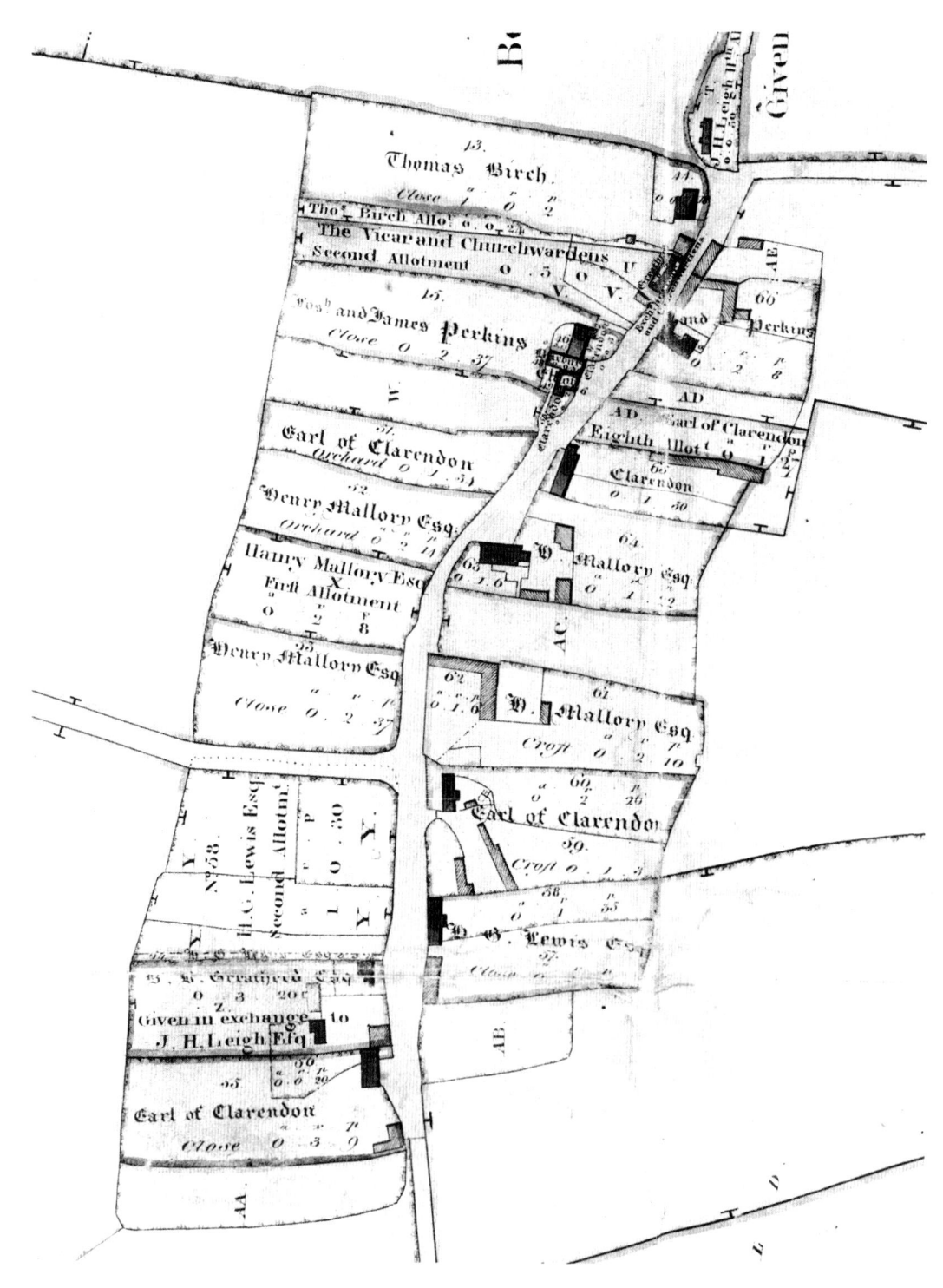

Extract from Enclosure Award, 1822, Hill Wootton
Warwickshire County Record Office, DR 38/13

The Story Begins

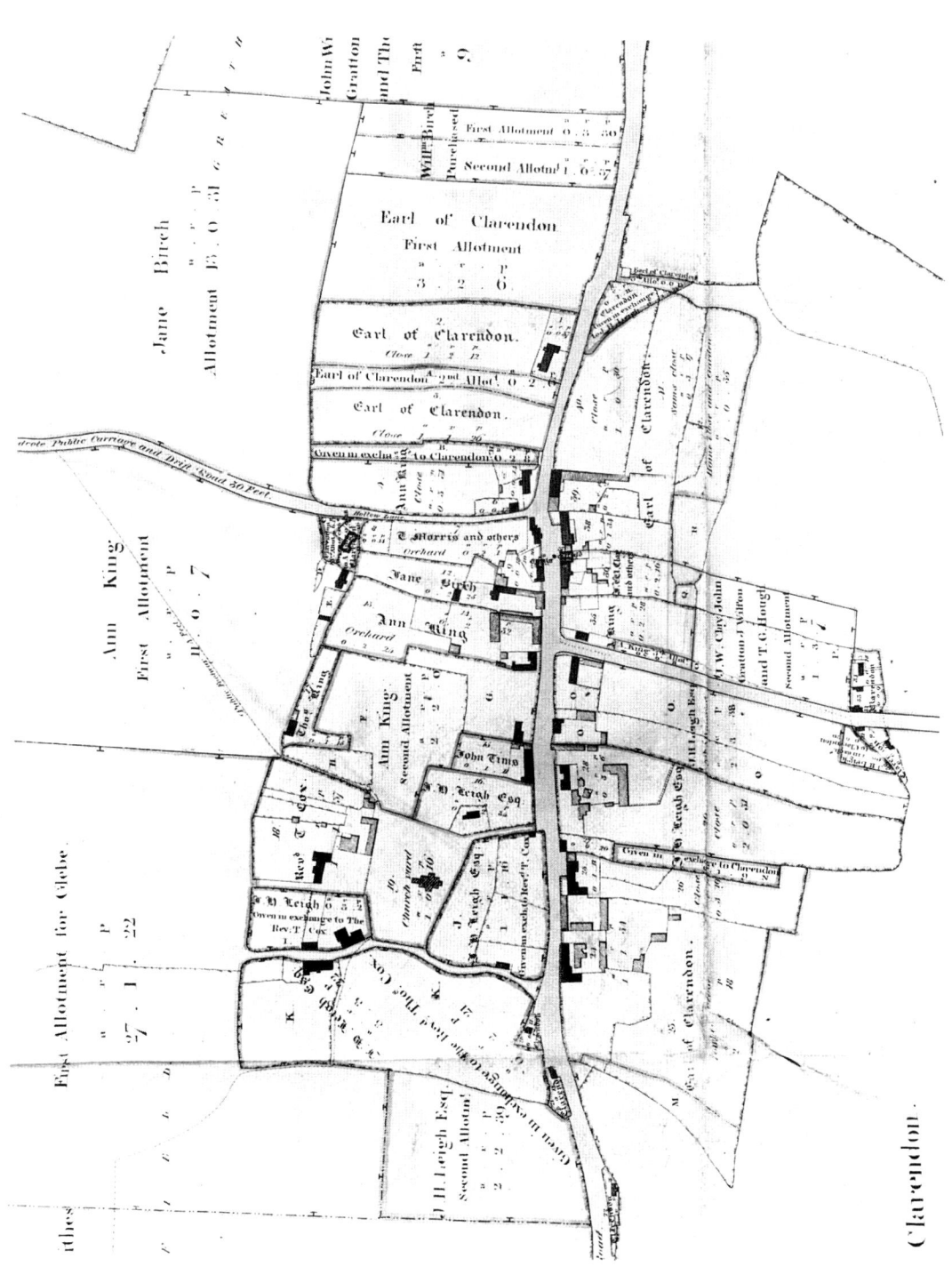

Extract from Enclosure Award, 1822, Leek Wootton
Warwickshire County Record Office, DR 38/13

Church and New Chancel, 1843
Warwickshire County Record Office, CR 351/237

2

The Parish Church of All Saints

A church has stood on or near the present site certainly since the year 1122 and probably longer, possibly preceded by a pagan temple. Little is known of the old Saxon/Norman church as it was pulled down in 1789, and all that now remains are some parts of the tower, a 12th Century tapered circular font, some mediaeval tiles and a 14th Century bell. It is known that the church had a short low nave, a high chancel with a clerestory* and aisles, a central tower and a small transept. The pulpit had a canopy. The pews were open except for two large square ones in the chancel belonging to Mr Greatheed of Guy's Cliffe and Mr Winter of The Grange, or Wootton Grange. It is possible that at least the lower stones of the tower were not destroyed but remain in the present tower.

The parish is fortunate to possess a manuscript history written during his tenure by The Reverend Frederick Leigh Colvile MA (Vicar from 1842 to 1880) and added to over the years by subsequent incumbents. In 1906 his son, Edward L M Colvile gave the 'History of Leek Wootton and its hamlets', written by his father, to the Vicar and Churchwardens for preservation in the parish chest. Frederick Colvile was the nephew of Lord Leigh, Patron of the church, and he came to Leek Wootton at the age of twenty-five, previously having been Curate of Ashow. His writings provide a brief history of the village and the church together with details of the communion plate, parsonage house, glebe land, charities and much else of interest.

It is from this volume that we learn that the wife of Thomas Schofield recollected that in 1789, at the demolition of the old church, a rope was tied round the 'spire' and the boys of the parish pulled it down. The Reverend Colvile imagined that they were allowed to take part in the demolition of the church so that the memory of the event would not be lost when the new church was finished. Mrs Schofield also recalled the clergyman and others throwing halfpence coins for the children to scramble for, and The Honourable Mary Leigh of Stoneleigh apparently sent each school child a present of a handsome prayer book. Other than these references and a pen and ink sketch from the manuscript history little more is known of the old church.

Leek Wootton was anciently the mother church of Leamington, Ashow, Lillington, Milverton and Cubbington. In the reign of King Henry I (1068-1135) the living at Leek Wootton was granted to his Chamberlain, Geoffrey De Clinton, as part of the Manor of Kenilworth. He gave the church of Leek Wootton to the Augustinian Priory at Kenilworth. In 1291 the living was valued at £5 6s 8d and it remained the benefice of the Abbey of Kenilworth until the Dissolution of the Monasteries in the reign of King Henry VIII when the church and land was seized by the Crown.

---
* The upper part of the nave, choir and transept of a church, containing a series of windows, clear of the roofs of side-aisles, admitting light to the central part of the building.

During the reign of Elizabeth I Leek Wootton and Stoneleigh Abbey's land passed to Sir Thomas Leigh, and the benefice of All Saints remained with the Leigh family until the late 20th Century, when it was suspended.

In 1638 Alice, Duchess Dudley, presented to the church of Leek Wootton, as well as to other parishes, a valuable set of church plate. This consists of a chalice with cover, bread bowl or tazza with cover, and a large flagon. All are made of elaborately decorated silver gilt. A condition of these gifts to the churches was that the sets must be used at least once a year in the communion service, or be returned to her estate. To this day the plate is used on special occasions. Every year Duchess Dudley and her daughter, Lady Alicia, are remembered in a sermon on Whitsunday. The communion plate at All Saints is one of the only treasures remaining from the ancient church.

The Present Church

This was built in 1790 on the same site as the earlier church. This was funded largely, though not entirely, at the expense of The Honourable Mary Leigh, who inherited the Stoneleigh Abbey estate from her brother, Edward Leigh, in 1786. She contributed £500. Other contributions are recorded from local dignitaries and parishioners including:

> The Earl of Warwick - 50 guineas
> Henry Wise Esq - £100
> Robert Mallory Esq - £50
> The Earl of Clarendon - 80 guineas
> Bertie Greatheed Esq of Guy's Cliffe - £40
> The Reverend Thomas Cox (Vicar) - £30

The church, designed by Hiorne of Birmingham, when first built consisted of the tower with a height of forty-eight feet and a nave forty-one feet by twenty-seven feet and eighteen feet high. The span of the chancel arch was ten feet and the height fifteen feet. The contractor for the stone work was Brown of Kenilworth who was assisted by his son, a mason.

Since the building was completed scarcely a decade has passed without some sort of extension or improvement being made. Fund raising committees and individual benefactors have knocked things down, re-built it and embellished it almost constantly over the past two hundred years.

At some time between 1789 and 1843 a west gallery was erected. The chancel was rebuilt and enlarged in 1843 at a cost of nearly £400, of which Lord Chandos Leigh gave £150, The Reverend Henry Wise (Vicar of Offchurch) £30, Earl Clarendon £20, the Earl of Warwick £15 and H C Wise £10. The Reverend Colvile wrote "The east window of three lights is filled with memorial painted glass, executed by William Holland of Warwick. The centre compartment represents our Blessed Lord in His Kingly Character, and on either side the two Apostles, Peter and Paul. The tracery is filled with a Barcelona Cross and angels bearing shields, with the emblem of our Lords Crucifixion. This window was erected by the trustees of the Bedworth Charity."

New Chancel, 1843
Warwickshire County Record Office, CR 351/237

The Church 1864

The Parish Church of All Saints

The Bedworth Charity had been founded by The Reverend Nicholas Chamberlaine who was Vicar of Leek Wootton from 1662 to 1664. For fifty-two years following he was Rector of Bedworth and at his death bequeathed large sums of money for the erection of schools, a hospital, alms houses and for the aged poor of that parish. He died on 14 July 1715, aged eighty-three, and was buried in the chancel of Leek Wootton church.

An organ was installed in the church and used for the first time on Christmas Day 1840. In 1844, at the suggestion of the Vicar, seventy-four parishioners each planted a lime tree alongside the churchyard paths, and these remain today. In 1845 a new font with oak cover was erected at the expense of Anne Amelia Colvile, daughter of Sir Charles Henry Colvile of Duffield Hall, Derby, and was sited at the base of the tower.

In 1847 various coats of arms were inserted in the extreme south and north aisle windows, funded by the respective owners. The coats of arms were those of Leigh, Duchess Dudley (paid for by Lord Leigh), Ricardo, Wise, Warwick and Clarendon. At a meeting in January of the same year the church heating was discussed. It was noted that "the interior of the church was very cold and damp during the winter season and many parishioners suffering inconvenience and discomfort". Later in the year a stove was installed at a cost of £17 12s 6d. Subscribers to this were Mrs Birch, Joseph Jaggard, Thomas Cook, John Ledbrook, Thomas Birch, Mrs Leigh Colvile, Mr King and Henry Wise. Others named were Mrs Burbury, Mr Harris, Mrs Perkins, Mr Tidmarsh, John Lane, Thomas, Joseph and Mrs Schofield. This last family must have felt especially cold.

In 1852 H C Wise presented a new reading desk of oak, made by Thomas Nicks, a local carpenter, and in 1885 George Wise presented to the parish a wheeled bier for use at funerals, as a thank-offering for "raising him up from his bed of sickness".

In 1864 the church roof was raised and the organ was placed on the west gallery. The roof was constructed by H Bevington and Sons of 48 Greek Street, Soho, London, of pitch pine and memel timber and was erected at the sole expense of H C Wise at a cost of £400. Four plaster arches were replaced with handsome stone arches, and a circular window, inserted with painted glass, was installed over the old vestry door (where the present font is sited). This window was in memory of Henry Wise's two sons. Further heating was installed with rows of pipes, heated by hot water, placed along each aisle, the cost of which was covered by voluntary contributions from parishioners. A new vestry and porch were also built at this time.

In 1897 a silver chalice and paten, which are still used on most Sundays, was presented in memory of Alan Edward Batchelor of Hill Wootton.

1889-1890 was a time for further major alterations. The architect responsible was W D Caroe (1857-1938) who undertook a great deal of church work in his role as Architect to the Ecclesiastical Commissioners. The alterations were:

- ❖ The nave was lengthened eastwards by the addition of one bay to allow for sixty extra seats, the chancel was removed and re-erected as the present vestry, with the Nicholas Chamberlaine east window, and a new chancel built with woodblock floor and patterned tiles (as today).
- ❖ The old box pews were removed and replaced by the present teak pews.

Coronation souvenir, George V and Queen Mary, June 1911

- ❖ The gallery was removed and the organ placed in the chancel.
- ❖ It is thought that some further form of heating was installed at this time. The Churchwarden of the day, John Nicks, wrote some letters complaining of the existing heating being very inadequate.
- ❖ It would appear that the plaster was taken from the walls of the nave at this time. Remnants of this can still be seen.

In 1890 the east window was installed, a gift of Mrs Hughes D'Aeth, and in 1894 the choir stalls, designed by W D Caroe, were erected in red deal, a gift of Lady Waller, in memory of her husband, Sir George Waller, Baronet, of Woodcote.

In 1923 the reredos* was a gift of Mrs Gilpin Brown, and in 1929 the oak chancel screen was erected in memory of Captain Sir Francis Waller, Baronet, who had been killed in action in 1914.

Electric lights were installed in 1931, the church having previously been lit by oil lamps. In 1938 a new pulpit was built and installed, using materials from the original one. There were repairs to the organ and an electric blower was installed, previously the organist having had to have an assistant pumping the bellows by hand. In 1940 seven seats were removed from the tower and sold at 5 shillings each for use in the cricket pavilion.

Interior, circa 1920
Helen Scott Collection

---

* An ornamental facing or screen of stone or wood covering the wall at the back of the altar.

In 1940 a bomb damaged some of the windows and the roof, and destroyed the stained glass in the Nicholas Chamberlaine window in the vestry. It was not until 1948, after years of discussion, that the windows were repaired with plain glass, at a cost of £215. The War Damage Commission paid £203, leaving £12 to come out of church funds.

In 1951 an iron gate to the porch, in memory to Mr Kevitt Rotherham, was given to replace the old one, and in 1952 the church was connected to the mains water supply, with two taps, one outside the vestry door and one in the stoke hole.

Pews were rearranged and some removed at the back of the church in 1981 to create standing room, and in 1989-1990 major repairs had to be made to the roof of the belltower and the pinnacles were restored, having been removed earlier in the century when they became unsafe.

In 1999 further major alterations were made inside the building. To commemorate the Millennium the rear of the church and base of the tower were substantially altered to create a kitchen, toilet and gallery above, with a room for meetings. The architect for this project was a parishioner and bellringer, Rod Wassell, and the building work was carried out by Clulee Construction of

The Millennium Room

Leamington Spa, under the direction of Peter van de Wiel, another parishioner who was appointed Clerk of Works. During the course of preparing the foundations for the balcony supports an area of red clay tiles was found some 75cm below the present floor level. The Warwickshire County Council Archaeologist was called in and in his opinion the tiles were of mediaeval origin. The tiles can now be seen at the base of the balcony support that is immediately above where they were found.

The excavation for the balcony on the south side revealed an even greater surprise when a large gravestone, about 50cm below the floor surface, was found covering a burial vault housing three adult coffins. Again the Archaeologist was called in and in his opinion these were of early 19th Century origin. Unfortunately there were no signs of identification. To enable the alteration works to carry on a reinforced cover was designed to cover the vault and the gravestone can now be seen set in the floor nearby. It is important to note that this stone is not considered to record the names of the occupants of the vault.

In the year 2000 the latest improvement to be made was the installation of an audio enhancement system and 'loop' to assist the hard of hearing.

There have been many gifts of money and ornaments to the church since 1790 (other than regular giving and covenanting), in addition to those described in this book, and all have now been recorded in 'The Book Of Benefactors' which is kept in the church.

Bells and Clock

The church tower contains five bells. The tenor was in the original belfry of the earlier church, and is of particular historical significance. It is the work of Johannes de Stafford, who lived in the 14th Century. The other bells originate from 1792. These bells were restored in memory of The Honourable Rupert Leigh in 1921, and in 1966 the bells were re-hung on bearings.

Will and Worton of Birmingham made the original clock mechanism which, together with the iron ringing gear, was installed in 1792. This is all still in situ together with an original clock face, now redundant, on the south side of the tower. Smiths of Derby installed an electric clock movement with electronic hourly striking device in 1968.

In the mid 1800s The Reverend Frederick Leigh Colvile presented the parish with a set of hand bells the ringing of which has been enjoyed over the years at concerts and social evenings. In 1950 the team of Golby, Terry, Gregory, Gurney and Legge completed an unbroken period of twenty-one years' ringing together. In 1996 the set was recast and missing bells replaced, all at the expense of parish benefactors.

Hilary David and Jill Corbishley

The Hand Bell Ringers
Ted Gurney, George Legge, Ern Gregory, George Terry, Will Golby
Courier Photographic Services, Leamington Spa

<u>Minutes of The Parish Council:</u>

"Proposed … that the Clerk record a report of various Parochial collections for the War Relief Funds:- viz

Jumble Sale at the Reading Room for the Wounded   £10 0s 0d
and
Working Party aided by friends in the Parish.
56 prs Socks, 50 shirts, 1 cholera belt, 1 helmet for Royal Warwickshire Regt.
22 Bed-jackets, 8 Nightshirts, 6 prs Red socks for Ch. Army Hospital in France.
12 Cholera Belts, 20 prs socks, 6 prs Mittens, 9 shirts for soldiers at the front sent to General Keir.
94 shirts, 156 prs of socks to Colonel Grundy for R. Warwickshire Regt. from Miss Beresford Wright also Weekly Hamper of Vegetables to Belgian Refugees and numerous money subscriptions for many relief funds from Mrs Beresford Wright of Wootton Court."

"A communication from the Weekly Dispatch concerning a bronze medallion to encourage recruiting in the parish was considered."

Wednesday, 27th January 1915

The Parish Church of All Saints

Vicars of Leek Wootton

The earlier names are taken mainly from Dugdale's 'Antiquities Of Warwickshire', but there are no records before 1316. The names of some of the earlier incumbents are worth noting because of their similarity to place names of today. Also, during the twenty years of the Black Death (1349-1369), it will be seen that there were five vicars, including two in one year:

Roger de Boyvill, 1316
Thomas de Coventre, 1328
Nicholas de Haselovere, 1349
William de Bradweye, 1361
John de Toucester, 1361
William de Stoneley, 1362
Thomas de Napton, 1369
Richard de Rossale, 1377
William Sprunt, 1380
Thomas Hulle, 1394
John Broun, 1401
John de Barston, 1408
Richard Crewe, 1409

The Reverend Edward Riley, Vicar 1905–1926

John Repton, 1409
Richard Ashby, 1416
John Racheford, 1417
Thomas Flynderkyn, 1425
Richard Browne, 1425
Thomas Weston, 1428
William Sutton, 1433
John Sokeling, 1439
John Clerke, 1456
John Furnevale, 1467
John Andeley, 1467
Thomas Prees, 1473
John Masty, 1487
Thomas Edwards, 1515
Henry Ellys, 1528

The Reverend Frederick Leigh Colvile, Vicar 1842–1880

The Reverend Sydney Ernest Longland, Vicar 1927–1943

Francis G Cholmondeley, 1880
Edward Riley, 1905
Sydney Ernest Longland, 1927
Richard G A Etches, 1943
John Reginald Ryecart, 1947
Andrew A Thomson, 1950
James Cornes, 1958
Charles Nettleship, 1965
James Clive Raybould, 1986
Keith Maudsley, 1989
Guy Cornwall-Jones, 1991
Brian Pearson, 2000

Robert Kinge, 1529
William Churchley, 1560
Anthony Offley, 1569
Humphrey Wilding
Nicholas Langridge, 1604
Humphrey Smallwood, 1627
Nicholas Chamberlaine, 1662
Richard Chamberlaine, 1664
John Jackman, 1701
John Mills, 1743
Robert Mills, 1754
John Clarke, 1767
Thomas Cox, 1782
Sir Henry Dryden, 1824
Leopold E Dryden, 1837
Frederick Leigh Colvile, 1842

The Reverend Charles Nettleship, Vicar 1965–1984

3

Alice, Duchess Dudley

Effigy of Alice, Duchess Dudley in Stoneleigh Parish Church

Alice Leigh, born in 1578, was the second daughter of Sir Thomas Leigh of Stoneleigh, Knight and Baronet. Her mother was Katherine, daughter of Sir John Spencer of Wormleighton, Knight. Alice married Robert Dudley, son and heir of the Earl of Leicester (favourite of Queen Elizabeth I) and they had four daughters, Alicia Douglas, Catherine, Anne and Frances. No two young people in England had better prospects, but events were to take a dramatic turn.

Robert Dudley's father, created Earl of Leicester by Queen Elizabeth I in 1564, had first married Amy Robsart who died by a fall down stairs. He then married Lady Douglas, daughter of William, Lord Howard and widow of John, Lord Sheffield, and Robert Dudley was born to them in 1574. However, the Earl soon conceived a violent passion for Lettice, daughter of Sir Francis Knollys and widow of the Earl of Essex, and he married her, disowning his former marriage and its unfortunate offspring.

Following the death of the Earl of Leicester, Lettice and others exhibited a Bill in the Star Chamber against Sir Robert and Alice, challenging Sir Robert's legitimacy and his rights to the Earldoms of Leicester and Warwick. He unfortunately lost the case, due in no small way to fraud, tyranny and the odious ministrations of the Star Chamber. The King seized his estates and Sir Robert, having experienced so much injustice, left the country and went to live in Italy.

The deserted Lady Alice from then on devoted her life to good works and, amongst other acts of charity, gave generously to the poor in the parishes of Stoneleigh, Mancetter, Leek Wootton, Ashow, Kenilworth and Monks Kirby. She bestowed lands from which rents are, to this day, distributed in these places. A condition of these gifts is that the vicars of the parishes must, on the feast of Pentecost, make a sermon in the parish church in her remembrance. In 1638 she also gave magnificent sets of silver-gilt communion plate to the same parishes.

In 1644 King Charles I, by Act of Parliament, created Alice a Duchess of England in her own right. In his Letters Patent, King Charles admitted to the injuries done to Sir Robert and the Lady Alice and their children. He stated that he was bound to honour her with the grant of the title of Duchess Dudley for her lifetime and to enable her to own her own property.

The Duchess Dudley Communion Plate

In a pamphlet produced in 1854 The Reverend Vaughan Thomas, Vicar of Stoneleigh, examined the probabilities of the Earl of Leicester's guilt. He did not entertain the slightest doubt of Sir Robert Dudley's legitimacy. He was convinced that he was the only legitimate son of the Earl and that the "Noble Imp", so gorgeously sculptured in the Beauchamp Chapel at St. Mary's Church, Warwick, his son by Lettice Knollys was in fact illegitimate.

Duchess Dudley died in 1668, in her ninetieth year, and in a funeral sermon preached in the Church of St-Giles-in-the-Fields, London, by The Reverend Robert Boreman on 14th March, the generous gifts made in her lifetime were listed. Among her bequests she left "£5 to every place her corpse should rest on its journey to Stoneleigh where her "noble monument" has long been prepared". She also left "six pence to every poor body that should meet her corpse on the road and £50 to the parish of Stoneleigh to be distributed that day".

Alice, Duchess Dudley is buried together with her eldest daughter, Alicia (who had died many years before her), in a vast ornate tomb on the north side of the chancel in The Parish Church of St Mary the Virgin, Stoneleigh.

Jane Pain

Minutes of The Parish Council:

"Distribution of Duchess Dudley's Charity ... was considered very satisfactory to the meeting

22 families with children received drapery
10 families without children received drapery
1 family with children received coals
10 families without children received coals
43 families and 50 children received the Charity"

Tuesday, 24th March 1908

4

Guy's Cliffe

The ruined mansion of Guy's Cliffe and its mill are situated just inside the Leek Wootton & Guy's Cliffe parish boundary at the most southerly point where it abuts with Warwick.

To the south is the parish of St. Nicholas, Warwick and to the north of the Warwick Bypass, just outside Leek Wootton village, is Blacklow Hill where Piers Gaveston was executed more than six hundred and fifty years ago.

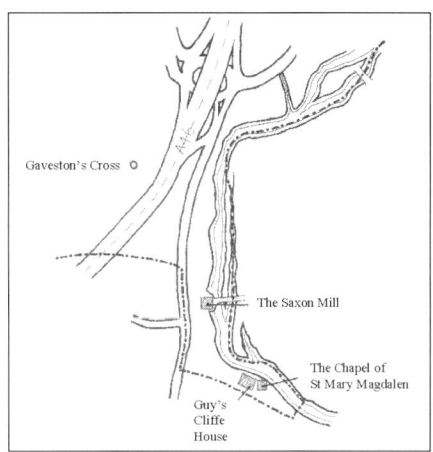

Guy's Cliffe Mansion and St Mary Magdalen Chapel

The history of the buildings and sites at Guy's Cliffe reflect the changing pattern of land ownership and events over a period of more than one thousand five hundred years. It is a story of peace and conflict, piety and profit, legend and legal documents.

Even before building began at Guy's Cliffe early historians had described the natural beauty of the situation. "There have yee a shady little wood, cleere and cristal springs, mossie bottoms and caves, meadowes alwaies fresh and greene, the river rumbling heere and there among the stones with his streame making a mild noise, and gently whispering, and besides all solitary and still quietness, things most grateful to the Muses" (Camden 1551-1623).

Such beautiful surroundings and their proximity to the old cathedral of All Saints, Warwick and the Augustinian Priory at Kenilworth were an incentive for men to worship there. John Rous, writing about 1440, records "that pious man St. Dubritius established an oratory at Guy's Cliffe dedicated to St. Mary Magdalen".

Dubritius came to Warwick from the south-west of England in the 6th Century. He established his episcopal see and erected his cathedral on a site now occupied by Warwick Castle. He died at Bardsey Island in 612 but this tradition suggests that Celtic Christianity was established in Warwickshire before Augustine re-introduced Roman Christianity in 597.

Guy's Cliffe became a favoured haunt for hermits, the first recorded being an unknown Christian who afforded "spiritual comfort" to Guy of Warwick around 929 AD. According to legend Guy was a Saxon thought to have been born in Warwick or possibly Wallingford. He fell in love with Felice the daughter of Rohund, Earl of Warwick. He was told to prove himself before gaining her hand and so embarked on a series of adventures. He slaughtered an enormous dun cow which was ravaging

Dunsmore Heath and a dragon which was terrifying Yorkshire. He fought Turks and brigands until it was finally agreed that he should marry Felice. However, after their marriage, he immediately set off for the Crusades and won countless battles against the Saracens.

Guy returned to England when the Danes were besieging King Athelstan at Winchester and demanding the surrender of England. It was agreed that the decision should rest on a single combat between the English and Danish champions. Guy, who had forsaken his previous bloodthirsty life and become a penitent palmer, agreed to one more battle against the Danish champion, Colbrand. Weary as he was, he fought and killed Colbrand and then resumed his life as a pilgrim. He returned to Warwick and received daily alms from Felice who did not recognise him in his penitent's robes. Guy lived for some years in a cave in a hole in the rocks by the river bank at Guy's Cliffe and, when he felt death to be approaching, sent his wedding ring to Felice, telling her that she would find him dead in front of the altar in the chapel of the hermitage. Felice followed his instructions and was so grief stricken upon realising that he was her husband and was now dead that she flung herself from the cliff adjoining the hermitage (Felice's Leap). Rous gives a date for their deaths of 929 but there is no record of a joint burial site. The legend is an interesting story but also provides interesting topographical details and descriptions of the caves at the hermitage.

Apart from a casual reference to "a small cottage where a hermit dwelt" there is no evidence that any building except a chapel existed on the site until the end of Henry VIII's reign. The first hermits were probably cave dwellers because even today the caves are dry and maintain an even temperature. 'Guy's Well' is an artesian spring which supplies clear water and has never been known to freeze.

Henry V visited Warwick and Guy's Cliffe in 1421 and was so impressed by the latter's serenity that he resolved to found a chantry with accommodation for two priests; but he died the following year and his friend Richard Beauchamp, Earl of Warwick, took over the responsibility. He received a licence in 1431 that he could grant the Manor of Ashorne with house and land and also land at Whitnash and Wellesbourne, producing an annual rental of £117, for the maintenance of two priests and their successors. Later, by the provision of his will, a chapel was rebuilt, two priests were established in ample accommodation 'upstairs' and the hermitage given an established foundation.

John Rous (1451-1491), who was a scholar, antiquarian and historian born in Warwick, became a chantry priest at Guy's Cliffe. Rous wrote the first 'authentic' version of the adventures of Guy of Warwick, 'The Antiquities of Warwick', and a history of Guy's Cliffe as well as many other valuable studies. A series of stained glass windows dedicated to Rous's memory and depicting his Roll of the Kings of England from King Egbert (802-839) until his day once filled the chapel. Bertie Greatheed installed these in the early 1800s but sadly vandals destroyed them all in 1974. As a chantry priest Rous led a peaceful and productive life, as did all his successors.

This was to change in the reign of Henry VIII who, as a result of his conflict with Rome, embarked on a policy of dispossessing religious foundations. The hermitage was eliminated, the priests and hermits banished, and all property confiscated. The resident priests were forced to grant the whole of the chantry's possessions to Sir Andrew Flamocke, his heirs and successors: "The particular lands belonging thereto being 15 messuages, 500 acres of land, 50 acres of meadow and 30 acres of pasture all situated at Guy's Cliffe, Ashorne and Whitnash".

Flamocke built what must have been a substantial mansion on land facing the present ruins, because there is evidence of extensive foundations on adjacent land now used as riding stables. He died soon after the house was built and his son, William, who died about 1560, left the property to his three year old daughter, Katherine. She married John Colbourne who thus acquired the estate but later sold it to John Hudson of Warwick. John Hudson's daughter married Sir Thomas Beaufoy of Warwick and it remained in that family until after the 1650s.

The house, lands and mill were sold in 1701 by Dame Charlotte Beaufoy and by 1720 the house had disappeared, only the chapel remained. The estate passed through the hands of a series of owners and lessees until on 9th August 1751 Samuel Greatheed purchased the property and a new period of prosperity began.

Samuel Greatheed was a Whig Member of Parliament for Coventry. He had family connections in the sugar plantations of St. Kitts, West Indies. He married Lady Mary Bertie, the daughter of Peregrine, Duke of Ancaster and built a new house in the classical style at Guy's Cliffe. However, The Honourable John Byng considered it "vile". In 1757 the property was described as being built of stone and brick with "convenient offices and Stabling for twenty horses and Standing for four Carriages, all hewn out of the solid rock never to be burnt or want repair". Mention was also made of a large triumphal arch and this still stands next to the ruins. Pleasure gardens were laid out, the chapel restored and the upper part of the tower built.

Samuel Greatheed died in 1765 but his widow continued to live there and befriended a young actress who had been sent to Guy's Cliffe by her father in order to break off an unsuitable attachment. Thanks to the good offices of Lady Mary the couple were reunited and married at Holy Trinity, Coventry. The actress was Sarah Siddons and she was to visit Guy's Cliffe frequently even after she became famous.

Lady Mary died in 1774 and Bertie Bertie Greatheed, her second son, succeeded to the estate. After Samuel's death Bertie had been placed under the guardianship of Brownlow Percy, 5th Duke of Ancaster. This resulted in half of the Duke's estate passing to Bertie and his wife when the Duke died in 1820. Bertie's only son died of fever in Italy when he was 22 and looking forward to a promising career as an artist. He had an illegitimate daughter, Anne Caroline, whom Bertie Greatheed and his wife adopted and brought up at Guy's Cliffe. Anne Caroline married Lord Charles Greatheed Bertie Percy in 1822, and after she died in 1882 the estate passed to the Heber Percy family who remained in occupation until 1939. They had close links with Leek Wootton both socially and as employers.

Bertie Bertie Greatheed was very much a man of his time: an entrepreneur associated with the development of Leamington as a Spa; the discovery of a saline well in the village opposite his estate in Leamington Priors increasing its value as a potential building site; a man of science interested in the latest inventions; and a writer. He wrote a play called "The Regent" in which he persuaded Mrs Siddons to take the leading part, but she miscarried on stage and the play was withdrawn. Soon afterwards England was to be ruled by George, the Prince Regent (later George IV) and Bertie observed "My Regent is a villain, the play can not be acted". Bertie found a great outlet for his creativity at Guy's Cliffe. With the wealth of his inheritance from his mother's family he began an extensive building programme to his own design. The house took on the romantic appearance that is still apparent. He created a new west front facing the avenue and also reconstructed the interior of the chapel. A handsome plaster ceiling was installed. All the leading intellectuals of the day were frequent visitors including Dr Johnson and Mrs Thrale, Samuel Parr, Walter Savage Landor and Mrs Somerville, a writer on astronomical and other scientific subjects.

Guy's Cliffe Mansion

For many years visitors were allowed to visit Guy's Cliffe and view the fine collection of paintings. One of these by Bertie Bertie's son had been exhibited at the Royal Academy and was entitled "The Cave of Despair". It was considered to be so horrific that it was covered by a curtain lest it should cause susceptible young ladies to faint with fear. Engravings of the house and gardens featured in countless guidebooks and on postcards.

With the coming of the First World War the house gradually began to fade. Lord Algernon Percy's only son died at the Battle of Jutland in 1916. The house was used as a hospital during the Great War and in the Second World War became a school for children evacuated from more dangerous areas. After the War there were plans to make the house into a hotel, and also plans for a housing estate on the site, but nothing came of these. The house fell into deeper disrepair and by the 1950s the mansion was in ruins. The final blow came in 1992 during filming by Granada Television when a fire scene got out of control and most of the remains of the house burnt down.

The house and chapel were leased by Freemasons of Coventry in 1974 and purchased by them in the 1980s. It is said that Mr Aldwyn Porter who then lived at the 'Saxon Mill' originally presented them with the property for a rent of two bottles of beer. The Freemasons continued the tradition established by Richard Beauchamp, the Greatheeds and the Percys of caring for and enhancing the beauty of the chapel and its adjoining rooms. Anne Caroline Greatheed Percy was particularly interested in the restoration and a brass plaque to her memory in the chapel concludes with the text "She did what she could". The chapel was adapted for use as a Masonic Temple and in 1979 was re-roofed.

The building may contain masonry from an earlier chapel but is largely 15th Century. It is oriented north-east to south-west traditional to that period, in keeping with Solomon's temple at Jerusalem. On the interior south-east wall and carved into the natural rock is a nine foot statue believed to be of Guy of Warwick and thought to date from the 14th or 15th Century. It has a shield but is missing a sword and right arm.

Guy's cave is situated to the east of the chapel and is thought to be the site of the original hermitage. It has an oval opening in the north side of the cliff, 750mm above the ground and overlooking the river. Facing this opening is an inscription, in Anglo-Saxon of a Mercian dialect, reading "Cast out, thou Christ, from thy servant this burden, Guy". A number of other rock-cut caves and features survive. These have been altered through the centuries and some adapted for domestic use. One was used as an ice house and another as a boat house. There are folk stories about passages leading from the caves to Warwick Castle but, whatever their history, anyone who looks at their location must envy Rous, who as Dugdale wrote, "Settled in a place on a hill near the bank of the River Avon, barely a mile distant from Warwick. This very lovely place is called Guy's Cliffe and is girt by a high wall. There in a kind of honest ease, he devoted himself to writing with all satisfaction and contentment. Thus he spent the rest of his life."

Guy's Cliffe Mill

Samuel Greatheed purchased the mill and land to the north of it and Bertie Bertie Greatheed purchased Gaveston or Blacklow Hill, which was highly romantic, being the place of execution for the treacherous Piers Gaveston. These two purchases illustrate the differences of viewpoint between father and son. They were both businessmen but Bertie was much influenced by the romantic ideas of his generation.

"Gibbeclive Mill" was the property of Kenilworth Priory in the 12th Century and remained in the possession of the Augustinian canons until the Dissolution of the Monasteries. The mill stands on the banks of the River Avon. Dugdale identified this mill as being the one mentioned in the Domesday Book but there is no historical proof of this. In the 16th Century there are references to two, and later three mills, under the one roof. On Reighton's map of 1725 the mill is marked as an "Oyl Mill". In 1782 the mill was leased to Thomas Perkins and is likely to have reverted to corn grinding by this

Guy's Cliffe Mill

The Miller's House, Guy's Cliffe

date. In 1822 the mill was rebuilt with ornate "Gothick timberwork", probably to present a pleasing view from the mansion. There was a succession of lessees in the 19th Century until Henry Summerton became the miller in 1892 and his family worked the mill until it closed in 1938. Mrs Summerton continued to live there until the 1940s.

In 1952 the mill and granary were converted into a restaurant and bar (the mill had been known as The Saxon Mill for many years by this time). The main waterwheel has gone but a smaller one still turns, and a solid wooden "spur wheel" is mounted on the wall just inside the restaurant. The original balcony of the mill has been extended across the mill and granary, which are now joined by a more modern stone building. From the balcony and terrace visitors can look out over the large pool to Guy's Cliffe and the trees and river which once so delighted Camden.

Blacklow Hill and Gaveston's Cross

In 1821 on Blacklow Hill Bertie Greatheed completed a project that he had been proposing for some time. He erected a stone cross to mark the execution of Piers Gaveston. His friend Dr Samuel Parr (the 'Perpetual Curate' at Hatton) composed the inscription, which reads:

> In the Hollow of this Rock,
> Was beheaded,
> On the 1st Day of July, 1312,
> By Barons lawless as himself,
> PIERS GAVESTON, Earl of Cornwall;
> The Minion of a hateful King:
> In Life and Death,
> A memorable Instance of Misrule.

Guy's Cliffe

The cross and plaque are sited above an earlier inscription on the rock face, as mentioned by Dugdale (1656) and Thomas (1730), which reads:

1311
P GAVESTON
EARL OF CORNWALL
beheaded here

Gaveston was a favourite of both Edward I and Edward II. He delighted in annoying the barons and encouraged Edward II in his despotic activities. He nicknamed the Earl of Warwick 'The Black Dog of Arden' because of his swarthy appearance, which so incensed the barons that he was first banished to Ireland and then to the Continent. He returned and with Edward II at his side fought a final battle at Scarborough. He was forced to surrender and was taken by the Earl of Pembroke to Deddington Castle, near Banbury. The Earl of Warwick surrounded the castle and he was taken bare headed and bare foot to Warwick Castle. The Earl of Lancaster agreed to take responsibility for his death and he was taken to Blacklow Hill to be executed. After his death four shoemakers placed his body on a ladder, some say they stitched his head back on, and carried him to Warwick. Four Dominican Friars finally transported him to Oxford.

Gaveston had been excommunicated but when this ruling was lifted Edward II gave his friend a magnificent funeral in the church of the Dominican Priory of King's Langley in Hertfordshire.

Blacklow Hill is the site of ancient settlements, and it was Lord Algernon Percy who recorded finding, in a drawer at Guy's Cliffe, four silver Roman coins "dug up on Blacklow Hill".

Gillian Bailey

5

Hill Wootton

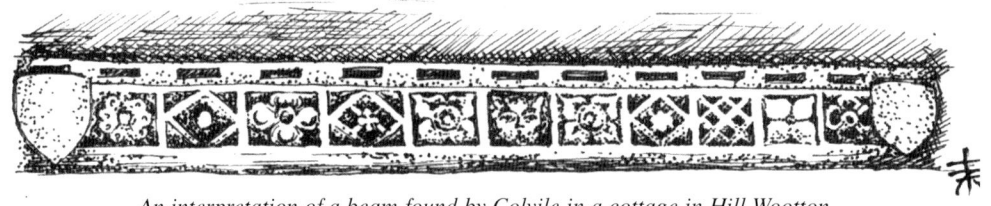

An interpretation of a beam found by Colvile in a cottage in Hill Wootton

To the east of Leek Wootton lies the hamlet of Hill Wootton, a small group of dwellings situated on a hill, surrounded by fields and meadows. It is bordered on three sides by the meandering River Avon and by the old Warwick/Stoneleigh road on the fourth. A thatched cottage, a half timbered house and a stone farmhouse hint at earlier beginnings, while a group of 1950s homes and a few of even more recent vintage complete the flow of architectural change from the 16th Century to the present day.

Over the years many well-known and important landlords owned property in the hamlet. Although there is no mention of "Hulle" (Hill Wootton) in the Domesday Book, an early document records a duel, fought in court in 1221, as a result of which Alan de Morcote conveyed to the Earl of Warwick and Prior of Kenilworth 3 virgates of land in "Hull" in return for twenty-four marks of silver.

In 1258 Thomas de Endesoure, Knight, gave to the church of The Blessed Mary of Stanleys (Stoneleigh) and the Cistercian monks there his land "in the ville Hulle next Wott(on)… his lands and rents, the tenements (dwellings) and his men, both free and villein".

Edward III was granted a special tax in 1332, on moveable goods, to finance his Scottish war. Goods under the value of ten shillings were exempt but Hill Wootton and Leek Wootton paid £1 13s 6d. Sixteen superior houses were taxed and this would indicate that there were about fifty dwellings in the two places at that time.

Life during the Middle Ages saw few changes for the inhabitants of Hill Wootton. They lived off the land, cultivating their strips and raising their stock, grazing their animals on common meadows. The woods and the river nearby provided firewood and, no doubt, supplemented their meagre diet with game and fish, and they paid their tythes to their lords and the church. Although it is thought there may have been a chapel in the hamlet at some time, the main place of worship would have been across the fields at Leek Wootton. From time to time the men were called to take up arms and fight for their masters.

Yet the villagers were not completely out of touch with worldlier goings on. They were within walking distance of Warwick Castle, one of the most important strongholds in the kingdom and Kenilworth Castle, a royal residence, was not much further away. There would have been a good deal of movement between the two places and news of foreign wars and loftier goings on at court would certainly have sifted through in some form.

In 1473 Beatrice Brome, widow of John, gave her lands in Hill Wootton to her son Nicholas in order to retain possession of the manor at nearby Baddesley Clinton.

During the reign of Elizabeth I, a glorious and largely peaceful era, which brought greater prosperity to many of her subjects, many brick and timber dwellings were built as cottages and farmhouses. The picturesque thatched cottage in the hamlet probably dates from this period.

During the 17th Century disquiet and unrest swept the country, culminating in the Civil War. After the battle of Edgehill in 1642 "a souldier, a poore fellow died at Hill and was buried in Wootton churchyard". The country was in great confusion at this time and no records were written in the Leek Wootton Parish Registers from this date until 1685. Dugdale records a strange and ghostly happening in Hill Wootton. "In 1669 there was much talk of a strange sound like the beating of drums in a march or call heard in a well belonging to one Nibbs…. which sound was said to have been heard in 1642 when it continued 14 days, and on his Majesty's return".

Deeds exist showing that John Smith, a Warwick baker purchased a half-timbered house in the hamlet known as Stud Farm, together with land and buildings, in 1674, for the sum of £238. As was common in those days he rented his property out to tenants, yeoman farmers, and left it to his "loving wife" Margaret in his will of 1693.

In the 18th Century and early 19th Century the stone building known as The Old Farmhouse was built and it is thought to have been part of the Stoneleigh Estate. An interesting feature of this property is its ancient yew hedge, parts of which are over ten feet wide. It possibly dates back to the late 18th and early 19th Century, and was the boundary between the Stoneleigh and Heber-Percy Estates.

Rose Cottage, originally the farmhouse of New House Farm, was built in 1769. At around this time Stud Farm, which is opposite, was owned by Henry Greswolde Lewis as part of the Malvern Hall Estate.

Up until the 19th Century the land in Hill Wootton was still being worked under the ancient open field system that had been in place since Anglo-Saxon times. Until the Enclosure Award of 1822 Hill Wootton was marooned in the middle of fields with only cart tracks and footpaths leading to Leek Wootton and Blackdown. There was a road at the south of the village leading to the river, now the closed lane, from which another lane followed the river to Guy's Cliffe. Among the people who received land at the time of the Enclosure Award was Henry Greswolde Lewis who had let Stud Farm and land to John Buckerfield in 1779 at a rent of £30; in 1821 George Hues was paying him rent of £100. He ensured that his right to "ride, hunt the land on horseback, or with guns and nets" was retained and his tenants were required to furnish him with "two good fat fowls or a good fat turkey" on New Years Day. Imagine how popular this must have been with the hard working farmers.

It is recorded that "In the year 1842 a fire broke out at Hill Wootton, through the carelessness of one Plummer, a poor crazy woman, whereby four families were deprived of a home. There was subscription set on foot for the sufferers and Lord Leigh presented £25 0s 0d (two of the cottages having been his Lordship's property)."

The coming of the railway revolutionised the transport of goods and people at a time of great industrial expansion. There was a vast railway construction programme throughout the country and in 1842 the London and Birmingham Railway Company proposed a single-track line from Leamington Spa to Coventry. This was to have a station at Leamington, later known as Milverton Station. Both Earl Clarendon and Lord Leigh opposed the plan along with many other prominent landowners; however, the line was finally completed in 1844. It included several bridges and a vast viaduct over the River Avon between Old Milverton and Hill Wootton. Land in the hamlet was purchased from Lord Leigh who agreed to receive payment in instalments for twenty-two acres of land, initially valued at £6,656 5s 6d. When recorded payments stopped in 1848 he had received over £1,200 in interest and a balance of £2,584 2s 0d was still owing.

On 11 June 1861 tragedy struck when the railway bridge over the crossroads between Leek Wootton and Hill Wootton collapsed, killing the driver and fireman of a locomotive hauling empty coal wagons to Victoria Colliery. Apparently the bridge was something of a local curiosity as it swayed and rumbled as trains passed over and local youngsters gave it the nickname of 'Crackley'. When the inevitable happened and the unstable bridge collapsed, the tender jack-knifed, crushing George Rowley and John Wade. It took several hours to remove the bodies, which were taken to The Anchor Inn at Leek Wootton where the inquest began later that day. A fractured bolthole from earlier repairs to one of the girders was held to be responsible. The London and North West Railway Company added a second track in 1884 but, as part of railway rationalisation in the late 20th Century, the line was reduced back to a single track.

Ruins of the Bridge on the Leamington & Kenilworth Railway where the Driver George Rowley and the fireman lost their lives by the Bridge breaking down as the engine was passing over on the 11th June 1861

Art Gallery & Museum, Royal Pump Rooms, Warwick District Council

A small bridge between the fields, where a private road formerly ran between Hill Wootton and the Warwick/Stoneleigh road, was blown up in 1981, as it was unsafe. Unfortunately, an ugly concrete bridge replaced the original, which was of mellowed stone and brick.

The Parish Registers record the births, marriages and deaths of many of the inhabitants of Hill Wootton, including poor Ann Pill, aged 20, who drowned accidentally in the River Avon in 1829, and early Census returns record the larger houses in the hamlet occupied by wealthy families who employed servants, labourers, stockmen and grooms to care for their farms and property. The Greens, Wests, Brittains, Jaggards, Pittaways and Perkins (the horse breaker) lived and worked in Hill Wootton in the early 19th Century, producing large families of children, many of whom did not survive infancy. It was a hard existence and while men laboured on the farms, their wives reared the children, tended their small vegetable plots, took in washing or worked as maids and cooks. There was a great disparity between the poor and the rich, with only the workhouse to look forward to for many of these people, if they became too ill or old to work.

In 1872 The Reverend Frederick Leigh Colvile discovered a beautifully carved beam ten feet long in the bedroom of the cottage of Thomas Freeman, a labourer, in Hill Wootton. He made a sketch and sent it to a Mr Edward Knowles of St Bees, enquiring whether it may have come from Kenilworth Castle. In his reply Mr Knowles suggested that this might be the relic of some manor house of the late 15th or early 16th Century but that it could not be identified in any way with the Castle. He went on to say that "..all that Henry VIII did has so utterly perished at Kenilworth as to give no clue". He also stated that the cottage in which it was found may be older than it appeared and may have a history of its own, or that the beam may have been brought from Warwick. Unfortunately there is no way of identifying the cottage in which the beam was found.

Just as today, disputes arose such as the one involving Lord Clarendon and Lord Leigh in 1892. Lord Leigh accused Earl Clarendon of building a cattle shed over his boundary. He wanted to build some pigsties but his dispute over four feet of land held him up and the solicitors, no doubt with an eye to their remuneration, exacerbated the situation. A series of irate letters flew between all parties. Lord Leigh was infuriated that his tenant's pigs had to be kept in calf pens, making a mess of the place. Eventually, realising that only the lawyers were gaining any benefit from the situation, the two wrote conciliatory letters to one another and negotiated a truce.

In the first half of the 20th Century the motor trade was booming in Coventry and wealthy car manufacturers and directors occupied several of the larger houses. Tower House was built in 1920 by the Riley family of Riley cars.

Although only a tiny hamlet, Hill Wootton did not escape the effects of two World Wars. During the Great War horses were requisitioned from the farms to help in the war effort. During the Second World War the railway line was a target for bombing and planes returning to Germany from Coventry jettisoned their bombs in the fields in the area. Bomb craters were found near Chesford Woods and a bomb dropped to the south of the hamlet by the river, which it was believed, did not explode. Attempts to dig it out from the wet, sandy and boggy soil proved fruitless as the hole kept filling with water despite efforts to pump it out. In recent years a fallen tree near the site was found to contain shards of metal, so perhaps the bomb had exploded after all.

Stud Farm, 1882
Warwickshire County Record Office, PH 458/14

Cottages, 1890, now the site of Hill Wootton Close
Birmingham Library Service

Hill Wootton

Village Children, 1890, Hill Farm
Birmingham Library Service

A Mumford Family Wedding
Stephen Mumford seated far right, Emily Mumford next to him, and Florence Payne their granddaughter next to her (Mrs James Francis) James Francis standing rear right

Following IRA activity before the Second World War that had led to Milverton Station being blown up, regular patrolling of the railway line and checking of bridges was begun. With the advent of the Second World War and the vulnerability to enemy bombing so close to Coventry, Mr Dee and Mr Hobbins, Special Constables from Leek Wootton, were required to continue the responsibility for carrying out these security measures throughout the War. Holes were also dug out and lined with sandbags in the fields bordering the river to provide surveillance points in case of invasion.

The farming community was working harder than ever to feed the nation. Prisoners of War from Goodrest Camp were sent to help and double summertime was in operation to enable the hours of daylight to be used fully. Food was scarce and rationed. After the bombing of Coventry the bakers in the area were required to bake bread twenty-four hours a day to supply the homeless. This must have put a great strain on bakers like Mr Dee at the bakehouse in Leek Wootton. John Semple, a young boy living in Hill Wootton at the time, recalls having to stay up late at night waiting for the family's bread to arrive.

The association with industrial Coventry continued after the War when Hill Wootton became home to other prominent figures. Mr Norman Spurgeon, a director at Lockheed, owned Hill Wootton House. Next door were several charming and well photographed half-timbered cottages, which had inspired the painter David Woodlock to paint them in the 'chocolate box style' so popular in the late 1800s. These were also owned by Mr Spurgeon and were demolished by him and replaced with Hill Wootton Close, into which he later moved. Mr McNeish of Triplex Glass, Mr Alick Dick, Chairman of the Standard Motor Company, Mr Leslie Kegan of KarRobes and Mr Walter Harmer of Alfred Herbert were other inhabitants. It was from this time that Hill Wootton began to change dramatically, away from a largely agricultural community to the one we have today.

In the 1950s land was sold and people began to build the individual houses which form a large part of the hamlet, as we now know it. Preserving historical buildings was not of such importance to the planners in those days. Stud Farm, the 17th Century farmhouse, was almost demolished in 1976 with the approval of Warwick District Council, but it was saved at the eleventh hour when it was listed as being of architectural and historical interest. The intention had been to replace it with a modern replica. The fashion for barn conversions did not pass the hamlet by and Belinda and Don Ellwood created The Old Barn in 1978 from the remains of another barn. Since then two new private houses and two farmhouses have been built.

Like all communities Hill Wootton has seen its share of suicides, love affairs, disputes and gossip. There have been many colourful characters, and one of them was Harry Mumford. The Mumfords were horse breeders who kept stallions at their stables at Stud Farm from the 1920s until the early 1970s. During

Harry Mumford and Mannion, 1972

that time the family made few changes to their farm, they never owned a tractor and their horse and buggy was always used to travel the farm. Mares were brought to the farm and stallions were taken to other farms. The house was totally unmodernised, except for connecting to water and electricity, until it was sold to George Smith after Harry died. Harry was well known for his booming voice and his punctuality. He died in 1973 and his gravestone in Leek Wootton churchyard reads "A dear lover of horses".

Mr Edward Hammond, who lived next door to Harry and owned Hill Wootton Farm, was another whose like will not be seen again. He was relentlessly cheerful and kind in all winds and weathers as he went about his farm, an old fashioned figure in his brown smock and cap.

Further down the lane lived Bill Watts and his sister Liz. They lived in one of the farm cottages, opposite Wootton Grange Farm, from the time it was built. Bill Watts was the village roadman or sweeper and he and his sister lived in a very simple way. There was no electricity, running water or sanitation in the house and as they had been brought up in a world without technology or mod-cons it was decided not to build them a bathroom when these luxuries finally arrived as "they would probably only use the bath to keep their coal in". The butcher would deliver their meat on a Friday and Liz would cook it; as they had no refrigerator she would then cook it again on Saturday and on Sunday and Monday.

Bill and Liz Watts

Peg and Jim Semple came to work for the Hammonds in the early 1940s. They came from Northern Ireland and arrived in the hamlet with their three children on a horse and cart with their few belongings. Everyone made a contribution to help out the young couple and Bernard Dee remembers his family donating a chair. At first they occupied a brick and timbered dwelling next to Thatched Cottage, which had a corrugated tin roof replacing the original thatch and a small garden which they cultivated to contribute towards feeding their family. As soon as the children were old enough they helped out with the gardening and on the farm. Mr Hammond and his mother regularly contributed extra provisions to help feed the growing family. Eventually the Semples raised six healthy children and they worked for Mr Hammond until Jim's death. Their son John continued to work for Mr Hammond and his partner and nephew, Alan Moore, until 1997.

Social events in the hamlet have helped to draw the community together and in recent years families in Hill Wootton and Leek Wootton would look forward to Christmas carols in the barn at New House Farm arranged by John and Brenda Semple, with the kind permission of Alan Moore. The Semples also started the Bonfire Night tradition when inhabitants of the hamlet took it in turns to host a bonfire night party for all their neighbours. Sadly these events no longer take place but trick or treating, Christmas parties, summer barbeques, swimming, tennis matches, plant sales and fund raising drinks parties are all regular events.

Hill Wootton has adapted and survived changing conditions throughout the ages while still managing to remain a small oasis in the sea of developed land that surrounds it. It remains to be seen if it manages to retain its status of "hamlet" far into the new century. Anyone who has been lucky enough to live there must surely hope so.

Joy Maisey and Brenda Semple

Christmas Carols at New House Farm, 1987
Heart of England Newspapers Ltd

<u>Minutes of The Parish Council</u>:

"Proposed ... that considering the great danger existing at the four cross roads under the Railway Bridge between Leek Wootton and Hill Wootton we respectfully suggest that danger boards be placed at proper distances on each road."

Monday, 29th March 1909

<u>Minutes of The Parish Council</u>:

"<u>Obstruction of Right of Way</u> on path leading from Hill Wootton to the Kenilworth-Leamington Rd. The Chairman reported that he had seen the notice re Pedigree Bulls but this did not constitute an obstruction."

Tuesday, 11th November 1941

6

The Wise Family at Woodcote 1832-1888

Warwickshire County Record Office, CR 26/5 (3)

In 1851 Henry Christopher Wise purchased the Ricardo Estate (part of the Mallory Estate), which included Woodcote House and most of the park and surrounding land, about one hundred and seventy-nine acres in all. He had evidently been renting Woodcote for some years before the purchase (several of his children were born there from 1832 onwards), but after Robert Hervey Mallory died in 1820 and his unmarried son Henry died in 1830, a division of the estate was made between the two daughters, Mrs Ricardo and Lady Williams. Eventually, in September 1851 Osman and Harriet Ricardo sold the house and land to H C Wise Esq for the sum of £31,273 16s 10d.

Henry Christopher Wise was born in 1806 in Offchurch. He was the son of The Reverend Henry Wise, Vicar of Offchurch 1805-1850, and his wife Charlotte Mary (née Porten). His great great grandfather was Henry Wise (1653-1738), Gardener to Queen Anne, whose career had begun at Brompton Park Nursery supplying trees and plants for large gardens and parks (including the royal parks) throughout the country, designing and laying out grounds, and sending skilled men to do the work. During his lifetime Henry worked at Blenheim Palace for the Duke of Marlborough, Windsor, Kensington Gardens, St. James's Park (where he was put in charge soon after the succession of Queen Anne), Hampton Court and Melbourne. There is a portrait of Henry Wise by Kneller at Kew. By 1709 Henry had amassed quite a fortune and his eye

Henry Wise, 1653-1738

fell upon the estate and mansion of The Priory in Warwick which he purchased and to which he retired in 1727. The Priory Estate included The Priory, lands lying between The Priory and the canal, and the farms of South, Middle and North Woodloes, together with the manors of Woodcote and Woodloes. So, when his great great grandson, Henry Christopher Wise, bought the estate of Woodcote in the parish of Leek Wootton in 1851 the family were by no means new to the area.

The Mallory family, from whom Henry Christopher Wise bought the Woodcote estate, had lived in the area for many years. Samuel Mallory leased Middle Woodloes Farm in 1684 and the parish records show many family entries at All Saints Church at the time. The memorial headstone of John Mallory was discovered under the floor of the church in 1999 during construction of the Millennium Room, which revealed that he was born in 1685, died in 1732, and was living at Woodcote when he died. John, Robert and Robert Hervey Mallory all occupied Woodcote during the 18th and early 19th century and in 1815 made improvements to enlarge the old house by adding to the south side and forming a new front. Their long occupation came to an end with the death of the unmarried son, Henry, in 1830. The estate was then divided up and Woodcote bought by Henry Christopher Wise.

When Henry Christopher Wise first came to live at Woodcote in about 1831 he was twenty-five years old with a young wife, Harriett, the third daughter of Sir Gray Skipwith, Baronet, from Alveston, Warwickshire. Henry Christopher and Harriett had married on 24th June 1828 and their first son, also Henry Christopher was born in Rome and baptised there on 12th April 1829. Before coming to Leek Wootton they had a second son, George, born at Tachbrook Grove, Bishop's Tachbrook in May 1830 and a third, William Naper was born at Woodcote in February 1832, followed by Harriett Mary in 1834, Frederick Gray in 1838, and Augustus in 1840. Two further children, Arthur and Celia, died in infancy.

A young friend of Henry's, The Reverend Ernest Adolphus Waller, became Curate of Bishop's Tachbrook in 1833 and in a letter to his brother in July wrote: "Young Wise lives about 6 miles from here, on the other side of Warwick at a place called Woodcote, so I was not perfectly without an acquaintance on my arrival and nothing in the world could have been kinder than they all have been to me. The beginning of next month they are all going down together to Dover for sun bathing and I dare say will make a long stay. This will be a great loss to me but it cannot be helped." Two years later Ernest Waller was to marry Henry Wise's sister, Louisa.

The Census of 1851 records Henry, his wife Harriett, and daughter Harriett

Mary living in Woodcote with ten servants (housekeeper, lady's maid, laundry maid, house maid, stillroom maid, scullery maid, kitchen maid, butler, groom and footman). There were also several outdoor servants living in cottages in the village.

Following his purchase of Woodcote Henry Christopher expanded and improved the estate. One of his first projects was to build a new road, Woodcote Lane, in 1852. The old road from Leek Wootton toward Rouncil Lane went along the old drive to Woodcote House and through the site of the present house, curved round to the north and west and joined Rouncil Lane just west of Keeper's Cottage. After the new road was built the old road continued to be used as a drive to the old house but in the vicinity of the house and garden it was removed. To the north-west of the house the old road continued to be used as a back road for some years, but this was eventually also removed.

Further to the land and buildings bought from Osman Ricardo, Henry Christopher enlarged the estate eastwards towards the centre of the village and the main road by buying Home Farm and its adjoining land in 1851, The Rock and a number of cottages from Edward J King in the same year, and in 1853 The Anchor Inn with adjoining cottages from T Morris. The Anchor Cottages were pulled down soon afterwards and new ones built on the same site. Three more cottages although originally four, together with a paddock and hovel alongside the road leading to Woodcote, opposite the Anchor Inn, were purchased from Edward King (now Ivy Cottage and Gypsy Cottage). Two cottages, now one known as Holly Cottage, near to Wootton Paddox and the Tink-a-Tank footpath were purchased from King in 1851, and The Stone Cottage (now The Old Post House) was also bought from King. Henry Christopher also purchased thirteen acres of land from the Birch family.

In December 1854 tragedy struck the family. Henry Christopher and Harriett's eldest son, Henry Christopher, then aged twenty-five, was fatally wounded at the Eureka Stockade in Ballarat, Australia. Gold had been discovered in the creeks and gullies of Ballarat in August 1851 and news of these discoveries had quickly spread throughout Australia and the rest of the world. During the next four years Ballarat's population increased to 45,000 and most were young men who hoped to find gold. Captain Wise was in Her Majesty's 2nd Battalion of the 40th Somerset Regiment, which had been ordered out from Melbourne to keep the peace. In the early hours of the morning of 3rd December 1854 a brief but violent battle took place between the gold miners and the Crown soldiers, and young Henry Christopher was mortally wounded. The armed insurrection at Eureka was a flash point that has become famous as one of the few armed battles in Australian history. A memorial was built thirty years later in 1884 thus Henry Christopher's short life is commemorated in Ballarat, so far from his home. There is also an impressive memorial erected by his Regiment on the south wall of All Saints Church.

Back in Leek Wootton Henry Christopher Wise set about improving the Woodcote estate and the Front Lodge was built around 1856. He also rebuilt some of the cottages on the estate. On Woodcote Lane, in what was called Park Garden, there were three old cottages which were pulled down around 1857 and three new cottages were built further back from the road in part of an orchard for tenants who were workers on the Woodcote estate (now East Cottage and Middle Cottage).

In 1856 Henry Christopher presided over the peace rejoicings at Leek Wootton to mark the end of the Crimean War. A contemporary newspaper article provides a delightful word picture of the occasion and is evocative of the era. It records that a meeting of all the "influential residents" had been called at the home of the Senior Churchwarden on 5th June when various duties were allotted. The names Wise, Jaggard, Perkins, Ledbrook and Hobbins appear on the various committees arranged to prepare for the celebrations. It reports that on 10th June "..the quiet little village of Leek Wootton was aroused from its usual daily routine by a parochial festivity in celebration of the happy return of peace to this country." "..it was decided that every one of every age and of both sexes in the parish should take part in them; accordingly all the children from the age of 14 downwards, were assembled at the school room at half-past two o'clock, whence they walked in procession with flags and banners, attended by the Schoolmaster and Mistresses, and accompanied by the Ladies of the parish, through the village. During their progress the Church bells sent forth a merry peal, and the eyes of all were fixed on the pretty scene exhibited, till they arrived opposite the Stone Cottage, the residence of the Curate of the parish; here the attention of everyone was arrested by the simple yet elegant decoration of the building, the gables of which were hung with French paper lamps of red, white and blue, and the lower windows were traced out with the same lamps of various colours, while the door-way was surmounted by the appropriate inscription – 'The Church the bulwark of the nation'. Passing by the Stone Cottage, the children proceeded through a series of flags and triumphal arches to the field set apart for the festivities, where they were regaled with tea, cake and bread and butter." "After tea the children were taken down to the entrance of the field, and arranged on either side to await the arrival of the procession of the adult population, which was being formed in another field on the Hill Wootton road." This second procession was accompanied by "Mr Wells's fine band, playing a lively march" and "The spectators in the dining field who saw this procession of about 250 people, marching closely up the hill to the strains of the music, asserted that it was one of the most touching scenes they had ever witnessed – old men and women, young men and maidens, all linked together in the bonds of friendship and unity, their faces radiant with the smiles of joy and happiness, and their mouths watering with the prospect of beef and plum pudding. On approaching the dining field we passed under several triumphal arches." "Exactly at five o'clock the procession entered the field and the band immediately on sighting the good old English fare, signified the same to its followers by playing the 'Roast beef of old England'." H C Wise Esq, Squire of the parish presided at one table, The Reverend C J Fuller, the Curate at another, and Mr Jaggard, Senior Churchwarden the third. "The dinner went off with the greatest spirit possible, and every one appeared joyous and happy." After many speeches ".. there were the usual sports, scrambling for nuts, running for oranges, and the women running for tea. The festivities finished with dancing."

In 1858 Harriett, Henry's wife of nearly thirty years, died aged fifty-two. Despite his loss Henry Christopher remained active and in 1861/2 the old house and buildings were pulled down. Unfortunately, during this operation a fatal accident occurred. On 3rd April 1861 Frederick Hodgins, aged only twenty-one, was killed by falling masonry. He was buried at nearby Ashow and on his headstone is written:

The Wise Family at Woodcote 1832-1888

> Mourn not for me my parents dear,
> I am not dead but sleeping here,
> my souls at rest my grave you see,
> prepare therefore to follow me.

The architect for the house was Gibson and the local paper reported: "On Wednesday July 10th 1861 the first stone of the new mansion about to be erected for H C Wise Esq was laid by his eldest son, George Wise Esq, in the presence of a select circle of friends. Mr Wise gave a suitable address to the workmen in which he expressed a hope that no accident might occur during the progress of the work, and at its conclusion he was widely applauded. The Reverend Mr Colvile then offered an appropriate prayer, after which the stone was laid. The workmen subsequently partook of a substantial dinner at the Anchor Inn, Leek Wootton, and greatly enjoyed themselves in the evening. Mr Trollope of London has been employed to build the mansion, and Mr Nicks of Wootton is clerk of the works." The new house was built in practically the same position as the old with stables, farm buildings and a kitchen garden in much the same place. The gardens and pleasure grounds were re-arranged, a reservoir built and five acres of the park were taken to enlarge the garden.

Helen Scott Collection

Henry Christopher had been Churchwarden at All Saints from 1851 to 1854, and in 1864 he again turned his attention to the parish church. At his expense the organ was placed in the west gallery, the roof of the church was raised and the church thoroughly restored. A large round stained-glass window was also installed in the north wall, paid for by George, Harriett Mary and Augustus Wise in memory of their late brothers William Naper and Frederick Gray Wise.

In 1867 the Back Lodge to Woodcote was built and a garden made.

Henry Christopher Wise

Jane Wise

Jane with Eddie & Alba

Alba

Henry was a Member of Parliament from 1865 until 1874, a magistrate for many years and Deputy Lord Lieutenant of the County. Happily within ten years of being widowed Henry was married again, to Jane Harriet (born 1828), youngest daughter of Sir Edward Cromwell Disbrowe GCG of Walton Hall, Derbyshire. Henry and Jane had two children, Henry Edward Disbrowe Wise (Eddie) born in October 1868 and Charlotte Albinia (Alba) born in June 1870.

In 1868 the first Horticultural Show was held in the village in a field adjoining Mr Nick's residence, the Stone House. Henry Wise's son, Augustus, had encouraged "useful and ornamental gardening in the village" and formed the Horticultural Society. He worked hard to organise this first show and persuaded people like Lord Leigh, Earl Clarendon and Lord Charles Percy to become patrons of the society. A large ornamental arch was erected at the entrance to the grounds on which were the words 'Leek Wootton Flower Show' in large letters. Flags were hoisted on the top of the church tower and at other places in the village. There were many prizes for Honorary Members, Blue Ticket classes, etc and extra prizes for the best cultivated and neatly kept allotment gardens were given by H C Wise. James Hancox was awarded 1st prize, 5 shillings and a spade, the 2nd prize was 4 shillings and a fork, 3rd prize 3 shillings and 6 pence and a rake, and the 4th prize 3 shillings and a hoe.

Henry continued his interest in village life and in October 1873 he laid the foundation stone for the new village school, which can still be seen today on the The Old School.

In 1877 the upper and lower pools were constructed in the grounds of Woodcote, and a number of the cottages in the village purchased in 1851 were altered around this time.

In the 1881 Census we read of Henry and Jane Wise living at Woodcote with their daughter, Charlotte Alba, aged ten. They employed fourteen indoor servants, including a governess, housekeeper, lady's maid, three house maids, stillroom maid, scullery maid, butler, footman, under butler and page.

On 15th January 1883 Henry Christopher Wise died aged seventy-six and was buried the following Saturday on a beautiful spring morning at All Saints Church. Those invited to join the relatives assembled at Woodcote at noon and the solemn procession wound its way down the long drive, and was reported to be an impressive sight. The coffin was of polished oak and bore the simple inscription on an engraved brass shield "Henry Christopher Wise Esq, born Oct 7th 1806, died Jan 15, 1883". It was borne on a wheeling bier and was covered with wreaths sent by numerous friends. Alongside the family and friends were various VIPs including the Earl of Warwick and Lord Leigh, also male and female domestic servants, labourers from the estate and a number of tenants. The Vicar, The Reverend Francis Cholmondeley, received the procession at the entrance to the churchyard, and Henry Christopher was interred in the family vault. The following vote of condolence was passed at a meeting that evening by members of the Leek Wootton Co-operative Society to Henry Christopher's eldest surviving son. "To George Wise Esq: We, members of the parish of Leek Wootton present at the quarterly meeting of the Co-operative Society, mindful of the many kindnesses received during so many years from the late Mr Wise and his family, and conscious of the loving interest they have also taken in all that might conduce to the welfare of this parish, desire to tell you how sorely we shall miss his kindly presence and good influence amongst us; at the same time we would respectfully assure you how very truly we sympathize with you and Mrs Wise at this sad time. That our Father in heaven may comfort and sustain you with His grace and mercy and that you may be long spared to be venerated and respected amongst us as your father was, shall be our heartfelt prayer. 20th January 1883".

The School Log tells us that on 21st February of that year "Mrs Wise left Woodcote". She took her two young children and returned to the Disbrowe family home, Walton Hall in Derbyshire, to live with her spinster sister, Charlotte, until she died there in 1908. Her son, Eddie Wise, married Katharine Mary Levett-Prinsep in 1896 and Alba married Gilbert Dolben Paul, died in 1959, and is buried in the family vault in the churchyard of All Saints. Her granddaughter recounts that Alba always had a special love for Leek Wootton. Alba's son, Digby Paul, was later to inherit Walton Hall and it is still in the possession of the family today.

George Wise, in his fifties and unmarried, became owner of Woodcote on Henry Christopher's death but he was frequently absent being at his family home in Charlwood, Sussex. During 1885 George presented to the parish a wheeled bier for use at funerals, as a "thank-offering to Almighty God for raising him up from his bed of sickness". The Vicar, in his Almanac, mentions George's "sad bodily affliction" but we know George was a "cheery and popular" character. Since 1876 he had been president of the Leamington and South Warwickshire Cyclists' Club.

In May 1887 the parish celebrated the Jubilee of Queen Victoria and on 25th May "upwards of 250 villagers (from the age of 13) sat down to a substantial dinner of cold meat and plum-puddings (hot and cold) at 4 o'clock in a spacious tent hired for the occasion, erected in the grounds of Woodcote by kind permission of George Wise Esq who was himself not able to be present". All the arrangements had been excellently planned and carried out under the direction of Mr John Nicks of the Stone House, the Churchwarden.

On 4th January 1888 George died at Charlwood at the age of fifty-seven and his body was brought from there to be interred at All Saints in an ordinary grave adjoining the family vault. Mr John Nicks, Agent at Woodcote superintended the funeral arrangements, and once again the cortège started from Woodcote and at the lodge gates was joined by a number of the tenants from Lillington and Warwick. Among the many mourners were H E D Wise, George's half brother Eddie, Mrs Wise, his stepmother Jane, Miss Wise, his half sister Alba, and George Waller, his cousin.

Under the terms of George Wise's will the Warwickshire estates, the London estates and other properties were left to his cousin George of Eaton Square, London, son of Sir Thomas Wathen Waller who had married George's aunt, Catherine Wise.

Jane Pain

7

The Waller Family at Woodcote 1888-1947

In his will, George Wise left Woodcote to his cousin, Major General George H Waller. George Waller was born in 1837 in Brussels, Belgium to Thomas Wathen Waller, a diplomat, and his wife Catherine (née Wise) and when he inherited the estate he was fifty-one years of age and had been married to Beatrice for eighteen years. They had two sons and two daughters, Margaret Beatrice born in 1874, Francis Ernest born in 1880, Wathen Arthur born in 1881 and Edith Sophia born in 1884.

George's grandfather, Sir Jonathan Wathen Waller, inherited the Waller estates from his maternal grandmother's family in 1814 and changed his name from Phipps to Waller. He was granted a form of the ancient Waller coat of arms. He was a fashionable and successful eye surgeon who was called upon in a professional capacity by the Royal Family and was created a baronet in 1815. Sir Jonathan was present at the death of George IV and in fact wrote an account of his death. Waller family history boasts a Sir Richard Waller who, during the reign of Henry V, took Charles, Duke of Orleans, prisoner at the Battle of Agincourt in 1415; a Sir William Waller, General of the Parliamentary Forces during the Civil War; and a Sir Edmund Waller, poet and parliamentarian during the 1600s.

At the age of seventeen George Waller went to fight in the Crimean War and returned home a distinguished hero. An extract from a dispatch from a Colonel of the 7th Fusiliers, dated June 1855, to the Adjutant General, Horseguards states: "The two officers, Waller and L R Browne, cannot be surpassed, that being Waller is the merest child to look at with the heart of a lion. In the repulse of the night attack on the garrison he with three or four men actually followed the column in its retreat, driving them before him by his shouting a long way beyond our lines, and if light had enabled the Moscovites to have seen what they were running from they would have seen a little boy, followed by a few more, which boys any one of them could have held up in one hand. This little fellow came out with the draft last Nov. and has never missed a duty,

Conservative Demonstration & Fete,
AT WOODCOTE PARK,
(By kind permission of General Waller,)

ON SATURDAY, SEPTEMBER 14, 1889.

Programme of Speeches, Sports, Entertainments, &c.

1-0. Admission by Ticket only, price 6d. each.

2-0. THE BAND of the Leamington Town Improvement Association, under the direction of Mr. BIANCHI.

1. ALLEGRO MILITAIRE
2. HUNGARIAN WALTZ.."Donan Wellen"
3. GRAND SELECTION from Verdi's Opera, "Ernani."
4. PIZZICATO GAVOTTE
5. A HUNTING SCENE (Descriptive)
6. RUSSIAN DANSE.."Les Patineurs"
7. NAUTICAL SELECTION.."Life on the Ocean Wave."
8. VOCAL WALTZ.."Little Gleaners"

Songs by Mr. ORCHARD.

2-15. Performance by the BIDFORD MORRIS DANCERS.

2-30. GRAND CRICKET MATCH between GENERAL WALLER'S and COLONEL SWYNFEN JERVIS'S Elevens.

2-45 till 3-45. SPORTS as per List.

4-0. GENERAL WALLER will take the Chair, and introduce VISCOUNT FIELDING and E. MONTAGUE NELSON, Esq., to the Meeting.

LORD FIELDING will move a Vote of Confidence in the Present Administration; which will be Seconded by E. MONTAGUE NELSON, Esq.

P. A. MUNTZ, Esq., M.P., will respond. H. TOWNSEND, Esq., M.P., will also respond, and be followed by BROOKE ROBINSON, Esq., M.P.

SIDNEY FLAVEL, Jun., Esq., J.P., Mayor of Leamington, will move a Vote of Thanks to GENERAL and Mrs. WALLER.

5-30. Continuation of SPORTS, and Exhibition by the BIDFORD MORRIS DANCERS.

6-0 till 8-0. Mr. BIANCHI's Band will play for DANCING.

SPORTS.

100 YARDS VETERANS' RACE,
For men over 45 years of age, for any Member of a Conservative Association or Working Men's Club, or a Member of the Primrose League. Entrance Fee, Sixpence.

150 YARDS RACE.
For men over 35 years of age. Conditions as above. Entrance Fee, Sixpence.

220 YARDS RACE.
For men over 20 years of age. Conditions as above. Entrance Fee, Sixpence.

BOYS' RACE (Open,)
For boys under 20 years of age. Entrance Fee, Threepence.

BOYS' RACE (Open,)
For boys under 14 years of age. Entrance Fee, Threepence.

SACK RACE (Open,) Free.   WHEELBARROW RACE (Open,) Free.

THREE PRIZES will be given for each Race, and the Entrance Money will be proportionately divided amongst the First Three in each Race.

Entries to be made on the Ground at the Secretary's Tent, where a Ticket will be given to each Competitor.

No Competitor will be allowed to take more than ONE FIRST, or TWO PRIZES ALTOGETHER.

Anyone found Betting will be immediately expelled from the grounds.

FIRST CLASS REFRESHMENTS AT MODERATE PRICES SUPPLIED BY Mr. H. MAYCOCK & Mr. B. BISHOP.

Price of Programme, One Penny.

sticking to the trenches during all the bad weather and has been out many a rougher hour. The men all call him 'little Waller' and I hear them telling one another stories of his behaviours. I regret to say that he got a crack on the head at last the other night from the splinter of a shell, it is however not much and he would be at it again if the doctor would allow him, pray make a good mark against this young gents name, he will do a good thing or two some day or I am mistaken."

Sir Thomas Waller, Bart, seated far left; Major General George Waller seated next to his father; Beatrice Waller next to him. Francis Waller in bowler hat, aged 11, in 1891.

George retired from the Army as a Colonel of the 7th Royal Fusiliers and he married Beatrice Katherine Tower, fifth daughter of Christopher Tower and Lady Sophia Tower of Huntsmoor Park in 1870. He inherited Woodcote in 1888, and moved there with his young family. One of the first things he was to do to benefit the people of Leek Wootton was to revive the cricket club. He provided a cricket pitch in the grounds at Woodcote and there were eight matches in 1889. He also "took the Chair" at concerts and penny readings held in the Reading Room. Admission charges for these were 3d for front seats, 2d for second row seats and 1d for back seats. He does not appear to have performed himself but clearly encouraged villagers to do so on the violin and pianoforte, and to sing songs, and give dialogues and readings.

The School Log tells us that both General Waller and Mrs Waller were regular visitors to the school and that cricket at Woodcote continued to be a popular pastime.

In January 1892, at the grand old age of eighty-seven George's father, now Sir Thomas Wathen Waller, Baronet, died and was buried in Leek Wootton churchyard, and George inherited the baronetcy. Sadly this was not for long, for in February of the same year George himself died, and was also buried in Leek Wootton churchyard next to his father, leaving Beatrice a widow with four young children.

In August of the next year Lady Waller, as she now was, once again invited the village schoolchildren to tea at Woodcote for their summer "treat". Miss Waller, together with Miss Wright from Wootton Court, also organised mothers' meetings in the village.

A happy occasion was to "rouse Leek Wootton from its wonted quietude" in July 1895 when Margaret Waller, George and Beatrice's elder daughter, now just twenty-one, married Captain Dennis Granville from Wellesbourne. The local paper reported that "many years have elapsed since a similarly joyous event was celebrated there, and certainly a prettier wedding could not have been imagined than that which united two such well-known and widely respected county families as the Granvilles of Wellesbourne and the owners of Woodcote". The parish church of All Saints was crowded with relatives and friends of the bride and bridegroom and the villagers "with a liberal display of bunting manifested their deep respect and cordial good wishes". The bride looked charming in her costume of white satin with long train, trimmed with chiffon and pearl, her veil being of Brussels lace and her hair adorned with orange blossoms. Bridesmaids were her cousin, Catherine Liddell, Mabel Granville, Dennis's sister, Edith Waller, Margaret's younger sister, and Averil Tower, another cousin. Lord Leigh proposed the toast to the bride and bridegroom and the happy couple went by train to Herefordshire for their honeymoon. The local newspaper listed every guest and wedding present and it is interesting to note that the Leek Wootton Football and Cricket Club gave them a silver tea set; the servants and workmen at Woodcote a silver coffee pot and silver-handled paper knife; cottagers on the Woodcote estate two china vases

Margaret Granville (née Waller), circa 1895

and the Leek Wootton schoolchildren a pair of cut glass scent bottles. Amongst the guests were Lord and Lady Leigh; the Marquis and Marchioness of Hertford; the Earl and Countess of Warwick; Jane, Countess of Aylesford; Lord Willoughby de Broke; Lord and Lady Algernon Percy; Mr and Mrs Fairfax-Lucy; Mr Mrs and the Misses Beresford Wright of Wootton Court; Mr and Mrs Donne from Leek Wootton House; and Mr and Mrs Smith-Ryland. There were many other familiar local names listed.

We read in the Vicar's Almanac for 1896 of "an addition to the east end of the church in memory of her brother" given by Miss Charlotte Louisa Waller, and the next year Lady Waller gave handsome new choirstalls, designed by W D Caroe, in memory of her late husband.

In December 1898 the family was to suffer another sad loss, that of their mother, Beatrice, Lady Waller. This left Sir Francis, aged eighteen, as head of the family. In the Vicar's Almanac we read that "the wise benevolence, ever-ready sympathy, thoughtful considerate kindness of Lady Waller can remain but as a precious memory now with those whose privilege it was to know her goodness". Beatrice was laid to rest in a grave beside her late husband in Leek Wootton churchyard.

The Waller Family at Woodcote 1888-1947

By this time the young Sir Francis Waller had finished his schooling at Harrow and had started his army training at Sandhurst. His younger brother, Wathen, was to follow in his footsteps.

The Boer War broke out in 1899 in South Africa and young Sir Francis left to fight with the Royal Fusiliers. His departure must have caused his younger sister, Edith, much sadness, as they were very close but he wrote numerous letters home to her from South Africa and Edith recorded them all in a journal. One such letter described in graphic detail the Battle of Colenso and was written from Chievely Camp on 16th December 1899.

It was not until Saturday 12th April 1902 that Leek Wootton was to welcome the young Squire back from the War "well recovered to all appearances from his wound". The church bells rang out and the village was gay with flags. More celebrations were to occur on 11th June when Sir Francis kept his coming of age and many were invited to enjoy his hospitality. Sadly, he was not to stay in Leek Wootton long as his career in the Army called him away and so later that year the house, grounds and land were let to Captain J Morrow for five years and The Rock became the family home. During 1903-4 the garden was enlarged by the inclusion and planting of grassland between the old north boundary of the garden down to the pools. Dicksons of Chester carried this out under the supervision of Mr Goldring of Kew Gardens. In 1905 Sir Francis left England once again with his regiment to serve in India, leaving the "kindly" tenants at Woodcote.

In 1908 Sir Francis retired from the Army because he felt it was his duty to live among his own people and take up what he thought to be his position in the county. He returned to Woodcote as a principal landowner, Patron of the living of Lillington church and lord of the manor. Sir Francis was one who thought more of the duties of his position than of any privilege it might bring him. The Vicar of Lillington wrote that "Time and again he was keen to offer his hospitality for the tenants and the children at the Christmas party, and his special charm was his personal touch. Nothing was too much trouble: he would go to the school and ask the children, and you could see him going from cottage to cottage inviting the elders, and when the day arrived there he would be from early afternoon until 9 or 10, chatting and making the thing go its very best. It was the same at the School Treat. He would hurry home to meet his guests, everything was carefully and generously thought out, a cricket ground and race-course prepared, and himself there all the while, starting races, and taking tea with the guests. And the prizes! He and his sister, Miss Waller were splendid. Duty to him meant a great deal and what was to be done was worth doing well. Beyond this, he was so unaffected and frank that he delighted in seeing the people happy and tried to make them more so. He was a man of few words and high principle."

Sir Francis Waller

Sir Francis became a magistrate, Deputy Lieutenant of Warwickshire, and in 1913 he held the second position in the county, that of High Sheriff. The officials spoke of his unfailing courtesy, the judges found him pleasant, conscientious, careful and diligent.

Over the years various parcels of land had been added to the estate. In 1893 the quarry field and cottages in the field on the main road were purchased from Lord Algernon Percy, and which had formerly belonged to Earl Clarendon. In 1908 land to the east of Terrace Hill Wood was purchased from the Vicar of Leek Wootton (glebeland) and also land to the south-east of the same wood from Beresford Wright (Wootton Court), and both were added to the farm.

Sir Francis Waller had two new cottages built in the paddock near Park Gardens about 1908, which we know today as Sunnyside Cottages (now off Home Farm). He had two more built in 1912 opposite the allotments near Woodcote Lane (now Honeysuckle Cottage and The Conifers).

On 24th July 1914 we read in the School Log that Sir Francis visited the school and invited the children to his annual tea party at Woodcote, and on 28th October "A War Office Telegram announcing the death of Sir Francis Waller Bart who was killed in action on Sunday 25th October cast a deep gloom upon the children". He was only 34. What a dreadful day for his sister Edith, who lived with him. A Leek Wootton child of ten remarked to her mother, when told that Sir Francis was dead "I am so glad I have got something to remember him by, the prize he gave me last July". A memorial service was held at Lillington church, where he was Patron, and also in Leek Wootton when the Vicar, The Reverend Edward Riley, officiated at a simple and impressive service in a full church. It was said of Sir Francis that the foundation of his character lay in his religion and he had that great blessing, a good mother. There was not an atom of pride or conceit about him. He was equally friendly with rich and poor. Sir Francis hated loafers. He could not understand why Warwickshire people were so fond of playing bowls rather than cricket.

Wathen Waller, brother of Sir Francis, inherited Woodcote and the baronetcy. He, too, had been educated at Harrow and Sandhurst, and served in the 5th Fusiliers from 1900 to 1905. He married Viola le Suer, who was from South Africa, in 1904. He soon took up his parochial duties and we read in the School Log that in January 1915 "a tea party was given in the School by Sir Wathen Waller, Baronet, of Woodcote and was followed by a magic lantern entertainment, which the children thoroughly enjoyed. Presents of various kinds were given at the close".

At the outbreak of the First World War Wathen had joined the Buffs, served with distinction and was awarded his triple stars in June 1916. In March 1919 he resigned his commission and devoted himself to public work. He was made a Deputy Lieutenant for Warwickshire in 1923 and served on the County Council and on Warwick Rural District Council. He was also a JP. Sir Wathen was a member of the Warwickshire and Leamington Divisional Conservative Association and also a member of Leamington Cricket Club and served as President at one time. In Leek Wootton Sir Wathen served for many years as Churchwarden at All Saints and was an active member of the Church Council. He was also Patron of the living at Lillington. He was President of the Leek Wootton Working Men's Club, the British Legion, the Horticultural Society and the Sports Club.

Sir Wathen had inherited considerable property holdings in London, which required management and attention. He was also a great collector of old deeds and documents pertaining to lands owned by the Wallers, Wises and other families in the general area around Warwick, Leamington, Leek Wootton, Kenilworth and of their London properties, dating back to the 13th and 14th Centuries. He spent a great deal of time in 1928 and 1929 recording much of this information from approximately seven hundred and sixty deeds and numerous other manuscripts into two bound books which contain some excellent information on the passage of land by death, marriage settlements, etc and the names and dates of the individuals involved in a chronological order.

In 1916, 136 acres of farmland belonging to Woodcote was let to E P Cattell, from The Elms, who worked the land until his death in 1943 when it was let to Tom Edgar, who purchased The Elms in the same year. Houses owned by Sir Wathen continued to be let to various tenants, i e The Rock, the Anchor Inn, and The Stone House. Areas of paddock and grounds were bought and added to The Stone House garden and the house was let to various tenants, including Captain G D Paul, from 1921-1926, and Commander Herbert, 1937-1939.

In 1927 Frank Graley came to Leek Wootton to work for Sir Wathen as a general handyman/odd job man. At the outbreak of War in 1914, at the age of eighteen, Frank had joined up and went to fight in France where he was captured and spent three years as a prisoner of war. When he arrived at Woodcote he joined a considerable staff working on the estate. The head gardener was Mr London who lived at the Front Lodge and he had four assistant gardeners under him, George Court, Albert Edwards, George Terry and Frank Bedding. The gamekeeper was Christopher Corby and there were two woodmen, Brown and Garrett. John Hobbins was waggoner with his horse Dobbin. The estate carpenter was Arthur Marriott and the chauffeur, who lived in the Back Lodge, was William Hayes. Later Ted Timmins became chauffeur. Indoors there were the butler, Albert Flood; the footmen; the cook, Mrs Bowie; kitchen maids;

Frank Graley

Christopher Corby

Helen Scott Collection

scullery maids and house maids. Hetty Lively worked in the house and was to continue as lady's maid until Lady Waller's death. Frank Grayley's duties included stoking the coke boiler and maintaining the ram, which was used for the supply of water to the house from a reservoir on the farm. Sometimes he helped the butler, cleaned the windows and exercised Sir Wathen's dog, Kim. He would also push Lady Waller around in her bathchair when she was unwell. Frank was provided with a cottage on the estate where he lived with his wife, Elizabeth, his son and two daughters. They received free skimmed milk and kindling wood; a large joint of beef at Christmas and his wages were something like 38 shillings a week. His working day was from 7 in the morning to 8 in the evening, but he did go home for breakfast, 'dinner' and evening meal. Frank was a member of the village branch of the British Legion, the Working Men's Club and the Sports Club. He was for many years a keen cricket umpire.

Other cottages were occupied by workers on the Woodcote estate. A line of cottages on Warwick Road opposite the old school were demolished in 1935 and three new ones, Rock Cottages, built in the gardens further back from the road. Two new cottages were built in 1926 on land adjoining those built by Sir Francis near to Woodcote Lane (Quarry Cottages), which were first occupied by E Brown and G Terry.

With the outbreak of the Second World War in 1939 Sir Wathen lent Woodcote to the Red Cross for use as a convalescent home, which was run by a matron called Miss Powlett. He and Lady Waller moved into The Stone House in 1940, giving up their large staff and making do with only a lady's maid, gardener, butler and chauffeur. Lady Waller worked very hard for the Red Cross during the War organising fund-raising events and supervising the knitting of balaclavas, socks, gloves, stockings etc for the troops.

The Waller Family at Woodcote 1888-1947

In 1946 Sir Wathen sold six of his cottages in the village along with the Anchor Inn. Ivy Cottage and Gypsy Cottage were among those sold. Ivy Cottage, which was built in the 17th Century or earlier, had been occupied by the Weston family since the 1860s and Henry Weston's daughter, Mary Clark, together with her husband, Joe, were the tenants. Joe Clark was a native of Westmorland and was the village molecatcher. He would often be seen returning home with a yoke over his shoulder with the moles hanging on it. They would be skinned and hung on the washing line to dry and he would sell the pelts to be made into waistcoats. Joe died in 1962 and Mary in 1974, after which the cottage changed hands and was extended.

After the War, Sir Wathen was refurbishing Woodcote ready to return, but in April 1947 he died suddenly at The Stone House. He was buried in the churchyard of All Saints alongside his father and grandfather.

Joe Clark

At about this time Frank Graley and Arthur Marriott were clearing out the Woodcote cellars when they discovered chests full of old and blackened Wise family silver, which had probably been lying abandoned there since the 1880s.

Village Cottages, 1914

In 1948 Lady Waller sold the house, grounds, and allotment gardens of Woodcote to Warwickshire County Council and, following conversion, it became the Headquarters of the Warwickshire County Constabulary in 1949. Frank Graley stayed

Sir Wathen Waller with his niece Judith standing to his left, and her husband, George Cole

on in his house as an employee of the police until his retirement in 1966. He had always loved Woodcote, even when sleeping there, on his own, during the post-war refurbishment. Frank died in 1967.

Lady Viola lived on at The Stone House until she died in 1962 and after her death Barry and Audrey Gillitt bought the house.

As Sir Wathen and Lady Viola were childless, the baronetcy was inherited by a cousin, Edmund Waller who died in 1954, then by another cousin, John Waller who died without issue in 1995, after which it became extinct.

A frequent visitor to Woodcote during the early 1900s was Judith Margaret Granville, only child of Captain Dennis Granville and Margaret, sister of Francis and Wathen. Judith was the only issue of all the children of George Waller and was a favourite of Wathen. She married George Cole and emigrated to Canada in 1930, and when John Waller died without issue, all the family papers, deeds and letters were inherited by their children.

Jane Pain

<u>Minutes of The Parish Council:</u>

"Proposed ... that the Parish Council send a vote of condolence to Miss Waller in consequence of the death of Sir Francis E Waller Bart. Who fell on Oct. 25th leading his regiment against the German Army."

Monday, 2nd November 1914

8

The Farms of Woodloes, Middle Woodloes and North Woodloes

Loes Grange

In 1709 Henry Wise bought the Priory Estate which included the farms of South, Middle and North Woodloes. In 1732 this property was settled on Matthew Wise, one of Henry's sons, and there is a deed of that date detailing: 'Woodlows House' and all the fields in or near 'Woodlows', 136 acres in the occupation of Wm Barnett, and also 'Woodcott' in the parish of Leek Wootton, comprising two "messuages, the Woodhouse and Whitehouse Farms, 223 acres in the occupation of Jn Nicholls".

All this land was, therefore, owned by the Wise family and later inherited by the Waller family, but always tenanted. Woodloes Farm is outside the parish boundary but is so involved with this story that it must be extensively referred to.

Between 1758 and 1760 a long hedge was planted from the great pool at Goodrest southwards for a mile and a half between the Wise estate and Wedgnock Park.

North Woodloes Farm

In the early 1700s North Woodloes Farm appears to have been separate from Woodlows and was in two parts, Woodhouse Farm and Whitehouse Farm. Woodhouse Farm was later to be known as North Woodloes Farm, now part of The Warwickshire clubhouse and course. The Whitehouse Farm was situated where North Woodloes Cottages and a barn later stood. These have completely gone but were located on the high ground between the 3rd and 9th tees of the North Course. The remainder of the land went with this farm. Between 1750 and 1800 the farms together became known as North Woodloes Farm and the tithe apportionment of 1846 refers to 357 acres representing the whole of North Woodloes Farm, and that part of Middle Woodloes Farm which lay within the then parish of Leek Wootton. The owner is given as The Reverend Henry Wise, Vicar of Offchurch, and the occupiers as T Cook and J M Ledbrook. By 1875 the tenants were Ann Ledbrook, now a widow, with Thomas and John Stanley Ledbrook, her sons, who also occupied South and Middle Woodloes Farms. In 1897 Thomas and John Stanley Ledbrook gave up North Woodloes Farm and it was taken over by P H Eykyn. In 1926 North Woodloes Farm was let to I Dodd.

Middle Woodloes Farm

A lease of 1684 refers to Middle Woodloes Farm being let to Samuel Mallory, and a survey of 1711 shows that he was still the tenant, but by 1732 Richard Smith farmed the 191 acres. By the early 1800s the tenant was William Birch and afterwards the tenants were T Cook and J M Ledbrook, together with North Woodloes Farm, see above. The Ledbrook family farmed Middle Woodloes Farm, together with Woodloes Farm, until 1917 when it was let to J F Lucas.

Woodloes Farm

Dugdale tells us that in the time of Henry I the Earl of Warwick gave The Woodloes to his cook, Richard, and from his son, Alan, descended the family of Woodlow. Eventually it came into the hands of the Brome family, Ralph, John, Nicholas and Robert, the latter occupying the lands in 1656. Ralph Brome erected the house in 1562. By 1711 the tenant was William Barnett together with 130 acres. In 1757 the farm was occupied by John Birch and in 1802 by Thomas Birch together with 143 acres. In 1854 the tenant was J M Ledbrook, followed after his death by his widow and sons, with a total of 533 acres including North and Middle Woodloes Farms, see above. Woodloes Farm, together with Middle Woodloes Farm, was let to J F Lucas in 1917.

Details of the Ledbrook family are recorded on a table tomb in the churchyard of All Saints. John Murcott Ledbrook died in 1875 aged 55 and his wife Ann lived on at Woodloes Farm until 1893 when she died aged 72. Mary Goule their daughter died in 1889 aged 40. Their son Thomas died in 1929 aged 77 and John Stanley died in 1933 aged 79. In his will John Stanley Ledbrook left to the Vicar and Churchwardens of Leek Wootton the sum of £500 towards the cost of a new pulpit to be erected in memory of his late mother. He also left money for the benefit of the poor of the parish and towards the upkeep of the family grave.

Despite the name, before 1850 there was very little woodland on any of the Woodloes farms. The original Terrace Hill Wood consisted of just a strip of trees along the western boundary called Shut Lane. At the northern end of the farmlands, near the

Cattle Brook, were two small plantations called The Knob and The Jutty. Between 1850 and 1900 Terrace Hill Wood was extended to about thirty acres taking farmland from North Woodloes Farm, Nine Acre Plantation was extended by seven acres, Gostee Spinney was extended to seven acres and Fox Covert was extended to about eight acres.

After the Second World War Sir Wathen Waller decided to sell the farms, which comprised the 500 hundred or so acres of land stretching from the canal in Warwick northwards up to Woodcote Park, which Henry Wise had bought in 1709 and had been inherited by the Waller family. At Woodloes Farm was an Elizabethan stone-built house with extensive outbuildings, and Middle Woodloes Farm comprised an ancient half timber, stone and brick built farmhouse which had been converted into three cottages, together with two modern cottages. The farm buildings included two yards with a six bay open-fronted shed. North Woodloes Farm comprised the stone-built farmhouse, farm buildings and two cottages adjoining the Nine Acre Plantation. George Corson had farmed the 200 acres of North Woodloes Farm since 1937 and Sir Wathen offered to sell the farm to him. John Lanc had farmed the 300 hundred acres at Woodloes Farm and Middle Woodloes Farm since 1932 and Sir Wathen also offered those farms to him. All of the farms were eventually sold at auction on 22nd March 1946 to the Sir Thomas White Charity for the sum of £17,000.

In 1952 Stanley Hattrell, a solicitor, acquired the freehold of all 500 acres from the Sir Thomas White Charity, and in the same year Aubrey Jones, a builder, purchased Wootton Court together with approximately 126 acres of the land. In the 1960s Messrs Hattrell and Jones bought the Woodcote Park land, with Tom Edgar as the tenant. John Lane continued to farm Woodloes Farm, with Middle Woodloes Farm, and in the 1960s Gordon Williams became the tenant of North Woodloes Farm. After the death of Tom Edgar, Gordon Williams also farmed the western half of Woodcote and Aubrey Jones farmed the eastern half. Mr Williams continued to farm until the late 1980s when he moved from the North Woodloes Farmhouse to Gaveston Wood Cottages.

Wootton Court was the Jones family home until the early 1970s when they moved to Sunrise Cottage and thence to Mulberry Cottage, Stone Edge. In 1973 M J K Smith the Warwickshire County and England Cricketer developed and ran Wootton Court as a country club, whilst the Jones family continued to farm the land.

Aubrey Jones envisaged the combined farmland as being suitable for a golf course and had approached Peter Alliss the well-known golf professional to undertake a feasibility study. However, it was not until the late 1980s, after Aubrey Jones's death that a sale was agreed whereby North Woodloes Farm, Wootton Court and the Woodcote Park land would be sold and developed as a course. Colin Snape of Snape Golf Consultancy, together with Golf Fund plc, acquired the site and The Warwickshire was opened in 1994 by Michael Bonallack OBE, Secretary of the Royal & Ancient Golf Club of St Andrews. The courses and ancilliary facilities cover an area of approximately 480 acres from Cattle Brook in the north to the boundary with Middle Woodloes Farm in the south. An entrance and driveway was created off a new roundabout on the Warwick Road near to Wootton Court just south of the village.

The three cottages at Middle Woodloes have been converted back into one attractive farmhouse, now Loes Grange, and the farm buildings were converted into two separate homes (Woodloes Barn and Covert Hall). The two modern cottages have been further modernised and extended.

The farm at Woodloes continues to exist but, as said earlier, is outside the parish although part of its lands may be within the boundary.

The properties in the area now referred to as North Woodloes, just off the main road close to the Blacklow roundabout and to the south of the village, were part of the Wootton Court estate.

Jane Pain

Minutes of the Parish Council:

"A paper issued by the Board of Agriculture & Fisheries respecting the formation of Sparrow Clubs was read. ... Proposed ... that the Sparrow Club be revived and subscriptions be invited for its support."

Tuesday, 7th December 1915

"In answer to a letter about the destruction of rats and sparrows, it was considered that the work is progressing satisfactorily in the Parish."

Friday, 12th January 1917

"Rats & Sparrows. Owing to the great amount of damage done in the parish by these pests ... proposed ... that the Clerk ask if the Parish Council can spend any money to help to destroy them.

"Rats killed during threshing were barred, but others were to be paid 1d per tail and sparrows, 4d a dozen."

Wednesday, 4th December 1918

Minutes of The Parish Council:

"A paper from Warwickshire County Council respecting 'Injurious Weeds Order' was read at the meeting."

Friday, 19th September 1924

By direction of Sir Wathen A. Waller, Bart., D.L., J.P.

IN THE BOROUGH OF WARWICK
and PARISH OF LEEK WOOTTON

•

Particulars, Plans and Conditions of Sale

of

VALUABLE TITHE AND LAND TAX FREE

FREEHOLD PROPERTIES

comprising

The Woodloes and Middle Woodloes Farms

with an **interesting Elizabethan Residence**

North Woodloes Farm

Fully-licensed Premises, "The Anchor Inn"

and

Six Cottages in Leek Wootton Village

Total Area, 536a. 0r. 32p. or thereabouts

in Five Lots.

TO BE SOLD BY AUCTION, BY

EDWARDS, SON & BIGWOOD & MATHEWS

AT THE COURT HOUSE, WARWICK
ON FRIDAY, MARCH 22nd, 1946
at 2-30 p.m. precisely.

•

Solicitors: Messrs. CAMPBELL, BROWN & LEDBROOK, 26 Jury Street, Warwick.
Land Agents: Messrs. WALTER P. EVANS & CO., 19 Eaton Road, Coventry.

AUCTIONEERS' OFFICES:
158 EDMUND STREET, BIRMINGHAM 3.

PRICE 6d.

Auction Particulars, 1946

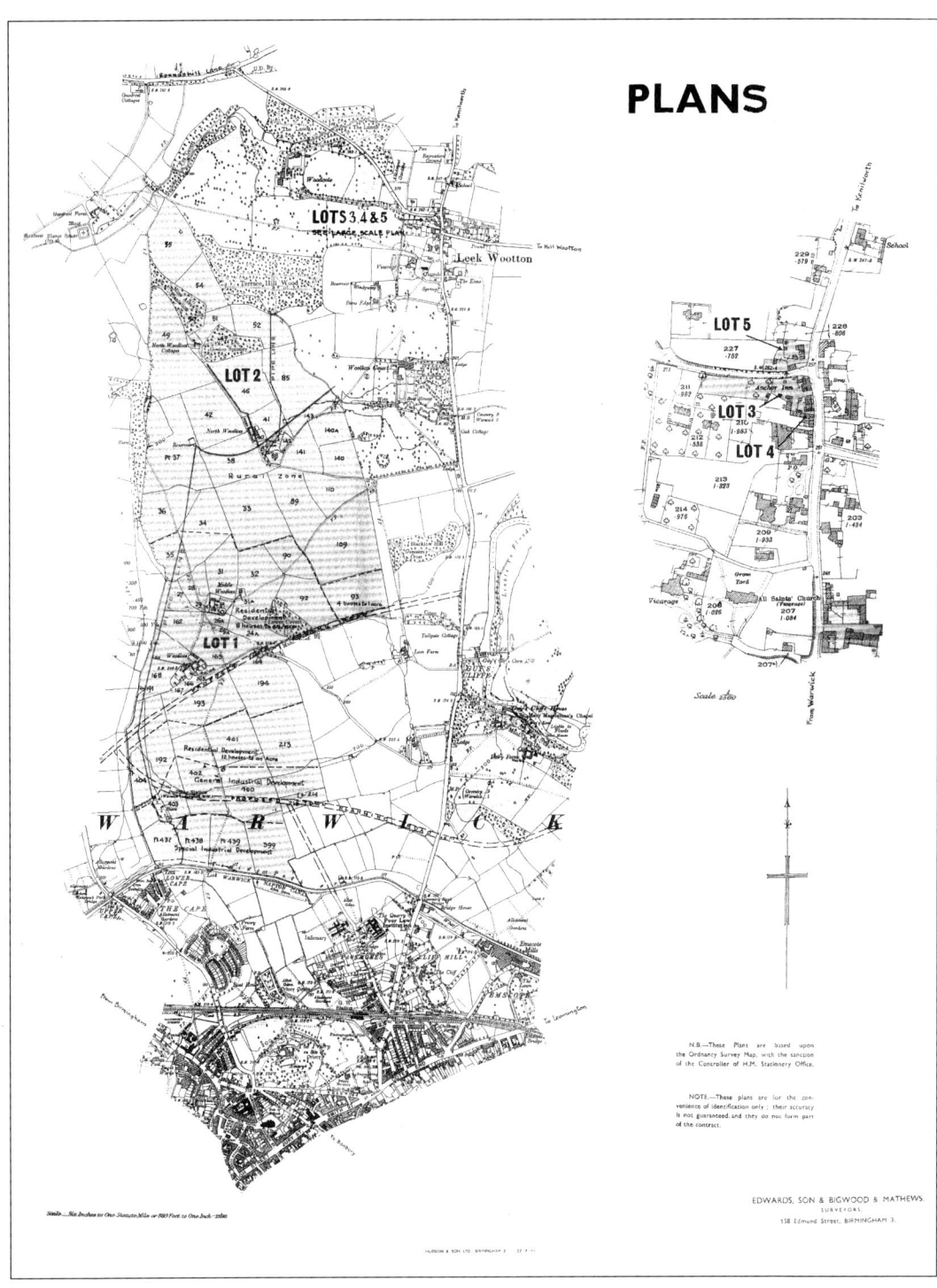

Auction Particulars, 1946

9

Wootton Grange and Broad Lane Caravans

Wootton Grange

Wootton Grange, on the northern boundary of Leek Wootton, has a long and interesting history having been a monastic property prior to 1536, probably owned by the Canons of the Abbey founded at Kenilworth by Augustinian monks in 1126-27. Indeed, in 1279 the Prior of Kenilworth was one of the four lords of Wootton, his portion being Cross Grange (by which name the farm was also known). The original parts of the house, dating from around 1547, could well be some of the oldest still existing in the parish. Following the Dissolution of the Monasteries by Henry VIII it was occupied for some years by Andrew Flamocke and his wife Elizabeth, and was purchased by Sir Thomas Leigh in 1561.

Parish records show that Thomas Winter and his wife Ann lived at Wootton Grange and had many children between 1693 and 1716. Thomas died in 1729 and his son Daniel, born in 1698, took over the farm in 1730. Daniel lived there with his family until his death in 1777 and in his will he left the interest of £200 to be paid yearly for the support of the school of the parish of Leek Wootton "for augmentation of the salary of the schoolmaster". The £200, and annual interest, was secured upon the tolls arising from the turnpike road from Stonebridge to Kenilworth. This endowment is now lost.

In the upper part of the tower of All Saints Church, on the south side, is an impressive memorial to Thomas and Ann Winter and their children with the inscription: "Blessed are the dead that die in the Lord". During alterations to the church in the time of The Reverend Frederick Leigh Colvile the graves of the Winter family were built over when the new chancel was constructed. This memorial was erected in place of the head and foot stones.

Following Daniel Winter's death the Burbury family lived at Wootton Grange and we read of many children being born to Thomas and Martha Burbury from 1783 to 1799. By 1822 parish records tell us that John, born in 1796, son of Thomas and Martha, and Ellen Burbury are now living at Wootton Grange. The records also show that they had children born between 1820 and 1832. John was Churchwarden at All Saints in the 1840s, donated a lime tree when they were planted in the churchyard in 1843, and gave £5 towards the new organ.

At All Saints Church we find two stained-glass windows in memory of Ellen Burbury, daughter of John and Ellen, who died in 1849 aged twenty-eight and of Elizabeth who died in 1841 aged twenty-one. There is also a memorial on the north wall of the church to Daniel Winter Burbury who died in 1857, another son of Thomas and Martha born in 1787, his wife Harriet and their only child Thomas who died in 1825 aged two months. In his will Daniel Winter Burbury left money stating "…whereas I am desirous of leaving a sum of money in aid of the funds for the support

By Direction of Messrs. Silk Brothers

Particulars with Plan of

"WOOTTON GRANGE FARM"
IN THE PARISH OF LEEK WOOTTON
KENILWORTH   WARWICKSHIRE

A MOST CONVENIENTLY SITUATED FERTILE ARABLE & STOCK REARING FARM IN A PRIME LOCATION

— equally suited for dairying —

comprising

2 EXCELLENT INDEPENDENT INDIVIDUAL CHARACTER HOMES EACH WITH GOOD FAMILY ACCOMMODATION

COMPREHENSIVE RANGES OF MODERN & TRADITIONAL FARM BUILDINGS
including Cattle Sheds, Dutch Barns, Milking Parlour, Dairy, Implement Stores, Grain Storage, Drying and Handling Equipment for approximately 200 TONS

PRODUCTIVE LEVEL ARABLE AND SOUND RICH PASTURE LAND including SMALL SPINNEY

225 ACRES

To be offered for sale by public auction — IN 6 INTERESTING LOTS AS DETAILED HEREIN — UNLESS PREVIOUSLY SOLD AS A WHOLE
With Vacant Possession and Subject to the Special and General Conditions as referred to herein
AT THE CASTLE SUITE OF THE DE MONTFORT HOTEL, KENILWORTH, at 6.30 p.m. on TUESDAY 10th MAY, 1983

Vendors' Solicitors
BRINDLEY TWIST TAFFT & JAMES, 3 THE QUADRANT, COVENTRY CV1 2DY (Ref JW) — Telephone: (0203) 51831 Telex: 312343 BTTJ G

AUCTIONEER
CHARLES R. PHILLIPS F.S.V.A.
For CHARLES R. PHILLIPS LIMITED
VALUERS, SURVEYORS, ESTATE AND LAND AGENTS

48 HIGH STREET, HENLEY-IN-ARDEN
SOLIHULL, WEST MIDLANDS B95 5AN
Tel: HENLEY-IN-ARDEN (05642) 4331/2
ALSO AT BANBURY BICESTER WARWICK AND STRATFORD UPON AVON

Auction Particulars, Wootton Grange Farm, 1983

of a School at Leek Wootton in the County of Warwick for the education of poor children there originally endowed by Daniel Winter ... £200 in 3 per cent Consolidated Annuities".

Below the altar step is a pavement given by John Burbury of Wootton Grange in memory of his father and mother, John and Ellen, which would have been laid in 1889 when the chancel was altered. This son John was born in 1826 to John and Ellen and continued to occupy Wootton Grange, with his wife Anne, breeding Warwickshire Longhorn cattle. He died in 1907.

The Georgian wing of the house, which was built at right angles to the original part, is believed to have been added around 1790. This was followed by the erection of a six-bay brick barn. In 1830 the wagon hovel in the farmyard was built, in 1850 the coach house, granary, bake and brew houses, whey pit and pigsties, and in 1858 the barn in Ancorns Field, near the pond. Wootton Grange Cottages, situated to the northern edge of the village, were built to house workers on the farm and have the date of 1866 on the front wall.

In 1906 the farm was the home of Madely Burman, a Shire horse breeder who, it is believed, was a founder of the NFU Insurance Company. His name appears in Parish Council records from 1902 until 1910. In 1916 the tenancy of the farm passed to the Silk family who were breeders of Large White pigs. In 1920 mains water was connected, in 1922 a telephone line was installed and in 1946 electricity was put in. Arthur Silk died in 1931 and in 1956 the freehold was purchased by his widow, Edith, and her sons Oswald and Edwin from Lord Leigh when he sold his interest, bringing to an end nearly four hundred years of Leigh ownership.

In 1971 the Silk family divided the original Elizabethan house and the later Georgian wing into two separate homes and undertook considerable restoration, particularly to the Elizabethan part. A fire basket for the inglenook in the main living room was made up from old bits and pieces collected from around the farm, and oil-fired central heating was installed.

In 1983 the whole farm of 225 acres, including the two homes, was sold by auction and in 1985 the barns and outbuildings adjacent to the two houses (Wootton Grange House and Wootton Grange Farmhouse) were sold off separately to be developed subsequently into separate dwellings as we see them today (The Byre, Coach House and Moo-Cow Cottage).

The Wootton Grange farmland is now owned and used by a number of different people.

Minutes of The Parish Council:

"A letter from Warwickshire War Agricultural Committee was read ... The Clerk was instructed to write that all farms in the parish are in a high state of cultivation and all gardens and allotments are let and being worked to their utmost capacity.

"A committee had been previously been [sic] called together in the parish to help cultivation by distributing the funds of the Parish Flower & Vegetable Show to procure labour for soldiers serving at the War."

Friday, 30th March 1917

Towards the southern end of the farm, adjoining Cattle Brook where it passes under the main road is a narrow valley. A very small part of this, 0.15 of an acre, has been occupied for many years by various woodmen. In 1938 approval was given to Lord Leigh for the establishment of a sawmill on the land. Today this area is still used for logging timber cut from the farms and woodland.

Broad Lane Caravans

Like Wootton Grange, a corridor of land in the valley alongside Cattle Brook of approximately three acres, was part of the Leigh estate, but was deemed unsuitable for agricultural use. It appears however to have had a varied history despite this. In the early years of the 19th Century there were allotments, and at one time a sheep dip. At some time before the Second World War there was a café run from a small building on the site by a Mrs Stacey who later married John Hobbins the waggoner from Woodcote.

From the findings of Lord Denning, Master of the Rolls, in a landmark Court of Appeal case in 1962, we learn that from 1926 to 1942 there was one residential caravan on the part of the land nearest to the road. In 1942 Coventry Steel Caravans Ltd was bombed out of its premises in Coventry and moved to Leek Wootton, and Clifford Dawtrey the Chief Designer, who was a renowned pioneer in the development of caravans, lived on and worked from the site. Mr Dawtrey is remembered for having entered into the life of the village at this time, helping to stage 'entertainments' at the WI Hut.

From the time of the arrival of Clifford Dawtrey and Coventry Steel Caravans Ltd the site was used for the repair, storage and sale of caravans and a timber prefabricated bungalow was used for a security man and his family.

In 1952, following the introduction of planning legislation, Coventry Steel Caravans Ltd sought to retain the residential bungalow and permission was given for this until December 1954 and subsequently extended until December 1956. In 1955, when Lord Leigh sold his interest in the land, it was a Mr Leonard Henry Miller-Mead

Site of Broad Lane Caravans, circa 1960

who purchased the freehold and from this time residential caravans began to appear on the site. There was one in 1955, two in 1959 and by 1960 there were four. These were not permitted and although Mr Miller-Mead was granted annual extensions to the permission for the residential bungalow, his applications for use of the site for residential caravans were always refused. In 1960 legislation was introduced allowing sites used for residential caravans to automatically be given a licence after four years use, but Warwick Rural District Council served an enforcement notice before the end of 1960 to stop this use on the site.

Extensive legal argument ensued which culminated in the Court of Appeal case in December 1962 when it was determined that the site had a long established right to be used for repair, storage and sale of caravans but residential use, in the Green Belt, was not allowed. The expansion of the use on to the land to the rear of the site was permitted by way of general development rights.

The bungalow was eventually abandoned, in about 1967, and fell into disrepair. Leonard Henry Miller-Mead continued to live in a permanent caravan on the site and his son, Richard Leonard, and his wife and three children, lived in another 'mobile home'. Jonathon Miller-Mead, one of the children, recalls living there and attending the village school before the family left in 1975.

In the early 1970s John Perkins who traded as Broad Lane Caravans in Broad Lane, Coventry bought the site from the Miller-Mead family and transferred his business to the village, although Richard Leonard Miller-Mead continued the storage of caravans and living at the rear of the site. In 1976 Colin and Jack Brown, who were already trading in caravans on a site near Daventry, bought the business from John Perkins and retained the name. Eventually the storage business was taken over by the Brown family and from the two bases they expanded the business, acquiring further sites and other businesses.

Broad Lane Leisure is now run from sites in Leek Wootton, Rugby, Alcester and Daventry. It is still a family business and Colin's son, Stephen, now manages the Leek Wootton site. Although the family has never lived in the village Steve made friends in the village as a boy, played on the recreation ground, and he and his wife chose to marry at All Saints in 1995.

Jane Pain and Paul Eldridge

<u>*Minutes of The Parish Council*</u>:

"A circular from Messrs Merryweather & Co offering to tender for the supply of a fire engine was discussed."

Thursday, 26th January 1905

"<u>Correspondence</u>: ... a letter from Kenilworth Fire Brigade giving their scale of charges outside the Urban District of Kenilworth."

Monday, 28th January 1924

"In consequence of surrounding towns deciding not to allow their fire engines to enter the parish in case of fire ... were appointed to represent this Parish at a General District Meeting at Warwick Board Room on the 20th inst."

Monday, 15th September 1930

10

Wootton Paddox

The village property now known as Wootton Paddox was previously The Vicarage and in the earliest parish register, in an entry of 1606, evidence of a parsonage house is to be found with a terrier* of glebe land and possessions belonging to the Vicar of "Leekewootton", The Reverend Nicholas Langrishe. This record mentions a mansion house with convenient barns for corn and hay with the benefit of the churchyard, orchard, adjoining croft and several fields. In these early days the parsonage was in fact a farm in miniature and the parson not only farmed his own glebe but also probably trundled round in his own cart to collect his tithes. A later terrier taken at the Bishop's Visitation in 1824 describes a mansion house, barn, farmyard, stable, garden and orchard etc, eighty-two acres of glebe land contiguous to the house with twenty-one acres in the hamlet of Hill Wootton. Little seemed to have changed over two centuries.

In 1824 the patron, Mr John Henry Leigh, presented the living to his kinsman, Sir Henry Dryden, Baronet, of Canons Ashby and he saw that the small vicarage which faced east towards the churchyard might be made into a fine country place. He pulled down much of it, forming a new south-facing front with views over the garden, enlarged the outbuildings and created a walled garden. This was a large undertaking, as there were cottages, a school house and farm buildings surrounding the

---

* A book in which the lands of a private person, or of a corporation civil or ecclesiastical, are described by site, boundaries, acreage, etc.

old parsonage that had to be cleared away, adding to the expense of the project. A borrowing was made upon the living and this was finally paid off in 1849. In 1842 a successor, The Reverend Frederick Leigh Colvile, also a Leigh family kinsman further enlarged the house, adding the library to the west end, with quarters for a butler.

An undated story entered into the Colvile manuscript history of the village reads: "In the middle of the Vicarage garden stood in former days a summer house built of stone (beneath which was a cellar) where three noble cavalier lords (friends of The Reverend Robert Mills, then Vicar of the parish) used to meet and carouse and drink to the memory of 'the little man in velvet', meaning by this the mole on whose hill King William III's horse stumbled and broke his royal rider's collarbone, which was ultimately the cause of death. One stone of this summerhouse still remains." The Reverend Robert Mills was Vicar from 1754-1767.

Legislation during the 19th Century was to change much for rural clergy. An Act of 1836 commuted all lay and ecclesiastical tithes into rent charges so that the parson could receive his due without the centuries-old squabbles that had attended the collection of tithe in kind. He could now look forward to an income in cash rather than haggling over the runt of a litter or the tenth and most maggoty pound of apples. In 1838 clergy were forbidden to take a farm of more than eighty acres without their bishop's permission, although they could still cultivate their own glebe. Clergy tended more and more to rent out the glebe, only retaining enough land to provide fodder for their own horses. In this way an age-old link with the land was being broken and the farming parson was disappearing.

The Vicarage continued to be occupied by Vicars and their families, The Reverends Cholmondeley, Riley, Longland, Etches, and Ryecart, until in 1953 it was

The Vicarage, circa 1910
Helen Scott Collection

sold by the diocese to Mr William C Harris for £5,000 and a new modern vicarage was built at the top of Hill Wootton Road on land which was formerly part of the garden to Leek Wootton House. Mr Harris, an estate agent, was Chairman of the Horticultural Society, a PCC member, a School Manager and a Rural District Councillor. After his sudden death in 1973 Wootton Paddox, as it was by now known, was bought by a Mr McCaughey, a builder, who added the swimming pool, enlarged the stables and built a cottage. Mr Hamilton Bland, England swimming coach and entrepreneur occupied the property after this and in 1986 Mr Quinton Hazel, later Sir Quinton Hazel an industrialist and entrepreneur bought it. Mr and Mrs Martin Clive-Smith purchased Wootton Paddox in 1995 and they are currently making further major changes to their home.

Jane Pain

Minutes of The Parish Council:

"*Highway Nuisance* The Chairman informed the Council that the Vicar had drawn his attention to the overflow of the Water-trough by the Highway at his entrance gate, asking the Council to look into the matter"

Saturday, 20th April 1895

"*Report of Sub-Committee on Water Trough* The Sub-Committee appointed at the last meeting to view the water trough at the end of the Vicar's drive reported that it needed repairing"

Monday, 15th July 1895

"*Reports* The ... trough was reported now to be all right having been repaired by the Vicar"

Monday, 20th January 1896

Entrance to Vicarage and Vicarage Lodge, now Paddox Cottage
Helen Scott Collection

11

The School

Records show that there was a school in Leek Wootton as far back as 1777. In that year Daniel Winter of Wootton Grange left the interest derived from £200 in his will to be paid yearly to support the school in the parish of Leek Wootton. This £200 was advanced on the credit of tolls arising from the turnpike road from Stonebridge to Kenilworth and the purpose of the bequest was for the augmentation of the salary of the schoolmaster. This endowment was at some time lost. In the 1857 will of Daniel Winter Burbury, also of Wootton Grange, he set aside a further £200 for the education of poor children in Leek Wootton, and this Consolidated Annuities Bond was left in the keeping of the parish. Village residents also supplemented the school income with donations.

The school is believed to have been in a building forming part of the old Vicarage and was pulled down in 1824 when Sir Henry Dryden rebuilt the Vicarage. In 1826 Lord Leigh lent to the parish a room with adjoining cottage for the school, and the cottage was the residence of the schoolmaster. It is believed that this was the property that later became known as the Reading Room.

Frederick Webb, who was appointed schoolmaster in 1838, had to sign his name to an agreement "to occupy the cottage and premises situated in the village of Leek Wootton allotted to him as master of the Charity School of the said village". He was not allowed to make alterations to the cottage or remove fixtures from the house or trees from the garden. He had to agree to leave at the request of the Vicar and Churchwardens, although twelve weeks' notice had to be given on either side. The premises had to be left in the condition he found them. In 1845 records show fifty-five children on the school register.

In 1873 Henry Christopher Wise MP of Woodcote laid the foundation stone for a new school on the east side of the Kenilworth to Warwick road. The following prayer was offered at the time:

"O Lord God, we beseech thee to pour thy blessing on the work on which we have this day entered and on all those concerned in bringing it about. Grant that these schools shortly to be erected for the training and education of the young in this parish may long be seminaries of sound and useful learning. We pray likewise that the religious instruction herein afforded may be in strict accordance with the Word of Life and accordingly with the faith of that pure and apostolic Branch of Christ's Church established in this kingdom, that it may influence the hearts and characters of those who receive it, causing them to grow up good Christians, loyal subjects and useful members of society. All this we humbly beg in the name and for the sake of Jesus Christ, our Lord. Amen"

The formal opening of the school was on 11th January 1875 when the Vicar, The Reverend Frederick Leigh Colvile, gave a tea. The school consisted of one large room with a smaller room off it, in the first week seventy pupils attended, and the first schoolmaster was Joshua Warner. The Vicar visited the school nearly every day, and his daughter inspected the work of the needlework classes regularly.

Some children walked long distances to get to school along rough footpaths, some from as far away as Milverton, and from the outset the weather dictated the level of attendance. Explanations for absenteeism were manifold. On 15th October 1877 the record reads "all children from Hill Wootton absent. They had gone out picking up sticks blown from the trees"; on 20th October 1880 "many children absent without leave picking up acorns"; on 23rd September 1884 "small attendance due to the Statute Fair, Kenilworth"; and on 1st March 1886 "two thirds children absent due to very snowy weather."

In 1896 Mr James Roberts came to the school as Master and his two daughters became his assistants.

Extract from School Log, 1879

11

1899–1900 List of Object Lessons for the Infants during the Year ending the 30th of April 1900.

1	Cat.	14	A Letter
2	The Rabbit	15	The Horse
3	Donkey	16	The Mole
4	Sheep	17	The Ostrich
5	Hen	18	The Frog
6	A Tree	19	Tea
7	The Apple	20	Cork
8	Clay	21	Soap
9	A Lead Pencil	22	Matches
10	Bricks	23	The Camel
11	Needles	24	The Owl
12	Pins	25	The Whale
13	A Knife		

Extract from School Log, 1900

May Day activities of singing, dancing and a tea party were held each year. An entry in the School Log on 6th May 1896 records "signs of carelessness among the children. This is always the case before May Day tea. Gave them a good lecture about it". May Day was a special celebration. The children were given an afternoon off school on the previous day to gather flowers. On the day they processed around the village and through Hill Wootton carrying the maypole, stopping at the big houses. Sometimes they sang and carried garlands, there were sword dances by the boys and a butterfly dance by the girls wearing white dresses with butterfly wings. There was often a big queen and a little queen, and some years a king and queen. A carriage was sometimes made for the queen with a wire frame decorated with paper flowers. The festivities concluded at Woodcote or the Vicarage where the children would perform and be rewarded by tea and a bag of sweets, and the Vicar or Lord Leigh would perform the crowning ceremon. The day would conclude with a dance at the school enjoyed by all. May Day was celebrated until relatively recently.

Later in the year the children were allowed days off for "gleaning and general harvesting with the family".

There were regular 'Her Majesty's Inspectors' reports, a notable one in 1899 stating "the school is steadily improving in efficiency. The children are more ready to answer and generally display more interest and intelligence in their work. The infants are successfully taught".

Lord Leigh crowns the Little May Queen . . .

. . . the Big May Queen . . .

. . . and Lord Leigh, May Day 1930

Helen Scott Collection

May Day, 1900

May Day, post Second World War

The pupil numbers increased to eighty and at one point to one hundred before the end of the 19th Century.

Diocesan inspectors also visited regularly and on 28th March 1904 it is recorded that "the school has been brought to a high level of attainment in religious knowledge and holds a high position in Class A. There was evidence throughout of earnest systematic teaching and no appearance of 'cram' work. The children by their intelligent and thoughtful answers shewed they had been taught to think for themselves. The spiritual lessons were well drawn and well adapted to the children's understanding. The infants were alert and bright and very interested in the work shewing that they had been prepared by an able and sympathetic teacher". The teacher of spiritual matters referred to was The Reverend Francis Grenville Cholmondeley who was an almost daily visitor and instructor to the school during his time as Vicar. At this time the school timetable seems to have been rigidly divided between secular and religious instruction. The schoolmaster, Mr Roberts, instructed pupil teachers for an hour before school and they also had a quarterly examination.

In 1902 there is the first mention of a Medical Officer of Health who closed the school for between ten days and a month during epidemics of measles, mumps and whooping cough. In September 1904 a boy died of "mumps and a severe chill". Outbreaks of scarlet fever in 1902 and diphtheria in 1914 are also recorded. During these closures the whole premises and furniture were scrubbed and disinfected. Any children found to be in a verminous condition were sent home.

At this time it was also noted that there was an Inspector for the Prevention of Cruelty to Children, and on an occasion when a child was inspected for a suspected verminous head and found to have bruises on his shoulders the matter was obviously reported because the child's guardian was ultimately sent to prison. The Inspector was, on another occasion, called to make enquiries about two brothers who were found subsequently "to be circulating falsehoods".

In July 1903 the school came under the management of Warwickshire County Council. On 1st June 1905 the County Council presented prizes for 100% attendance and half-day holidays were regularly awarded for 95% attendance. Holidays were also granted to celebrate royal occasions and important national events. Mrs Beresford Wright presented a forty-foot high flagpole to the school in 1907, which was erected in the schoolyard. Empire Day was marked on 22nd May each year when the scholars all saluted the flag and sang 'God save the King', and lessons were given on the theme of the British Empire. This custom continued until the early 1930s.

In 1909 and in subsequent years it is recorded that nature specimens were sent to schools in London in spring and autumn, and examples of woodwork were sent back in exchange.

In 1911 there were seventy-five pupils on the roll and the school began teaching gardening as an extra subject. Eleven plots were laid out in the grounds and the gardens were regularly inspected.

The proximity of the school to the road was always a cause for concern. On one occasion a gang of youths on their way to Warwick races threw stones at the children in the yard, injuring one boy seriously. The culprit was apprehended and was later sentenced to one month's imprisonment at Milverton Police Court. On another occasion a boy was run over by a baker's cart at the bottom of the school steps.

The School, 1890s

The School, 1920s

At this time The Reverend Edward Riley supported the school, not only in his capacity as Vicar, but also by his generosity. On various occasions he provided ships' biscuits, butter and cheese, clothing and strong clogs because he was concerned that many of the children were underfed and badly clothed. He also gave a rocking horse to the infants' class. He would sometimes bring a jar of sweets to school on a Monday that he had bought at the village shop. Another treat for the children was when he hid a sixpence in a wall and the child finding it could keep it. He had a white beard, black top hat and silver cane and was always popular with the children.

In 1914 when the First World War broke out school life changed. It was recorded that the death in October 1914 of Sir Francis Waller of Woodcote "cast a deep gloom

The School, late 1930s

over the children". In Easter Week of 1916 four dozen new-laid eggs were collected by the children and sent to the National Egg Collection for wounded soldiers in London. Instead of the usual May Day activities the children collected money for the Red Cross with the girls dressed up as nurses and the boys carrying flags and assisting by singing suitable songs. They raised £5 1s 0d.

The children were also absent on many occasions working in the fields. They collected blackberries to make jam for soldiers and sailors. On one occasion seven hundredweight of chestnuts was collected and sent from Kenilworth station "to make munitions". They also collected eight hundredweight of waste paper and a half-hundredweight of cardboard. In September 1918 they spent five days blackberry picking for the Ministry of Food. The school was also closed for potato picking and the children were paid half a crown ($12\frac{1}{2}$p) a day.

On 19th July 1919 the children attended peace celebrations at Woodcote where they had tea and sports. Each child was presented with a bronze medal as a gift from The Reverend and Mrs Riley. An additional week's holiday was also given to celebrate the signing of the peace treaty.

School was closed on 19th April 1920 "for the death of the wife of the Master and mother of the assistants", and on 31st August 1921 James Roberts and his daughters left the school. Lord Leigh presented Mr Roberts with a testimonial of twenty guineas and an illuminated address, in appreciation of his twenty-five years of faithful service.

In October 1921 lessons were given on the value of cleanliness and caring for the teeth. £4 10s 0d was raised to purchase twenty pairs of shoes and stockings so that the children didn't stay all day in wet feet. In that year games and physical exercise were introduced and the boys played football matches against Kenilworth school. Cricket was introduced in 1924 with some success and the girls were taught rounders. The keeping of chickens was introduced and proved a great success. Mr Harvey, the head teacher in 1923, introduced private study for history, geography and recitation and recorded his observations that children over twelve years old benefitted from this method as they developed initiative and self reliance. In 1924 a new method for arithmetic teaching was tried, mechanical work alternating with individual work. At this time the children were educated in the village school until the age of thirteen and then transferred to school in Kenilworth for further education.

The girls' needlework was regularly inspected and it is recorded in 1924 that Miss Jenkins, on behalf of the County Council, found that the needlework teacher at Leek Wootton School was inexperienced, tending to favour decorative work at the expense of useful garment making. The teacher was advised to teach children the latter before they left school. In 1927 the school was to become a pioneer in sewing machine classes organised by Singer & Co.

Numerous outings were organised to the theatre, the circus and a lecture in Warwick by Lord Baden-Powell. The school was closed on 3rd July 1924 to enable the children and teachers to visit the British Exhibition at Wembley. Money was raised to provide hot drinks for the children for their midday meal and the chosen drink was hot chocolate.

Sadly, towards the end of 1926 the headmistress records the following in the school records "the Vicar, who assisted the headteacher so wonderfully by taking scripture every morning except on Mondays had been ill since the end of October and his kindly interest and influence has been greatly missed by all in this school". The Vicar, The Reverend Edward Riley, died on Christmas Eve 1926.

In 1928 electricity was introduced to the school.

Music took a new turn in 1927 with the introduction of the gramophone, and featured very strongly on the curriculum. Beethoven's centennial was celebrated in March and the school choir competed in the Leamington County Festival and in the Folk Dancing Festival. In 1928 they took first place in the School Choir Festival. They also competed in the Northampton Eisteddfod and they won first place and were awarded the Arnold Challenge Trophy Shield. The adjudicator wrote of "a delightful little choir, not such developed voices as some, but quite beautiful". In June 1935 the choir won the Joseph Riley Shield for the fifth time in succession at the Leamington Spa Music Festival and obtained the highest marks awarded to any school, town or county, secondary or elementary. They shared the Purcell Warren Memorial Shield with Graisley Senior School, Wolverhampton. Also at this time collective piano lessons began.

The money won from the Eisteddfods paid for special day trips that were sometimes given as rewards. Trips included a visit to the Regents Park Zoo; outings to Bournville and Weston-super-Mare were also recorded, along with others to Oxford and Abingdon, and the gardening boys went to visit an exhibition of insects at County Office.

On 11th January 1937 the school changed to cater only for Junior and Infant pupils, which left just fourteen children on the register. The older children were sent to Kenilworth Senior and Coten End schools. At this time Mrs Davies took over from Mrs Jordan as headmistress.

In 1939 when the Second World War started the school received nine boys evacuated from Chislehurst in Kent. More children arrived from Aldeburgh, and by 1940 there were forty-two children on the register. The summer holidays were shortened and the curriculum modified to allow as much recreation as possible. The school building was adapted for wartime conditions with the windows being protected from splintering with strips of adhesive tape and wire netting. Following a three-month long saving drive to provide money for a Bren gun the savings group contributed £56 10s 0d, and the Officer in Charge at Budbrooke Barracks permitted one of these guns to be brought to the school for the children to inspect. The children also collected five shillings for the troops and 'cog badges' were awarded to those who had collected salvage. Conditions at the school were still fairly basic with outside toilets and cold classrooms, heated only by 'pot-bellied' stoves. Washing was with carbolic soap and in cold water whatever the weather.

In May 1945 the children were given two days' holiday in thanksgiving for Victory in Europe and in June 1945 there was a 'V Day" party for the children. Cards were distributed bearing the King's 'V Day' Message and a tea with a Punch and Judy show was held at the WI Hut. In September 1945 when the War was fully over, the domestic science organiser began providing school dinners.

Sir Wathen Waller was a School Manager for many years and he and his wife were very generous to the school children, and in particular Lady Waller arranged each year for the children to visit the pantomime in Coventry.

In the early 1950s the Fire Brigade inspected the school premises which was the beginning of Safety Regulations as a fire extinguisher was bought and fire drill practised. Safety first talks by the local police constable featured regularly in the school calendar and a Traffic Warden was appointed in 1960 to assist with children crossing the by now very busy main road outside the school gate.

The school went through some very difficult times with staffing after the Second World War. At times there was only one teacher but by 1957 the situation had significantly improved. An HMI Report speaks of the children being friendly and responsive and of higher intelligence than is usual in a small rural school. It predicted a "promising future" for the school. In 1957 there is the first mention of Woodcote being used by the Warwickshire Police and this is reflected in the frequent changes of pupils in the school as they moved in and out of the village with their fathers' work. By 1963 the school consisted of two Junior classes and an Infant class.

In 1968 there were meetings to discuss comprehensive education and French lessons. In the months of December and January from 1968 to 1970, because of changes to British Summer Time, a policy that resulted in dark mornings, school started at 9.30 am. On 19th May 1970 the Junior children went on a walk to Blackdown Hill using the spinney footpath as part of a Conservation Year project to survey the footpaths in the village.

At the beginning of 1971 considerable inconvenience was caused as a result of industrial action by power workers, fuel tanker drivers and postal services. In June 1971 discussions were taking place regarding the development of houses on land adjoining the school which proved to be a great asset because it brought new children to the school to swell dwindling numbers. In 1974 there were discussions concerning the proposed re-organisation of schools due to take place in 1976, and the Parent Teacher & Friends Association (PTFA) was formed. By 1972 the Kenilworth Bypass (A46) was under construction and the children visited the archaeological sites which were revealed at Blacklow Hill.

Centenary Celebrations

The school centenary was in January 1975 and all the staff and children dressed in period costume. Local press and television were present and the parents came in the afternoon. The children were dismissed by the Vicar and given an orange and a bun, "Onward Christian Soldiers" was sung, and a "Memorable Day" was recorded.

The summer of 1976 was very hot and "the children walked in the woods where it was cooler". The school session times were changed to 8 am to noon and 1.30 pm to 2.30 pm as the temperature was 100°F in the 'terrapin' classrooms which by now provided accommodation in addition to the original school building. Various outings were organised including picnics in Stratford-upon-Avon, visits to the theatre, Twycross Zoo and West Midlands Safari Park.

A conservation garden was constructed in the late 1980s and an afternoon gardening club was formed. The much-loved beech tree that had stood in the school grounds became so diseased that, sadly, in 1995 it had to be felled. It had provided welcome shade over all the years of the school's existence on this site.

In 1993 the school was threatened with closure. The government of the day put pressure on local councils to reduce surplus places and the policy of Warwickshire County Council was to close several village schools in order to save money. In the view of many this policy was flawed, as the surplus places were in the urban schools and not in the popular village schools. The residents of the parish were outraged and a school action group was formed supported by both the church and the Parish Council. A survey showed that 97% of the community was in favour of keeping the village school. The new requirement was for a school for pupils between the ages of four and eleven and the existing premises could not accommodate this proposal.

November 1993

The Coventry Diocesan Board of Education came to the rescue with a proposal to build a Church-Aided Primary School. Unfortunately a site that had been acquired and held by Warwickshire County Council since the 1960s for a new school had been sold by the Council in the 1980s for the residential development of Quarry Fields. A green field site off the main road adjacent to the southern fringe of the village was identified and special consent was obtained for its development with the new school, despite it being outside the village envelope, and in the Green Belt. Money was raised by selling the old school for residential development and conversion, the government paid 85% of the remaining cost and the diocese and the village together funded the final 15%. The community raised its share by covenanting, donating and organising fund-raising events. The Right Reverend Simon Barrington-Ward, Bishop of Coventry opened All Saints Church Of England (Voluntary Aided) Community Primary School in 1996. Since its opening the school has been so popular that it has been necessary to add extensions, the last of which was completed in the year 2000. The school now has one hundred and seventeen pupils on its register and continues to go from strength to strength.

Celebratory cake by Greta Bowyer

The sources for most of the information in this chapter have been the School Log Books and Registers, which make fascinating reading and reflect vividly the life of the community from which the children came. When the first purpose-built school opened in 1875 all the children came from households where the adult occupations were associated with service and a rural way of life and this remained virtually unchanged until after the Second World War, when the nature of the village began to change to the present-day commuter village.

Jean Singleton and Roselyn Commander

The School

Minutes of The Parish Council:

The list of candidates for Leek Wootton Parish Councillor included a woman for the first time – "Jordan, Bertha Leek Wootton Schoolmistress".

Monday, 5th March 1934

School Register 2000

Children registered at the school in the academic year 2000–2001 are:

Kamron Ahary	Courtney Field	Lewis Noakes
Sharlee Ahary	Curtis Field	Amy Pardo
James Allen	Jonathon Fox	James Parris
Katie Allen	Daniel Gardner	Rachel Parris
Hazel Anderson	Robert Gardner	Natasha Pollard
Jordan Asghar	Jamie Gibson	Rebecca Pollard
Saul Asghar	Jordan Gower	Lauren Quilter
Ciaran Bailey	Edmund Green	Angela Renshaw
Connor Bailey	Natalie Green	Jamie Ridley
Charlotte Ball	Martha Greenbank	Joseph Ridley
Kathryn Ball	Samuel Greenbank	Elena Russell
Rosie Ball	Charlotte Greger	Joseph Russell
Edward Barber	David Greger	Shaun Ryan
Holly Barnes	Sophie Hall	Ben Sidaway
Kimberley Barnes	Adele Heritage	Sophie Skinner
Luke Baylis	Frazer Heritage	Jack Slinn
Jessica Beards	Kimberly Hill	Jack Smailes
Emily Benton	Alison Hines	Kenneth Smailes
Harriet Benton	Charlotte Holder	Jacob Stockton
Jack Bridges	Giselle Hynes	James Stuart-Finch
Edward Burman	Andrew Jackson	Laura Stuart-Finch
Oliver Burman	James Jackson	Helen Taylor
Emily Cannings	Dafydd Jones	Emily Thelwell
Steven Cannings	Kathryn Jones	Elaine Thomas
Faaizah Chishty	Matt Jones	Robert Thomas
Fahrid Chishty	Megan Jones	Rosemary Thomas
Tiffany Clark	Stephanie Jones	Samuel Thomas
Garry Clarke	Zoe Jones	Alexander Thompson
Emily Coleman	Alexandra Keay	Elliot Thompson
Samuel Coleman	Charlotte Lane	Joe Thompson
Andrew Cooke	Molly Lane	Kenneth Thompson
James Davies	George Marlow	Daniel Trundle
Laura Dayman	Heather Marshall	Nicholas Trundle
Jessica Digby	Mark McCorquodale	Max Varney
James Donovan	Philip McCorquodale	James Wilkins
Rebecca Draper	Daniel Metcalfe	Martin Williams
Timothy Eldridge	Jennifer Metcalfe	Mathew Williams
Harriet Fellowes	Rachel Murphy	Nicholas Wiliams
Oliver Fellowes	Jacob Noakes	Joe Yeomanson

12

Wootton Court

The Wootton Court estate lies to the south of the village and is now part of The Warwickshire but its history goes back to the 19th Century and through its owners it is linked with the huge expansion and wealth created by the Industrial Revolution. Through the stories of the people who owned it or worked on the estate we get a glimpse of the history of Leek Wootton and of the estate, from the purchase of the house by gentry at the close of the 19th Century, through the Second World War, right up to its present commercial use.

At the time of the Enclosure Award (1822) the lands at the southern end of the village were apportioned to the King family. The origins of Wootton Court date from the 1860s, although it was not originally known by this name. Margetts of Warwick sold the newly built house and fifty-one acres of land at auction at the Warwick Arms Hotel on 1st September 1860 on behalf of Edward King, and it was purchased by a Carl Frederick Trepplin. Of Prussian descent, Carl Trepplin had made his money in Cheshire as a cotton broker before moving to Warwickshire. He added a new wing to the house, which was then known as Green Hayes, laid out the general design of the gardens, created the arboretum and built three new properties for his staff on the main road. The South Lodge was for his butler, Henry Reece, the North Lodge (later Avenue Lodge) for Joseph Murdoch his gardener, and Keeper's Lodge for the gamekeeper, Charles Stanley. Keeper's Lodge was later known as Oak Tree Cottage and now as Gaveston Lodge. In the Census of 1881, he is listed as a gentleman farmer, aged 63, born in Prussia but now a naturalised British subject, known as Charles Trepplin. His household is listed as seven servants and two gamekeepers and the estate comprised one hundred and sixty acres.

Eventually Charles Trepplin moved to Kenilworth where he became a pioneer in market gardening. He was an efficient and astute businessman and built up connections in Leamington, Coventry and London. He was also at the forefront of new ideas; for example he started turning his grass to silage. We also know that he raised the ire of the local farming community by his success, through the higher wages he paid his men, and by selling milk at 3d a quart whilst they were charging 4d a quart.

He sold the Green Hayes estate to Francis Beresford Wright in 1882.

Green Hayes, 1860
Warwickshire County Record Office, CR 1596/Box 82/26

The Wright Family

The earliest recorded member of the Wright family was John Wright, a yeoman with a small estate, who died in Stowmarket, Suffolk in 1592. The family prospered, including a Thomas Wright who was made a Freeman of the City of Nottingham and was recorded on the City Rolls as being an ironmonger at the time of his death in 1730. He left two sons, Samuel, a merchant, and Ichabod who traded in timber, iron and hemp out of Kingston-upon-Hull.

In 1760 Ichabod and his son John founded a bank, Ichabod Wright & Son, which remained in family hands until 1898. Many family banks failed at this time but Ichabod Wright & Son was to play an important part in the industrial expansion of Nottingham when there was a huge demand for capital to fund the Industrial Revolution. Their most important banking venture was to back Richard Arkwright in his ambitious scheme to advance the design of roller spinning machinery. Ichabod Wright agreed to finance him, not on a fee basis, but for a share of the profits, which shows that Wright was a very astute businessman.

By 1790 the Wrights, although non-conformists, had moved by a series of marriages from the merchant classes to the gentry. In 1790 Ichabod's son, John Wright, founded a new company with three partners, which was to establish an ironworks and exploit the coal deposits on the Butterley Hall estate in Derbyshire. It later became known as the Butterley Company. During the Napoleonic Wars (1793-1815) the company received large orders for naval cannon. In the 1820s it expanded rapidly, many more mine shafts were sunk and more furnaces were built, and eventually Butterley became one of the leading mining companies in Nottinghamshire and Derbyshire. It also made steam engines for both the home and export markets.

In 1830 John's son, Francis, took over the company. Francis Wright was a man of great energy. During the frenzied development of the railways from the 1840s onwards, the company built engines, railways, viaducts and bridges both at home and on the continent. By 1870 the Butterley Company employed 8,000 people and was recognised as one of the great enterprises of England. Francis continued his father's tradition of being a caring employer, he built schools, churches and a library for his workers and created a model village at Ironville that eventually accommodated 1,500 people. When he died in 1873 his son, Francis Beresford Wright succeeded him.

Francis Beresford Wright purchased Green Hayes from Charles Trepplin, as he believed the Warwickshire air would be beneficial for the health of his wife, Adeline. The couple and their surviving family of four sons and a daughter (four other children had died in early childhood) moved to the estate in 1883.

Francis immediately expanded the house, enlarged the lake and improved the garden. The name of the house was changed to Wootton Court, as his cousin already owned a property called The Hays. The family often abbreviated the name, referring to the estate as just 'Wootton'. In 1900 he built Sunrise Cottages and Avon Cottages for his staff.

Francis Beresford Wright remained Chairman of the Butterley Company and also served as a Justice of the Peace at Warwick. He was a strong family man and a

Francis Beresford Wright

Adeline Wright (née Fitzherbert)

devout Christian. Prayers were said daily at Wootton Court, a tradition that his son continued up until 1951. Three of his sons played football at Woodcote for the Leek Wootton team in the 1890s; they were also members of the village cricket team. The estate was run on traditional mixed lines and centred on a small herd of Jersey cattle. In 1900 Wootton Court had an indoor staff of seven to look after Francis, Adeline and their daughter, and there were seven cottages for outdoor staff.

Francis was a keen botanist and horticulturist and was President of the Kenilworth Horticultural Society. The gardens at Wootton Court were magnificent and received favourable comments in the magazine of The Royal Horticultural Society 'The Garden' in 1902. It described how the mansion was completely covered with honeysuckles, magnolias, jasmines, ampelopsis, banksian and other climbing roses and "presented a beautiful picture". He kept very detailed records and listed ninety-nine different wall climbers, forty-five types of orchid, seven types of lily and six types of rhododendrons. On his fruit walls he listed apricots, cherries, peaches, pears, quinces, figs, mulberries, nectarines and plums. John Huckvale (1863-1937) the head gardener was congratulated on his skills as a plantsman.

Later Francis employed two brothers, Isaac Forrest (1898-1976) as a gardener and Tom as cow man who lived in Sunrise Cottages, William Gregory who lived at Avon Cottages, and William Neale as a gardener who lived in Avenue Lodge. In 1904 Francis enlarged the estate by purchasing some of the glebe land from the church for £4,551. Conscious that his son would inherit Wootton Court when he and his wife died, Francis built a property on the edge of this land in 1908 for his unmarried daughter, who was also called Adeline. The house was built with stone quarried from the Wootton Court estate and he called it Stone Edge, the name it retains today.

Francis Beresford Wright died of a heart attack in 1911 and an obituary recorded him as "a liberal and unostentatious helper of charitable and philanthropic societies and institutions" who was "regarded with high esteem by all who were acquainted with him".

When War was declared in 1914 the estate horses were requisitioned and estate families suffered their share of casualties. The gardener, Huckvale, lost both his sons in battle. Corporal Mathew Forrest and Sergeant J Morgan, who had close family links with the estate, also lost their lives. All four are listed on the Roll of Honour in the church.

Romance blossomed on the estate. Isaac Forrest married Daisy, daughter of John Huckvale the head gardener and bailiff, in 1921. Isaac later succeeded his father-in-law as head gardener and went to live at Oak Tree Cottage. In 1924 Edith, daughter of William Gregory, married Oliver Holmes, who by now lived next door in Avon Cottages.

Adeline Wright remained at Wootton Court until her death in 1924. Despite always suffering from delicate health she reached the age of eighty years.

Wootton Court was inherited by her son, Arthur FitzHerbert Wright, who served as both Secretary and Chairman of the Butterley Company between 1888 and 1937. He moved into the house with his wife Daisy in 1927, along with eight of their nine children who ranged in age from 8-25 years.

Oliver Holmes and Edith Gregory, December 1924

To improve facilities and staff accommodation a pair of semi-detached cottages was built near the entrance to the main drive, known as Lime Villas. One of these housed the laundry on the ground floor and the two laundry maids lived upstairs. The other cottage housed Harry Skelton, the chauffeur, his wife and their two children, Gordon and Margaret. The Skelton family had moved with the Wright family from Aldercar in Derbyshire. Stone Edge remained occupied by Adeline, Arthur's unmarried sister, and two bungalows were later built for retired members of staff. Of the seven cottages on the estate for the outdoor staff, one was made available for Strickland, the retired head gardener and his family from Derbyshire.

The indoor staff in 1927 included a governess, Mrs Pierce; nursery nurse, Louise Strickland (who came from Aldercar and stayed with the family until she died in 1986); cook (Miss Partridge, but given the courtesy title of Mrs); kitchen maid (Margaret Jackson); parlour maid; two house maids and two laundresses (Emily and Alice Morgan). The outdoor staff consisted of the chauffeur; the bailiff, who was Huckvale who had been gardener to Francis; four gardeners (who were also expected to help with the harvest when needed) and three farm workers. Hector Chapman was a gardener, Sam Bullock cow man and Tom Lane waggoner. The estate carpenter was Oliver Holmes who, with his apprentice, was responsible for all the maintenance on the estate. The kitchen garden, the orchard and the dairy supplied all the needs of the family and indoor staff. Mr Dee the village baker delivered bread, and honey came from the bailiff's bees. This level of staffing continued until the outbreak of War in 1939.

Relations between the staff and the Wright family were always friendly, each taking an interest in the other. Mrs Daisy Wright and her daughter, Hilda, were Godparents to Gordon and Margaret Skelton respectively, the two children of Harry Skelton the chauffeur.

Wootton Court was a very happy family home, with the older children keeping an eye on the younger members of the family. The children were expected to show good manners to each other and to be polite to members of staff at all times. Arthur and Daisy instilled in their children the philosophy 'that from those to whom much has been given, much would be required', in other words, privilege meant responsibility. Arthur did not allow a telephone in the house as he believed that the children would always be speaking to their friends, a sentiment that many of us may still share, so they had to use the telephone in Mrs Dee's shop in the village.

Servants at Wootton Court, circa First World War
Mr Huckvale standing centre, Mrs Partridge seated left and Miss Foot standing far left

A resident governess taught the younger children until the boys left for boarding school at around the age of nine or ten years, and the girls a little later. The boys were sent to Harrow with one of them, Robert, going on to Cambridge University. The girls were educated at Malvern Girls College.

Arthur FitzHerbert Wright was a gentle and compassionate man with a dry sense of humour and to his many house guests he was a generous and relaxed host. There were virtually no formal dinner parties and the men did not change for dinner, although the women would tend to change for the evening.

Wootton Court played an important part in the local community. There were pageants and church fêtes held in the grounds and Scouts and Guides camped there during the summer. The Wrights were a very sporting family. During the 1930s hockey, lacrosse, cricket and tennis matches were played in the grounds. Robert Wright captained the village cricket team for which his grandfather, father and uncles had also played. This cemented many lifelong friendships. He also set up the Leathercrackers Cricket XI with friends and relatives of the family. The team had fixtures in different parts of the country, and regularly played the village team. These matches became highlights of the local sporting calendar.

The Wright Family at Wootton Court in the 1930s

Robert Ronnie Bardie Mahler Arthur Doreen Ida Gilbert Fred Laurie Artie (almost hidden)
              (Husband of Hilda) Fitzherbert (wife of Gilbert)   Norah (Husband Judy
                                              holding Nicholas   of Norah)

       Geoffrey   Hilda   David   Rosamund Judith Daisy
                                Mahler   Laurie   Laurie

Church Fête at Wootton Court, early 1950s

Villagers' Memories

One of the best insights into life at the house comes from Margaret Angless (née Jackson, and sister to Charles) who worked at Wootton Court as a kitchen maid and is now living in retirement in Kenilworth. Margaret was born in 1913 in the Lodge at the foot of the drive to Wootton Court. Her father, William, was coachman to the family, working for both Francis and Arthur. Margaret was one of seven children, all of whom were born at home.

Her father served in the Army during the First World War and he developed epilepsy on his return, which his family believed, was the result of an injury. His job as coachman had gone, as the estate horses had been requisitioned for military transport, so he became an odd job man on the estate.

Margaret recalls that they had a happy childhood although they did not have much money. They were never hungry as her parents kept chickens and grew fruit and vegetables in their garden. The family was allowed one pint of full milk, and as much skimmed milk as they needed, from the dairy per day. Each child had a Saturday job to do in the house, but they were not allowed to play on the front drive. Sometimes the older children would be allowed to walk to Kenilworth or Warwick to visit the shops or a fair such as the Warwick Mop. When the children were much older they would be allowed to go to dances in the WI Hut. This was also the venue for the weekly whist drives, which were organised by her brother, Charles, and were popular with all members of the family. Margaret's mother, Ethel, helped with the refreshments. Hurdy gurdy players used to visit the village as well as gypsy peddlers selling ribbons and pegs.

After leaving the village school at the age of fourteen, Margaret went into service at Wootton Court for one year as a kitchen maid. On an average day she was out of bed by 6 am to light the fires and she did the washing up after all meals. Margaret's other duties included scrubbing the floors, blackening the grates, and preparing the vegetables and fruit for cooking, brought to the kitchen each day by the Head Gardener. As Wootton Court was a working farm, she also worked in the dairy turning the butter and her day ended at about 8 pm when she had finished the washing up after dinner, which was usually taken at 6.30 pm. She was entitled to half a day off each week, plus half a day on every other Sunday.

Margaret recalls that she was very happy working at Wootton Court; the Wrights were a considerate family and she was treated very kindly. She married Frank Angless in 1936 and later lived at the Hunt Kennels in Rouncil Lane where Frank was Huntsman with The North Warwickshire Hunt. Her parents lived at the Lodge, which was a tied cottage, until William died in 1937 when her mother and the two youngest children together with her eldest son, Charles, who was twenty-five and supported the family, had to move to Kenilworth. The Lodge then became home to Oliver Holmes, the estate carpenter, and his family.

Gordon Skelton recalls that his father, the chauffeur at Wootton Court, always had to ensure the petrol store was full and he would fill up the cars of overnight house guests before their departure. Gordon also remembers how Gilbert Wright, one of Arthur's sons, was mad about cars and would race his Sunbeam around the village with his brother Robert who drove a Riley Kestrel. Gilbert became an aircraft engineer after serving an apprenticeship with the Blackburn Engineering Company in Lancashire. He later opened a garage in Buckinghamshire with one of his friends, and he took part in many car rallies and trials.

William Jackson, Coachman, and Isaac Forrest

Kevin Meredith, who moved to the village in 1922, recalls a great friendship with the Wright boys. He can remember how Gilbert, who was a skilled pilot and member of the RAF Volunteer Reserve in the 1930s, flew into the grounds of Wootton Court in his Tiger Moth, known as 'Moses Aloft'. Gilbert was keenly interested in cars, planes and cricket.

Audrey Jones (née Holmes) was born in 1931 at Avon Cottages. Her father, Oliver Holmes, was a skilled carpenter and was a highly valued member of staff who could turn his hand to any task. She recalls the Christmas parties that were held for all the estate children. Each party had a theme and one year it was boats, so her father built a very large replica of a boat that was at the centre of the festivities. The house was decorated with holly and evergreens and a large pine tree would be cut down from the grounds to be decorated as the Christmas tree. In the nursery were trunks full of fancy dress clothes for the children to wear, and they had an exciting time followed by tea and a magic lantern show. Audrey used to play with the grandchildren of Arthur who often stayed at the house. As there were three staircases and a lift, they had plenty of places to hide. She remembers the Wright family with great affection.

Margaret, Bertha, Charles, Nancy and Frank Jackson, 1920s

Bernard Dee, son of the village baker, tells the story of how some lively young members of the Wright family went to the railway station to collect two recently engaged house guests with a farm horse and dray*. On their arrival at the station, as a joke, they laid out a long strip of red carpet. When their guests alighted from the train, they walked along it and boarded the cart to great shrieks of laughter all round. The carpet was then rolled up and the family members climbed on to the dray and drove back to Leek Wootton. The incident had afforded great amusement for watching bystanders.

Wootton Court and World War II

Arthur FitzHerbert Wright was a prodigious letter writer; particularly to his son Robert who had joined the Colonial Service in Nigeria in 1937, and through these letters Robert became aware of his father's foreboding that war would shortly break out. The charmed life at Wootton Court was coming to an end.

Arthur was seventy-four when War was declared on 3rd September 1939. His letters describe the build-up, from his description of Germany's bullying behaviour in January 1937, to the need for strong leadership as events became 'more grim', and in July 1939 he wrote "We need a Dictator, Churchill say!" He supervised the running of

---

* A low cart without sides for carrying heavy loads.

the estate with his usual good humour and was determined to do all he could for the war effort. The lawn at Wootton Court was dug up and replanted with buckwheat. Sometimes he helped with the feeding of the animals, chopped wood, carried coal, when some was available, or worked in the kitchen garden.

Three of his sons, Gilbert, Artie and Geoffrey, joined the armed forces. In 1942 Robert became the Personal Secretary and ADC to the Governor of Cyprus and held the rank of Captain in the Cyprus Regiment. Another son, Ronnie, was a farmer in Scotland. Judy and Ida, his two youngest daughters, who lived at home, became nurses at the new war hospital in Warwick when it opened in 1940 and remained there until 1945. Mrs Daisy Wright, who had very bad arthritis, organised working parties for the war effort. This was something she had done in Derbyshire during the First World War, and she was a tower of strength.

At Wootton Court they produced over 3,000 items including jerkins, quilts and bandages, and Oliver Holmes made wooden splints for the Red Cross. In June 1940 the cellar was opened up as an air raid shelter. Rationing of food, coal, petrol and household items was introduced and the country went on to a total war economy.

Many of the people working on the estate were directed by the government to take part in the essential war work. This included Harry Skelton, the chauffeur, and some of the maids. One of the house maids left to do the washing up at the army barracks at Budbrooke, near Warwick. Arthur later commented that she earned more than a skilled agricultural worker did. When Isaac Forrest, head gardener, Church Warden and Air Raid Warden, was called upon to register for essential war work Arthur declared "...it would be ridiculous to take him; besides working like a slave in the kitchen garden and on the farm, he is invaluable in filling up forms and sticking on stamps: if I have to do it, there will be some muddles." In the end Isaac remained on the estate.

Arthur's letter to Robert of 26th May 1940 carried worrying news "Gilbert is 'reported missing' in France but we still have hope he is all right. …We hear he was seen coming down 'under control' near Arras, and two others who did the same have since turned up … We have looked out the 'elephant gun' and find it has a dozen cartridges left so I hope to be able to perforate at least a dozen parachutists, possibly more if two could be got in line."

On 15th June 1940 he wrote "200 or so wounded, Scotties mostly, have just arrived at Warwick and so Judy and Ida are hard at it: just in the middle of chicken hatching too! … Just heard that France has collapsed. Words fail."

On 1st September 1940 "We have had no bombs nearer than Hill Wootton and I expect we shall get used to them in time."

In 1940 Gilbert's wife, Doreen, their three children under the age of four and a nanny moved into Wootton Court and took over the nursery wing. Doreen was very energetic and became involved in voluntary work for the war effort. When Coventry was blitzed Doreen would collect bread from the village bakery and soup made by WI members and transport them to the city where she worked in an emergency canteen. She also helped at Woodcote, the convalescent home. Doreen, who is now 93 years old, remembers "making football boots out of old car tyres to protect the plaster from breaking while the wounded soldiers played football". She also recalls that "blackcurrant and rhubarb was the best jam to meet Lord Woolton's* jam quota".

Wootton Court gave shelter to many people during the War, especially to nurses who worked at Warwick Hospital, usually in groups of fifteen, and when relatives visited the injured servicemen convalescing at Woodcote they often stayed overnight at Wootton Court.

When Coventry was bombed many people, often with children, would walk out of the city into the countryside after work, to escape the night-time bombing. Arthur would stand at the bottom of the drive and invite them to come in for shelter for the night. He would not normally select men on their own, but families with children, women or old people. Sometimes the house was so crowded that people even slept under the billiard table.

On 28th November 1940 he wrote "Then we had a bomb on the Stone House, near the church, and Holmes has been mending windows ever since. Glass was broken all over the village and tiles 'lifted', including some on Stone Edge Barn. Our numbers are still averaging 40-45 and we have cleaned out the old apple rooms; if the village is attacked, they might come in useful. Of course there is practically no feeding to be done, so matters are very much simplified."

On 13th April 1941 "Poor Coventry is catching it again. ... A good many of 'our' nurses came from Coventry when their hospital was bombed and their patients sent to Warwick; they were going back by degrees but some are among the last casualties. I do think they are marvellous, many not much more than children. ... when they have to see their patients under dropping bombs whose noise alone is terrifying, marvellous is a mild description of their courage. Even at this distance the noise is bad enough. Our nearest bombs this time were a couple in the hollow beyond the cricket field which killed a rabbit and broke some windows ... another small bomb or anti aircraft shell exploded in Hays meadow near the brook: it made a crater about 9 feet diameter and 3 feet deep and hurled turf over a diameter of about 50 yards. ... We really have nothing to complain of."

In 1941 the coal ration was further reduced and the house was too cold for the nurses and evacuees. Arthur responded by ordering the chopping down of another large tree. He was supposed to have a licence to do this, but he could not stand all the bureaucracy. It was a miracle that the arboretum survived.

In 1942, when there was virtually no petrol, he put the last car in the garage and used the pony and cart. The garage now housed six cars but no petrol was available.

Whilst Robert was ADC to the Governor of Cyprus he met Winston Churchill and General DeGaulle. They both stayed overnight at Government House on their way back from the Casablanca Conference in January 1943.

In April 1943 Arthur's daughter-in-law, Betty, heard that her husband Geoffrey had been severely wounded when his troop ship was torpedoed off the coast of North Africa. He had been rescued and spent seven months in hospital.

In August 1943 Robert Wright enlisted in the RAF in Rhodesia and he trained as a pilot, earned his Wings and was Commissioned. Despite asking for a posting to the Far East to fight and to avenge his brother's death, he actually served in Palestine and

---

* Minister of Food

Egypt. When he later captained a Wellington bomber he served with 575 Transport Command.

That November, Barbara Wright received news that her husband, Artie, who was in the Army, had been listed as missing. She was relieved to be told later that he was alive, although a Prisoner of War in Oflag VII.

On 9th January 1944 Arthur wrote "I suppose you have seen in the papers about the new 'propellerless' aeroplane? The inventor seems to have been a Coventry man educated in Leamington, another bit of reflected glory." This was a reference to Frank Whittle, the inventor of the jet engine, who was educated at Leamington College.

The 6th of June 1944 was D-Day, the Allied invasion of Europe.

On 11th June Arthur wrote "Ida and Judy are on days now, and after coming home at 8 had to go back at 10 for a convoy of wounded from France; about a 100 turned up at 10.20. They got back about 1 a.m. and Judy had to be off again at 7.30 and missed her breakfast. ... If they were in tip-top shape that sort of thing wouldn't matter so much. I think they expect about 200 in all."

As more convoys of wounded men were coming into the area, Wootton Court was in more demand for overnight accommodation for their relatives. The War continued with bitter fighting across Europe until Germany surrendered unconditionally in May 1945, and the Japanese surrendered three months later.

Towards the end of the War Gilbert's widow, Doreen, and the three children moved back to their home in Buckinghamshire. Nicholas, her eldest son, who had developed bovine tuberculosis whilst at Wootton Court tragically contracted scarlet fever on his return and died in April 1944 aged eight years.

Artie was released from the POW camp and came back to his family. Geoffrey returned but a leg injury was to trouble him all his life, and curtailed his sporting activities. Harry Skelton resumed his role as chauffeur and worked for the family until he retired.

Robert rejoined the Colonial Service in Nigeria in 1946 and the following year he transferred to the Education Department. By 1952 he was the Chief Education Officer for Northern Nigeria. In 1955 he was appointed the Permanent Secretary at The Ministry of Education. Robert had promised his father that he would take care of his mother and two sisters, and this was one of the principal reasons that he decided to retire in 1956 and return to England.

The End of an Era

The 1945 election saw a Labour government sweep to power and the start of a new post-war society. Arthur, who was ill, was very worried about the future of the estate because of the likelihood of high death duties, and he feared that the estate would have to be sold to pay these when he died.

The Nationalisation of the coal, iron and steel industries had a major impact on the Butterley Company and the Wright family. Its collieries and iron interests were taken over by the government, although the family did receive compensation.

Arthur's health deteriorated which resulted in a fall down stairs, and an injury to his leg. Oliver Holmes, his loyal employee and friend made him a wooden hoist so that he could lift himself up in bed. Arthur FitzHerbert Wright died in 1952, aged 86 years, and was mourned by his family and employees. He had lived through times of great change.

In 1952 the Wootton Court Estate was sold to Aubrey Jones, a Coventry builder, ending the Wright family's history at 'Wootton'. Arthur's widow and his two daughters, Ida and Judy, and Louise Strickland moved to Stone Edge, where Robert Wright joined them in 1956. This house became the centre of their family life. Robert joined both the Parish Council and Parochial Church Council and was the County Chief Warden in the Civil Defence. He was also captain of the village cricket team and a superb gardener.

Daisy Wright, Arthur's widow, died in 1957. Sadly, the family moved out of the village in 1977 due to the ever-increasing cost, both financial and physical, of maintaining a large house like Stone Edge. They are recalled as "So kind and thoughtful. If someone was ill or in need a member of the family would call on them with eggs or food, or whatever was necessary. There was no fuss; it was all done very quietly. We will never see the likes of the Wright family in this village again."

Following Aubrey Jones's acquisition of the estate in 1952, it was efficiently managed as a mixed farm with traditional crops, and once again it became a focal point of the local community. Isaac and Tom Forrest, Oliver Holmes, Sam Bullock, Hector Chapman and Tom Lane continued to work for the new owner. Marjorie Jones carried on the gardening tradition, and Wootton Court continued to be the venue for church fêtes, barn dances and other village functions. The beautiful gardens were also opened for charitable causes, as were the gardens of Stone Edge.

Wootton Court Gardens

In 1972 the house and seven-acre walled garden were sold to M J K (Mike) Smith, the Warwickshire County and England cricketer, who converted them into a country club with both squash and tennis courts, whilst members of the Jones family continued to run the farm. The club became very popular with a large membership, including many people from the village. In 1987 the property changed hands again, when it was sold to Gordon Barrow, a local hotelier.

In 1990 Wootton Court Country Club and Wootton Court Farm were sold, together with other farmland and woods, to eventually become The Warwickshire, which fulfilled one of Aubrey Jones's original ideas of building a golf course. The original plans to erect an associated 150-bedroom hotel are no longer being pursued, and The Hayes is now to be converted into apartments.

This is the history of the Wootton Court estate, from its creation as the home of a 19th Century Prussian to its current use as part of a leisure facility. For much of its history it was the family home of the Wright family and it is through their records and the recollections of the villagers who worked at 'Wootton' that we see a picture of estate life during some of the most momentous years of the 19th and 20th Century. For all their privileges, the Wright family lost a son in the Second World War, as did many other families, and the post-war world was a very changed place which brought to an end the era of many such estates.

The village has never lost its close links with Wootton Court and even now residents can enjoy the 'estate' by walking the public footpaths over the rolling countryside of The Warwickshire. As they do so they might spare a thought for all the people who lived and worked at 'Wootton'.

Catherine Sandwell

As this book was nearing completion news was received that Robert Hepburn Wright, the last surviving child of Arthur and Daisy Wright, who had kindly and enthusiastically contributed to this chapter with personal reminiscences, had died at the age of 88. At a Service of Thanksgiving in All Saints Church the Easter altar cloth made in 1951 by his sister-in-law, Doreen, from the dress his grandmother wore when she was presented at Queen Victoria's Scottish Court, was used.

Minutes of The Parish Council:

"Proposed ... the following letter be sent to Captain A Eden MP, member for Warwick and Leamington, 'The Parish Council of Leek Wootton regard the act of the Valuation & Rating Bill contains in it proposals which are likely to be both costly and inefficient. Since the present Overseers receive no emolument and are from their position persons but able to judge of the capacity and obligations of the rate payers. This Council begs that the most strenuous opposition should be made to these proposals'."

Tuesday, 2nd June 1925

13

Elms Farm

Elms Farmhouse, barn and cottages
Helen Scott Collection

The farmhouse and outbuildings of Elms Farm were situated in the centre of the village, opposite the church, where The Elms development is to be found today. John Samuel Perkins (1829-1893) farmed the Elms in the latter years of the 19th Century. He was married to Katherine (née Jaggard) and in the 1871 Census he was described as a landowner/farmer with 478 acres, employing thirteen men and six boys. Lord Algernon Percy bought the farm from Earl Clarendon in 1890. After the death of John Perkins in 1893 Ernest Pate Cattell (1869-1943) rented the farm and from 1916 he also leased Woodcote's Home Farm. Ernest was a large man with a ruddy complexion and his wife was Adela, a tiny lady who died in 1965, aged 92. Their daughter, Julia, was in the Women's Land Army during World War II. Mr Cattell read the lesson in church each week and when he walked into church all his farmworkers traditionally had to file in behind him.

After Ernest Cattell's death in 1943 Tom Edgar took over the farm. Tom came from Cryfield Grange in Coventry and was one of four brothers, who all farmed locally. The family continued to farm at Cryfield until Warwick University was built on the land in the 1960s.

Tom's great interest as a young man was horse ploughing and he would travel all over the country entering ploughing competitions. There was great excitement in the

Ted and Liz Edgar
Kenilworth Citizen

Aerial View of Elms Farm, early 1970s

village in the 1940s when one of the first combine harvesters in Warwickshire was acquired by the Edgars. In addition to the farm buildings at Elms Farm the Edgars also had the use of those at the Home Farm, Woodcote.

Fred Wilson, a long time employee of the Edgars, came to Leek Wootton in 1954 as head cowman to the dairyherd at Elms Farm. His brother, George, had been cowman before him in the 1940s. At that time the Edgar family employed several other men including a shepherd, a waggoner, a stockman, grooms and a horseman, and most of them lived in tied cottages in the village, some of which have long ago disappeared. At potato harvesting time twenty or so women would be collected from Warwick and Kenilworth and brought to the farm to assist. Tom Edgar was very involved with the Warwick and Kenilworth Agricultural Societies, showing animals at the Kenilworth Show and others. He took part in many village activities including giving a barrel of beer for the celebrations at the end of the Second World War and donating a pig for the bowling prize, and giving milk for teas at the annual Horticultural Show. The old farmhouse to Elms Farm was demolished in the 1960s and a bungalow was built at the edge of the village on Hill Wootton Road to which Tom and his wife, Ethel, retired. Ethel died in 1968 and Tom in 1969.

Towards the end of Tom's life he had abandoned dairy farming to concentrate on sheep, and the fattening of beef and pigs which were sold to the Coventry Co-op or taken to Warwick market.

Tom and Ethel had two children, Ted and Marge, who were brought up with showponies, taking part in showjumping and point-to-point. Ted married Liz Broome and much of their lives have been devoted to world-class showjumping. Before their move to the Ponderosa, later Rio Grande, on Hill Wootton Road in the early 1980s Ted and Liz lived in a bungalow that replaced the Elms Farm farmhouse in the heart of the village. This bungalow and the farm buildings were eventually demolished to make way for the new houses of The Elms.

Fred Wilson is still working for Ted Edgar on a part time basis, looking after the sheep, with extra help at lambing. He has lived with his wife, Edna, in their cottage on Hill Wootton Road since they came to the village in 1954, where he is a keen gardener growing prize-winning dahlias. Fred has seen many changes over his years in the village. When he came to Leek Wootton he had no back garden but cultivated a patch of land adjacent to the old Pound across the road. Next to the pair of farm cottages, one of which is his home, there were two very old cottages, known as the Hamlet, with outbuildings and about half an acre of garden. Reg and Joan Lynes occupied one of these. Reg's father, Bill, with his sister Emma, had lived there before them and there had been earlier generations of the Lynes family in the village since the 1850s. The old cottages were lost in the 1960s with the development of modern homes on Hill Wootton Road. It is said that the Lynes family once wrote a record of the village history but this is now lost. It was understood from that old record that where The Forge Cottage is now, there was once a village green and at harvest time a fiddler would play on the green to entertain the farm workers who would bring their haycarts, stop for drinks at the Anchor Inn and enjoy the merry-making.

An employee at Elms Farm who became a resident of Leek Wootton in the 1940s arrived by a quite different route. Paul Smolin was born in Opole, East Germany in 1922 and conscripted into the German Army at the age of seventeen. After training as a Wireless Operator he was sent to Russia for a year, was wounded and sent back to Germany and then to the south of France. When the Allied invasion began he was sent to the Caen area in Normandy, where he was captured by an Irishman and brought to England as a Prisoner of War. Upon his arrival at Southampton Paul was sent to a POW camp at Moreton in Marsh where he was set to work on farms and in gardens and later in a sugar beet factory. Later he was transferred to Banner Hill Camp off Rouncil Lane, and he was put to work for Tom Edgar. When Paul was released he decided to stay in England. His father and five brothers had perished during the War and his mother died soon afterwards. Eventually, Paul met his wife-to-be, Ethel Smith, and they were married in 1952. He worked as part-time Caretaker at the village school and undertook other work locally, was Churchwarden at All Saints for seventeen years, and he and Ethel lived in the village until Paul's death in 1998.

Jane Pain

Minutes of The Parish Council:

"Suggested ... that owing to depravity, indecency and damage done, that a Policeman stationed in the village was needed."

Monday, 3rd November 1919

Minutes of The Parish Council:

"Proposed ... that an urgent appeal be made to the County Council Surveyor of the state of the road between the Elms, Leek Wootton & Guy's Cliffe owing to the greasy nature of the road surface when wet. Cars and motor-bikes are continually upset into the ditch. Three or four a day have been turned over. Can anything be done to remedy this death-trap?"

Friday, 19th September 1924

Minutes of The Parish Council:

"Proposed ... that the clerk inform the County Council Surveyor of the danger of the telegraph posts beside the footpath and ask if they can be painted white to prevent travellers stumbling against them on dark nights"

Friday, 25th October 1926

14

Village Houses

83 Warwick Road

Ronald Simpson bought 83 Warwick Road, or 83 Church Lane as it appears in old records, in 1968 from a Mrs Gibbs, a policeman's widow. The property is a 16th or 17th Century workman's cottage, built on the site of an old quarry, evidenced by dramatic sandstone cliffs rising sharply to the field behind and above. Today it is situated on and even below the main road through the village, but even before the advent of the motorcar it would have witnessed many comings and goings.

In ancient days the track through the village wound up from the river bank along the wall forming the southern edge of Elms Farm. On reaching the site of number 83 it turned north for a few yards before continuing up the drive of Wootton Paddox, then a public lane called Back Lane, along to the Tink-a-Tank and to Woodcote Lane, up what is now the drive to Woodcote, round and north to Rouncil Lane.

In earlier times the cottage had been owned by the Guy's Cliffe estate, as was Elms Farm opposite, and would have housed a workman's family. It was in a sorry state when Ronald bought it and he spent thirty years carrying out what was to become his hobby of restoration and improvement, with Peggy creating her treasured garden, importing stone to form the colourful, flower-filled terraces. A natural spring emanating from Spring Cottage next door provides a permanent dribble of water, creating a striking grotto-like effect amongst the moss-covered rocks and stones behind the property. The cottage still retains its ancient wells, one inside the house itself, built of bricks and dating back to the time of Queen Anne, with another underground well outside.

On an April evening in 1997 a stray spark in the thatch of the cottage caused a disastrous fire and Ronald, then eighty-four years old, and Peggy were homeless. However, refusing to consider defeat they immediately set about repairing and re-roofing the cottage, moved back in August of the same year, and spent the next few months finishing the work.

Farriers and Aymestrey

These two houses on Warwick Road were built in the 1920s behind the forge or smithy. A Mr Isaac Cottrell came from Stretton-on-Dunsmore to build the semi-detached houses, and lodged with Mrs Golby on Woodcote Lane. He quarried stone for the building from the village quarry on Warwick Road and used second-hand bricks and timbers. It took him twelve months to complete the project and whilst he was in the village he was employed to cut a hole in the wall of what is now The Old Post House for the post box

> <u>Minutes of The Parish Council:</u>
>
> "The Clerk read a letter from the RDC Surveyor as to the name 'Warwick Road' to be given to our main road, and that numbering of its houses would follow."
>
> *Friday, 20th March 1970*

The Forge Cottage

When the village smithy was demolished in 1945, the last blacksmith having died in 1942, the adjoining cottage was left standing. In 1955 Billy (or Mick) Nicholls who attended the village school from 1929 until 1937, worked for the Post Office, and was a faithful church sidesman, bought the cottage. He recalled that the cottage had been owned by a Mrs Plevins and was rented to an old shepherd, Tom Wrighton, who lived there with his Airedale, Bruce. After Mr Wrighton died it was let to various tenants, and when Mrs Plevins died the cottage was left to her housekeeper, Mrs Rose, and her son. As a schoolboy Billy had worked the hand-bellow for the forge furnace, when Harry Billington was the village blacksmith, and his reward had been sixpence and a

beef dripping sandwich, and he recalled the great experience of seeing the farm horses lined up ready to be shod.

Billy Nicholls retained many of the original features of the cottage such as the cooking range and the bacon wedges for hanging home-cured bacon which, being upstairs, indicated that the dwellers lived upstairs and that the cattle, pigs and fowl had access to the cottage. Fodder was stored in what later became the dining room. He continued to live with the earth floor, the original staircase and the elm first floor boarding. In 1981 the roof was investigated and new oak beams were installed before John Warner of Brandon carried out a complete re-thatch.

Billy Nicholls sold The Forge Cottage in 1987 to Phil Sylvester, a local jeweller, and retired to Kenilworth. Phil set about a major restoration and sympathetic modernisation of what is a fine example of a thatch cruck building, one of only about six examples left in Warwickshire. This type of cottage evolved from a simple 'A' frame structure built during the Anglo-Saxon period designed to produce a strong framework which would support the thatch and hopefully withstand the worst excesses of weather. During the restoration work sheep or goat jawbones were discovered in the earth floor of the cottage, together with a halfpenny piece dated 1749.

Leek Wootton House

Leek Wootton House appears originally to have been two separate cottages, one built in the 17th Century and one in the 18th Century, with a substantial central block added in Victorian times. Henry Donne, Land Agent to Lord Leigh, came to live at the house in 1871, aged twenty-three, and at that time there were seven acres of land with the property. The 1881 Census records that he was married with two small children, both born in Leek Wootton. Henry Donne's eldest daughter, Mary, married Richard Beresford Wright of Wootton Court in 1899. On the departure of the Donne family from Leek Wootton House in 1898 'The Hunting Box', as it was referred to in the popular press, became the home of Francis Dudley Leigh, son and heir to the 2nd Lord Leigh, and his wife the wealthy American heiress Helene, a society beauty.

Francis Leigh inherited in 1905, and it is likely that his brother, Rupert, moved to Leek Wootton House in 1906 since it is understood that his son, Rupert William Dudley Leigh, was born there in 1908. Rupert Leigh became the 4th Lord Leigh upon the death of his Uncle Francis.

For a period that covered the Second World War Leek Wootton House was occupied by the Rotherham family, owners of a renowned watch making business in Coventry that had been established in 1750, and magistrates. During the War the garage was utilised for the production and packing of small munitions, and a number of village women were employed there. Mrs Rotherham was a Parish Councillor and, with her daughters, an active member of the Women's Institute, and allowed a number of Parish Council Meetings and other gatherings to take place at the house. Leek Wootton House was sold by Lord Leigh in January 1954.

The present Vicarage in Hill Wootton Road was built on what was once part of the garden as was the next door bungalow (2 Hill Wootton Road), and the two bungalows on Warwick Road to the south of the house (Charisma and Cedar Gable). Various barns and outbuildings are still partly used by Leek Wootton House for garaging and part has been converted to create Pen-Y-Bryn.

The Lodge

The Lodge on Hill Wootton Road was built in 1879 for Leigh Delves Broughton, a solicitor from Jersey, and his wife, Elvira. In the 1881 Census he is stated as being forty-two with a wife and three servants. Legend has it that he died in a hunting accident and a year later Elvira died from a broken heart, aged only twenty-nine. The property originally extended to four acres, from the corner of Hill Wootton Road with Warwick Road down as far as some old cottages known as the Hamlet, now demolished. Included were a lodge cottage and outbuildings/garages that existed before the development of The Lodge, plus a tennis court, kitchen gardens and extensive ornamental gardens.

Mrs S D Hughes D'Aeth was the second owner and in 1890, when the church was enlarged and the new chancel built, she gave the new east window. She died in 1894,

Helen Scott Collection

left the property to her nephew, and in 1913 the house was sold to W F Mitchell. The Mitchells were the owners of a pen knib factory in Staffordshire and their son, Lieutenant F G Mitchell was killed in the Second World War. Frank Golby, a long time village resident, was chauffeur to the Mitchells for some years and they built Quarry Lodge on the west side of Warwick Road for him to live in. They also built Rockside on the east side of Warwick Road for their gardener. Mr Mitchell died in 1950 and Mrs Glover occupied the house until 1959 when the Philpot family bought it. Mrs Marjorie Philpot took the west end of the plot with the garages and outbuildings and built Broadlands; the company of Glyn Philpot Ltd took the remainder. The house was divided into two (The Lodge and Westside) and four houses were built on the gardens to the east of the house (White Gables, Firlea, Hillcrest and The Mumblies) with accesses being cut through the old Lodge wall. The Lodge was sold on to Mr and Mrs Davies with a frontage to Hill Wootton Road of eighty-five feet and the 'nursery strip' behind the properties was retained by the Philpots. The Lodge was sold again in 1984 to Nigel and Ann Hill and subsequently to Piyush and Janneke Patel who live there today.

Peter and Pat Wartnaby bought Broadlands from Mrs Philpot and have in their turn built a bungalow to the west of Broadlands (Tremayne) and a house to the east (Hedgerows). Parts of the original outbuildings were incorporated into the Wheelwright Mews development, but the remainder is still part of Broadlands. In the late 1990s a chalet bungalow (Cranleigh) was built behind, between Broadlands and the properties on Tidmarsh Road, on the part of the 'nursery strip' that went to Mrs Philpot when the west end was separated off.

The Old Post House

The Old Post House was formerly Stone Cottage, and it is said that it was built around 1570. This is only partly born out by a survey of 1950 when a building society traced its history back at least 250 years.

The cottage was constructed of sandstone, believed to have been quarried in the village, ships' timbers from Worcester, with wattle and daub walls and a vaulted cellar, and it had a thatched roof. Tradition has it that the cottage was built by the church to house one of its members, as the villagers were not behaving themselves to the satisfaction of the clergy.

The cottage is shown on a map of the village dated 1818 alongside the property now known as The Rock. At that time it was owned by Mr Edward J King and was used as the Curate's house. The Reverend Colvile wrote "Mr John Shuckburgh, a man of some notoriety in his time, and of whom one may see many engravings in his nightcap and dressing gown, was Curate here between 1760 and 1770". The cottage was purchased by Henry Christopher Wise from Edward King, together with his other acquisitions in 1851, and continued as a Curate's house for the next twenty years.

The Reverend Colvile's manuscript history of the village also records that in 1855 a deep hole was sunk behind Stone Cottage and a coffin handle and a pair of 17th Century scissors were dug up. A Mr Bloxham suggested that they had belonged to someone who had died of the plague and was buried with their implements of housewifery outside the churchyard. The Reverend C J Fuller became the tenant in 1857, followed by The Reverend M E Browne. Following its use as a house for the Curate J Jaggard used it as a farmhouse.

J Burbury became the tenant in 1872 followed by the Leek Wootton Co-operative Society in 1881. In 1904 H Summerton took over the cottage and ran a grocers and general store. The Summerton family also owned Guy's Cliffe Mill, milling flour and animal feed and Miss Summerton taught at the village school.

The first Post Office in the village was opened in 1848 in a shop near to the Anchor Inn, but by 1932, when the Dee family purchased the general store and bakery, the village Post Office was also at Stone Cottage (see Chapter 15).

There were bread ovens at the rear of what is now the kitchen but during the War new ovens were installed to the rear of the building. A trap door was put in to let down the sacks of flour, stored on the upper floor, by a hoist. The Dee family closed the shop and bakery in the 1970s and the cottage remained empty for several years. In 1978 Tom and Ros Commander purchased the property, refurbished the derelict cottage, extended it to the rear, added a garage to the side and turned it into a family home.

Minutes of The Parish Council:

"It was noted that the Street Lamps were being installed in the Village."

Wednesday, 1st March 1950

The Rock

The Rock is believed to have been built in the 17th Century, or possibly as early as the 16th Century, as a small timber-framed cottage and, like many other older properties in the area, has ships' timbers in the roof, probably obtained from the breakers' yards in Worcester. The house has been substantially enlarged over the centuries. The Enclosure Map of 1822 shows that Ann and Thomas King owned several acres of land and The Rock. E J King sold it to Henry Christopher Wise in 1851. It remained in Wise/Waller ownership probably until the late 1940s and was home for Sir Francis Waller and his sister Edith from 1902 until 1907 when Woodcote was let while Sir Francis was so frequently abroad in the Army.

A particular feature of The Rock for many years was 'The Weather Tree' which grew in the garden of the property. This tree, which was a variegated elm, was given its name by local people who believed it was able to forecast the weather for the ensuing summer. The legend was that if the leaves were mainly white there would be a hot summer while if they were mainly green a wet summer would follow. It is said that farmers came to consult the tree to help them decide which crops to plant.

There was believed to be only one other similar tree in the country and it was of such local fame that in 1952 the Parish Council asked Warwick Rural District Council to place a Tree Preservation Order on it, although the then owner had no intention of cutting it down. This request was initially refused on the grounds that it was not of sufficient merit to justify singling out. However, on recognising the level of local interest in the tree, an Order was placed on it in 1957. Sadly, by 1970 the tree had become diseased and, despite all efforts to save it, it had to be felled in 1975. The variegated leaves can still be seen in the hedge that grows on the boundary wall from shoots that have sprouted from the roots of the old tree.

The Weather Tree at The Rock, 1932

Reading Room Cottage

The first school house in the village was pulled down in 1824 during the rebuilding of the old vicarage, so Lord Leigh lent the parish a room for a school "added onto an old farm house" where the schoolmaster lived. When Frederick Webb came to Leek Wootton as schoolmaster in 1838 his residence is referred to as a "cottage" in the agreement which he signed upon occupying "the cottage and premises". However, these buildings could not be specifically identified from the church records.

More than thirty years later, when the new school opened in 1875, a new schoolmaster was appointed and the 1881 Census reveals Frederick Webb, ex schoolmaster, now 78 years old, living at "The Old School House, joining the Reading Room". It is therefore assumed that it was to the Reading Room on the lane by the church, which was owned by Lord Leigh at the time, that the school moved in 1825.

During the 1880s, 'Penny Readings' were held at the Reading Room, hosted by either Francis Beresford Wright or General George Waller, and designed for those wishing to listen and learn how to read. Concerts of music and readings performed by villagers were also held there. Later the property became a working men's clubroom with bagatelle, an air rifle team, billiards and a bar. Bernard Dee, son of the baker at Stone Cottage, remembers delivering bread and cheese for the men and finding the room "full of black smoke and stinking of beer."

In 1940, Sir Wathen Waller bought the clubroom together with the adjoining cottage and cottage garden from Lord Leigh. At that time Owen Wain occupied the cottage and it continued as a Working Men's Club. Owen died in 1950 but Mrs Wain, who was cleaner to the Club, continued to live there. Long time resident of the village, Les Jones, recalls the day a Jim Billington was enjoying his mug of beer and smoking his clay pipe and Les was playing darts, when a dart ricocheted off the board and smashed into Jim's clay pipe, shattering it. Les generously bought him a replacement. Whilst at the Reading Room the Club was strictly for 'Men Only'.

In the early 1960s, possibly after Lady Waller's death when her estate was sold, Joseph Henry Fox bought the property, renovated it and converted it into a house. The Working Men's Club moved to a purpose-built clubhouse on the recreation ground. Mr Fox sold the house to Judith and Tony Coltman in 1966 and in 1972 they bought a small part of the adjoining Stone House garden, added a 'granny annexe' and garage, and all is now known as Reading Room Cottage.

Minutes of The Parish Council:

"Bus Shelter It was reported this Shelter was again being used as sleeping accommodation .."

Thursday, 8th May 1958

Spring Cottage

Little is known of the history of this cottage. It is known that the water trough at the foot of the Vicarage drive was sited close to Spring Cottage, and a boar's tusk was found in the earth floor during renovation. When the garage was constructed the natural spring, after which the cottage is named, was disturbed and ran freely across the road. The spring may well have fed the trough, but has now been contained except for a small trickle that supplies the water feature in the garden of the adjoining cottage (83 Warwick Road).

The Stone House

Records of the site of The Stone House begin in the early 1700s and in about 1780 the site owner was Bertie Greatheed of Guys Cliffe who sold to a John Tims. About fifty years later Tims' executors sold the site to a Thomas Rawlins and it was occupied by George and Hannah Jaggard. In 1859 the property was sold to John Nicks who was Clerk of Works at the building of the new house at Woodcote. Up until this date there had been four or five houses on the land, which was some 1,600 square yards in extent with a frontage to the main road. John Nicks proceeded to pull down some of the houses and he added on to the principal one, using stone and materials from the development of the new house at Woodcote. John Nicks was Agent for the Woodcote estate to both George Wise and Major General George Waller and he lived at The Stone House he created until his death in 1894, when he bequeathed the house and land to Eddie Wise, son of Henry Christopher and his second wife Jane.

Late 1870s

In 1909 Eddie Wise sold The Stone House to Sir Francis Waller and it was then leased to various parties over the next thirty or so years, including for a few years Captain Gilbert Dolben Paul, who was married to Eddie's sister Alba. Half an acre of extra garden south of the house was purchased from Lord Leigh in 1940 and Sir Wathen and Lady Waller moved to the house in July of that year when the Red Cross occupied Woodcote. Lady Viola continued to live at The Stone House after Sir Wathen's death and she died there in 1962. The house was bought by Barry and Audrey Gillitt, who had a bungalow built to the south-west of the main house (Stonefield). In subsequent years they have made various other alterations both to the house itself, and in selling off the stabling/garage block on the main road for the development of Stone House Mews.

Jane Pain, Roselyn Commander, Ian McAllester, Jean Singleton

Minutes of The Parish Council:

"Mrs Rotherham raised the question of the poor service rendered to the public of Leek Wootton by the Midland Red Bus Company and it was resolved ... that the Company be asked to arrange for additional buses ... in order that residents might have public transport to and from the evening performances of the cinemas at Coventry, Kenilworth, Warwick and Leamington."

Friday 25th February 1946

Minutes of The Parish Council:

"The Council felt Hill Wootton Rd. houses should now all be numbered ..."

Thursday, 20th September 1962

Village Houses

117

View of the Village from Church Tower, 1960s
Courier Photographic Services, Leamington Spa

PROGRAMME
OF
CONCERT & PENNY READINGS,
TO BE GIVEN IN THE
READING ROOM, LEEK WOOTTON,
ON THURSDAY, OCTOBER 28TH, 1886.

F. B. WRIGHT, Esq., in the Chair.

1.	OVERTURE	*The Fairy Queen*	THE MISSES FITZHERBERT.
2.	SONG	"Long, Long ago."	MR. J. ARCHER.
3.	SONG		~~MISS WRIGHT~~ H?
4.	SONG		MR. J. JENKINS.
5.	SONG		MR. TAPSFIELD.
6.	SONG	"Home Rule."	MR. F. JENKINS.
7.	SONG	*I've got a little list*	MISS C. FITZHERBERT.
8.	READING	"The Chameleon."	MR. FRIER.
9.	SONG	"The Muffin Man."	MR. J. HUCKVALE.
10.	SONG		MR. FREEMAN.
11.	SONG	"People will talk."	MR. T. TAPSFIELD.
12.	RECITATION	"How I gained my Victoria Cross."	MR. J. LYNES.
13.	PIANOFORTE SOLO	"Silvery Waves."	MISS H. WATERS.
14.	~~SONG~~ Banjo	*Go & put your bonnet on Betsy*	MISS H. FITZHERBERT.
15.	SONG		MR. CAVES.
16.	SONG	"Only one."	MR. J. ARCHER.
17.	READING		MR. WILKINS.
18.	SONG		MISS WATERS.
19.	SONG	"All very fine and large."	MR. A. WESTON.
20.	DIALOGUE	"Generally Useful."	MESSRS. J. & W. LYNES.
21.	SONG		MR. J. JENKINS.
22.	~~SONG~~ Trio	*The little maids from school*	Messrs Wright & Fitz Herbert MR. FREEMAN.
23.	SONG	"Ten Little Niggers."	MESSRS. KEYTE, LYNES, PITMAN.

GOD SAVE THE QUEEN.

DOORS OPEN AT HALF-PAST SIX. TO COMMENCE AT SEVEN.

ADMISSION:—Front Seats, 3d. Second Seats, 2d. Back Seats, 1d.

RULES OF THE
LEEK WOOTTON WORKING MEN'S CLUB,
With
Reading Room and Air Gun.

Patron - - - Rt. Hon. Lord Leigh.
President - - - Rev. S. E. Longland.
Secretary - - - O. W. Holmes.

1.—That the Institution be called "The Leek Wootton Working Men's Club with Reading Room and Air Gun" and its objects shall be Reading, Recreation and Refreshment.

2.—That the Committee consist of a President, Secretary and Treasurer, and two other members to be nominated by Lord Leigh, and of five members to be chosen annually at a meeting held in October, Committeemen must be residents in the parish and over 21 years of age.

3.—All members shall pay an entrance fee of sixpence, and a quarterly subscription of ninepence to be paid in advance, and no member shall be entitled to any privilege of the Institution who is in arrear with his subscription. Quarter nights fall due in the first week of January, April, July, and October.

4.—No person to be admitted as a member who is under sixteen years of age.

5.—Strange workmen may be admitted as members on payment of an entrance fee of 3d. and a weekly subscription of 4d., after being proposed and seconded by members with the consent of the Secretary and two Committeemen in addition. A meeting to be called for their election to be voted on if they are objected to by any member. Their names must be posted up as in rule 10.

6.—The funds shall be applied towards paying the expenses connected with the working of the Club; no surplus being divisible among members individually.

7.—All games are allowed which do not interfere with the quiet and good order of the room; but no gambling of any sort to be permitted.

8.—No newspaper or periodical to be detained more than fifteen minutes after it has been asked for by another member. This rule applies to games. No newspaper, less than two days old, or periodical to be taken away without the sanction of the Secretary or Caretaker.

9.—Any member may introduce a friend as a visitor, but the same person shall not be introduced again until after the lapse of 14 days except by payment of one penny a night. No payment shall be made by a visitor for any goods, and no refreshment shall be carried off the premises by any person who is not a member of the Club.

10.—Persons may be nominated at any time by posting up their names with the names of proposer and seconder in the Club but they shall not be members until (after an interval of not less than 48 hours) their admission has been approved by the Secretary and two Committee men.

11.—No refreshment shall be purchased by, or given to any intoxicated person.

12.—No intoxicated person shall be admitted at any time and any member using bad language shall be fined sixpence, and be suspended from the benefits of the Club until such fine is paid. Any misconduct, if persisted in, to be punished by expulsion.

13.—No member shall be allowed to vote at any meeting who is in arrear with his subscription.

14.—The Caretaker shall attend on Monday from 8 to 8.30 p.m. to exchange Books, &c. Non-members may have books on payment of 1d. a volume. After a book has been borrowed 14 days, a warning will be given and then a fine of 2d. enforced if it is not returned.

15.—A list of newspapers shall be hung in the Club and also articles sold, and the price of them.

16.—Members shall be supplied with a copy of the rules on joining the Club.

17.—The Committee shall make such bye-laws as may be necessary for the working of the Club.

18.—The Annual General Meeting shall be held in October, when officers for the ensuing year shall be appointed and any proposed alterations of the rules put to the meeting for consideration. Arrangements for working the Club and alterations of the rules to be subject to the approval of the President.

19.—Annual donations of not less than five shillings entitle to Honorary Membership, after the name has been posted up as in rule 10.

20.—Six days per week the Club shall open at 10 a.m. and close at 10 p.m., except when a reasonable extension has been sanctioned by the Committee and approved by the president.

The Castle Press, Printers, Warwick.

Leek Wootton Working Men's Club Football Team

Leek Wootton Working Men's Club Shooting Team
Warwickshire Air Rifle League, 1925

Standing l-r: – Chapman; Charles Holmes; Percy Lawson; Oliver Holmes; William Golby
Seated l–r: Ernest Gregory; Reginald Gregory; Tom Forrest; – Coleman

15

From the Stable to the Bakehouse

The recollections of Bernard Dee, long time and much-respected resident of Leek Wootton, on the life of his family and the Village Stores.

    The Village Stores was run by members of my family for over forty years and included a shop, Post Office and bakehouse. The property, Stone Cottage, was rented from the Waller estate and was situated on the Warwick Road, opposite to the junction of Hill Wootton Road. It is now a family home and known as The Old Post House.

    My father William was born in Fulbrook near Sherbourne in 1893 and his family later moved to Alveston. This is where he started his working life as a stable boy for a Lady Muntz, and where he met my mother, Dorothy, who was in service to the same family. She was born in London in 1894.

    William's duties included exercising the horses, and he told the story of one stallion that was particularly high spirited and which he sometimes had to lead to Stratford and back to visit the blacksmith. He was strictly forbidden to ride the horse but on one occasion my father saw a workman with a handcart who agreed that he could stand on the cart in order to mount the horse. He rode back to Alveston feeling very pleased with himself. Unfortunately Lady Muntz saw him ride into the stableyard and sacked him on the spot.

    He then started work at Alveston bakery, and after serving in the Irish Guards in the 1914-1918 War, he married my mother and lived in Ullenhall, and then Evesham, where he managed a bakehouse, and I was born in 1923. In 1932 the family moved to Leek Wootton.

    My father purchased the business and goodwill of the Village Stores, bakery and the delivery round from a man named Hancocks who played a dirty trick on him and 'sold him a pup'. When Hancocks showed my father his books, his list of customers looked impressive. However, when my father took control of the business, he discovered that Hancocks had a relation who was also a baker in Cubbington and this man had taken over many of the customers, leaving my father with just twenty-three, but not for long. Father was a good baker and a very determined character; and soon customers came to him to buy his crusty bread. Eventually his delivery round covered not only Leek Wootton and Hill Wootton, but also Blackdown, Chesford, Ashow, part of Warwick and most of Kenilworth.

    The secret of his breadmaking was to burn a bundle of faggots (twigs) in the oven before the dough was put in, giving a wonderful flavour to the crust. He baked both white and brown bread, and he also made cakes, pork pies and hot-cross buns. At harvest time he baked three loaves in the shape of stooks of corn for the church, and he would cook poultry and joints of meat in the bread oven on Christmas Day for the village people, a practice which we continued until the mid 1960s.

    My mother was in charge of the shop and Post Office whilst my father baked the bread and did the delivering. He would be out of bed by 5.30 am and a sack of post

Dorothy and William Dee

would be delivered to the Post Office once a day at 6.00 am. This post had to be sorted by members of the family and then delivered around the village. This system continued until the late 1950s. Occasionally the post was delivered with the newspapers, which was against Post Office rules but was a practice that often happened in the countryside. Deliveries were first made by a carrier bicycle but later we used a motorcycle and box sidecar, and from 1938 we used a motor van.

My brother Dennis, who later ran the village Scout Troop, and I delivered the newspapers locally whilst my father delivered them to the outlying areas. Dennis also helped with deliveries during the War as well as working long hours in a factory.

I started at Leek Wootton School in 1932 and moved to Kenilworth Secondary School in Priory Road in 1934. I left school in 1937 when I was fourteen years old to work in the family business.

Before the Second World War my father was a Special Constable, along with his friend John Hobbins. When the IRA was active in Coventry, they used to patrol the railway lines that passed through the parish, from Milverton at one end to Kenilworth at the other. He was also on the Parish Council from the mid-1930s until 1950, and was Chairman for a time.

When Woodcote became a convalescent home for wounded troops during the War, our bakehouse supplied all their bread, which was quite a substantial order. Bread was not on ration during the War although it did go 'on coupon' for a short time afterwards.

When Coventry was blitzed, some bakehouses were damaged and much of the city was without gas, electricity and water for a while. So, along with other bakers in the county, we had to bake extra bread every day, which was collected and taken to feed the people of Coventry. When a bomb was dropped near The Stone House in the village, its impact weakened the bread ovens and, although they remained usable, they eventually had to be replaced. There were many evacuees in the village and I remember a London boy who went to the school who, each morning, would knock on the bakehouse door and ask in his London accent "Got any stale bans?" He was always given a fresh bun and was known affectionately by the family as 'stale bans'.

The shop was at the centre of village life, where villagers often exchanged news about the local lads who were away fighting in the armed forces. Most days a member of the Wright family, often Doreen, whose own husband Gilbert was missing in France, would call in to ask about them.

In 1942 I joined the RAF, trained as an Aircraft Fitter, and was posted to India. The sea journey took three months, apart from the two weeks spent in a transit camp in Durban in South Africa. When my mother told Doreen Wright that I was in Lahore, she sent me a letter of introduction to a friend of hers who lived there. I was invited to lunch and asked to bring a friend from the base. The lady was very friendly and put two young aircraftmen at ease, the meal was a great success, and it was definitely an improvement on the camp food. I returned home in 1946 and was demobbed the following year.

I started work again in the bakehouse and went on day release to Coventry Technical College for two years and then on to Birmingham Catering College where I studied baking, confectionery and bread making, and gained a first-class award in my City and Guilds Exams.

Bernard Dee, 1942

When the Waller estate was sold in 1947, the family wanted to buy Stone Cottage, but a representative from the Abbey National Building Society inspected the building and refused to grant us a mortgage because the building was in too bad a condition. Stanley Hattrell and Aubrey Jones then purchased it, but the family continued to run the business. When my parents retired I took over the business, and I was helped by my wife Anne and by our three children.

I followed in my father's footsteps by becoming a member of the Parish Council and also served as Chairman. We eventually stopped baking bread in the mid-1960s because the oven flues needed replacing, which would have been very expensive and we had no security of tenure. The shop finally closed in the early 1970s, although we continued delivering newspapers twice a day until 1992 when I sold the round to Guy Sullivan, who continues to operate it today. My parents had moved to a cottage in the village, and my mother died in 1975, my father in 1982. Anne and I still live happily in retirement in Leek Wootton.

Cake of Village Church by Bernard Dee

Bernard Dee

The Village Stores

<u>Minutes of The Parish Council:</u>

"*it was mentioned that some means of showing the next clearing of the Post-Office letter box would be a benefit to the Public.*"

Thursday, 5th September 1912

"*…seen the Post Office Mistress … She informed him that the Post authorities do not supply indicators to any Sub-post offices.*"

Thursday, 24th October 1912

"*Proposed … that the Clerk write to the Post-Master of Warwick to inform him that much inconvenience is experienced – especially on Thursdays by the smallness of the Leek Wootton Post-Office Box*"

Thursday, 23rd September 1914

"*Proposed … that the Post man's half holiday be given on Saturday evenings.*"

Wednesday, 21st January 1923

16

Chesford Grange

No. 3011. Chesford Grange.

Joseph Hinks was a very successful lamp manufacturer from Birmingham whose family appears in the 1881 Census in Milverton, Leamington Spa. He and his wife Frances had seven children, the last two Bertram aged six and Ernest aged two, having been born in fashionable Leamington Spa. Joseph and his father James ran their business from 91 Great Hampton Street, Birmingham, and they were described as 'lamp, incandescent, gas and electric fittings manufacturers'.

In 1900 Joseph leased land from Lord Leigh and built Chesford Grange for his large family and accompanying servants. The house was built with no expense spared. "When Chesford was built only the best materials were used, all the rooms had fine plaster ceilings moulded with bunches of flowers, many of the walls were panelled in oak or mahogany and the fireplaces were of carved wood. A coach house with a glass roof ... provided room for four cars and stalls for a number of horses."

The family continued living at Chesford Grange until, in 1908, the name of Hinks can no longer be found in local records. Although Joseph's father had died in 1905 aged eighty-nine, this did not appear to be the reason for the family moving away, as they were at Chesford for some three years afterwards. An entry in the Kenilworth Advertiser for 7th February 1907 merely states:

> **Chesford Grange**
> Chesford Grange, near Kenilworth, built by
> Mr Joseph Hinks and occupied by him since
> leaving Leamington Spa, has been sold by
> Messrs. Walter Collins and Son, of Leamington,
> to Lord Algernon Percy. Mr and Mrs Hinks will
> shortly remove to the neighbourhood of Windsor.

CHESFORD GRANGE RESTAURANT, KENILWORTH.

By 1911 Joseph is to be found living in Marlow, Berkshire but by 1915 their house there has new occupiers and Joseph and his family cannot be traced.

Chesford's new owner was Lord Algernon Malcolm Arthur Percy from nearby Guy's Cliffe. He was the second son of the 6th Duke of Northumberland and had been educated at Eton and Oxford. His career included the Grenadier Guards and he eventually became an MP. He bought Chesford for his daughter Katherine Louise Victoria who, in 1904, had married her distant cousin Josceline Reginald Heber-Percy. Katherine and Josceline are recorded at Chesford Grange in 1909. Lord Percy was no doubt delighted to have purchased such a suitable house for his daughter and son-in-law so close to his own. Josceline served in the Northumberland Fusiliers and life may have been lonely for Katherine had she not had her parents so close by at Guy's Cliffe.

Josceline Heber-Percy had a distinguished career in the Army, serving in the Great War before becoming Deputy Lord Lieutenant of Warwickshire in 1923, and a JP. There were three children of the marriage and the family moved from Chesford Grange to Guy's Cliffe, certainly before 1924, probably to help Katherine's elderly parents run the estate.

By 1924 the new owner of Chesford Grange was Henry Pratt, the son of Henry Pratt JP, of Dukinfield, Cheshire. Born in 1881 and educated at Giggleswick, he was married with two sons and two daughters. Whilst occupying Chesford he was Sheriff of Caernarvonshire in 1928. It is believed that Henry Pratt made his money through BP Oil.

Chris Jackson remembers, as a young girl in the village, the Pratts as a benevolent family. When she was growing up in the 1920s the Pratt family used to give a Christmas party for all the local school children, some seventy in total. There would always be a large Christmas tree reaching up to the ceiling of the big hall, and they would put on a cinema show and tea party for the children. It was the Pratts who gave chairs for the WI Hut. Chris also remembers, perhaps a few years later, a charabanc being laid on from the village to go to the theatre at Chesford Grange, and even the play that was produced, 'Outward Bound', which she says she "couldn't make head nor tail of".

The Pratt family was still at Chesford in 1935 but in 1938 Henry Pratt died and the Hames family, who had to move from The Gatehouse at Kenilworth Castle, heard that Chesford was empty and successfully took up residence in late 1938. They found that the property had been uninhabited for some time but having been built of quality materials simply required lots of 'elbow grease' to make it good again. The family lived in part of the house, using other areas as a hotel/restaurant. Regular dances and visits from day-trippers ensured they did well.

Soon after the start of the Second World War Chesford was requisitioned by the War Department and used as the Rover design centre. Rover was one of the companies involved in the development of gas turbine engines for aircraft, and there is an interesting rumour that parts of one of Frank Whittle's early jet engines were dumped in the Avon at Chesford.

Shortly after the War, with his family all gone, Philip Hames was allowed to return to his former home but the sight of the carnage in this once beautiful house devastated the young man and he left. Some time later the house apparently became a Borstal institution before reverting to a hotel and, by 1956, Chesford Grange Hotel was being run by a Mr Richardson.

By 1965 the occupier, perhaps manager, is Mr Eckersley whose daughter Nicola was baptised at All Saints Church on 29th December 1968.

In recent times ownership of the hotel has changed several times, and in the mid-1980s it actually changed hands four times in six years. Successive owners have continued to expand the property and who would recognise the place described in this 1960s guide?

> "The residential facilities are second to none…
> and offer 40 bedrooms…
> all with radio and intercom, over half of them also having
> private showers or baths, and toilets."

There is now a leisure club and there are plans for a conference hall and more bedrooms. Many problems have been overcome since the devastation of the occupation during the Second World War, and a fire on New Year's Eve 1994, and the hotel is thriving. It provides employment opportunities for local people and brings business and leisure users into the area. Joseph Hinks would certainly not recognise his old home but he would have to acknowledge that a house designed to represent his success to the outside world had certainly gone from strength to strength. One successful enterprise has helped generate another, one hundred years apart.

Caroline Gath

<u>Minutes of The Parish Council:</u>

"Mr England drew attention to the fact of Public Bathing in the day time near Chesford Bridge. The Chairman undertook that steps should be taken to put a stop to it."

Monday, 21st July 1895

17

The Anchor

The Anchor Inn, 1907
Warwickshire County Record Office, PH 420/14

A naval connection so far from the sea? A symbolic name maybe (the anchor is, for example, a Christian symbol of hope)? Or does it represent something unchanging? Certainly the first appearance of the name dates back a long way, at least to 1813, when Thomas Morris promised to "keep good Order ... and suffer no unlawful Game in his house". The site remains largely unchanged from the 1822 Enclosure Award which shows three or four cottages joined together with a gap and more buildings, comparable to the existing driveway and Anchor Cottages, whilst the land at the rear is marked as orchards in 1822. Many pubs had their own brewery at this time and perhaps the orchard provided fruit for this purpose.

Thomas Morris and his family owned the pub until selling it to the Wise family in 1853. The Morris children were baptised at All Saints between 1813 and 1818 and they appear on the Censuses of 1841 and 1851. Thomas, his wife, and daughter Sarah all died within just over a year of one another in 1854-5 and were buried together in the churchyard.

Four years later, in 1857, Henry Wise pulled down the Anchor Cottages, replacing them with new dwellings on the same site. The Ragsdale family, originally from Nottingham, were employed as tenant licensees. John and Elizabeth Ragsdale and their niece Sarah were also to have long-lasting connections with the village. Elizabeth was still Landlady of The Anchor when she died in 1884, aged 81, but John carried on until retiring, with Sarah, to Leamington Spa. The Vicar records the event in the Parish Almanac, "the chief [change] has been the departure of our old friends Mr and Miss Ragsdale from The Anchor. We cannot help missing them though in Mr and Mrs Caves they have found, I trust, worthy successors, anxious to retain for The Anchor its good name as a thoroughly respectable well-conducted village inn". John, Elizabeth and Sarah are buried together at All Saints.

Like their predecessors, Joseph Caves, his wife Harriet and their four children, who took up residence in 1887, were also to inhabit the pub for a long time. Joseph was also a wheelwright and became a member of the Parish Council in 1907 and remained one until his death in 1916. Harriet died suddenly in 1893, aged forty-four, and Joseph re-married. He is buried with his second wife, Mary, in the churchyard, the grave overlooking that of Harriet and their daughter Alice (later Higham). On Joseph's death Alice and her husband John took over the pub, keeping it in the family until her retirement in 1936. By all accounts she was a real pub owner, very smart and fun. She was a good businesswoman and it is thought that she might have done bed and breakfast. Her husband used to take a pride in the pub's appearance, keeping the steps white and joking that he had "half a bed to let" when she went away on trips.

Billy Bass took over in 1936/7 and ran the pub until at least 1948. It was probably around this time, in pre-National Health Service days, that the 'Second Dividend Society' was run from The Anchor, with people paying a little money in each week to fund unexpected doctor's bills or absences from work.

Sir Wathen Waller sold lands including The Anchor and Anchor Cottages at auction in 1946 to Atkinson's Breweries of Aston for £13,150. In the auction particulars the Anchor Cottages are described as having detached washhouses and electric lights.

Between about 1950 and 1961 Frank C Martin was the landlord. Frank, a good looking man, would put on his blazer and play the piano in the lounge on a Friday or Saturday night, Ivor Novello tunes were a speciality, and he is remembered with great affection to this day. It is believed that he retired to Bournemouth.

Jack and Lily Gibbs took over from Frank Martin in the early sixties. Paul MacMahon, who was later himself the licensee, but in those days an area supervisor for the Mitchell & Butlers Brewery, remembers that Jack came to The Anchor from the King's Arms and Castle (latterly Drummonds) in Kenilworth. Jack Gibbs died pulling a pint and, unusually for those days, the brewery agreed to the tenancy being transferred to his widow Lily, in recognition of her long and loyal service. In those days it was a pub for regulars, and outsiders were strictly vetted. After Jack's death, one regular remembers of Lily that "she became more and more nocturnal, so that after-hours drinking increased. Since the Constabulary Headquarters then had no bar, the Anchor was the local watering hole for the police and so late drinking was no problem. However, precautions were taken to avoid too much advantage being taken. When time was called the regulars would sneak quietly into the snug, which was hardly ever used, and there we would sit quietly in the cold and dark until Mrs G called us out to resume drinking."

Lily was a fascinating character in her own right. The same regular remembers "...down the stairs Mrs Lily Gibbs would make her usual dramatic entrance. She had been a widow for a good many years but remained slim, handsome, tall and statuesque.

LOT 3.
(Coloured Pink on Sale Plan.)

THE VERY VALUABLE

Freehold fully-licensed Premises

known as

"THE ANCHOR INN,"

occupying a prominent position on the Warwick to Kenilworth and Coventry main road at the corner of the road leading to "Woodcote," in the centre of

LEEK WOOTTON VILLAGE

with Garages, Car Parking space, Lawn and Garden at the rear.

Let on lease to Messrs. Hunt, Edmunds and Co. Ltd., for 21 years from 24th June, 1936, at a rent of

£130. 0s. 0d. per annum

both parties having the option by giving six months' notice to terminate the tenancy at **24th June, 1950.**

The Lessor covenants to insure, do structural repairs and outside painting—the Lessees covenanting otherwise to keep the premises in good and tenantable repair and to insure the Licence.

THE PREMISES are brick built, with tiled roof, and contain :—

ON THE GROUND FLOOR: Entrance passage with wood block floor ; **Tap Room**, with brick arched fireplace and wood block floor ; **Bar** with brick built fireplace ; **Smoke Room**, 13ft. 3in. by 12ft., with fireplace, dwarf cupboard and outer door ; **Lounge**, 20ft. by 12ft., with tiled fireplace and cupboards at side, a covered yard off which is a Ladies' lavatory, connects with the **Living Kitchen,** having sink (h. and c.) and "Triplex" grate with airing cupboard at side; Pantry and Washhouse with copper and sink.

ON THE FIRST FLOOR : Four Bedrooms and Bathroom with porcelain enamelled bath (h. and c.), basin (h. and c.) and cupboard.

There is a capital rock hewn Cellar and adjoining the Washhouse a Bottle Store similarly formed.

Electric Light, Main water, Main drainage.

OUTSIDE are Coalhouse, a lean-to **Greenhouse**, 18ft. by 7ft. 6in, **three open fronted Garages** with Loft over ; paved car-washing space with drain ; **Garage** and Ladies' and Gent's lavatories.

Adjoining a Lawn at the rear are a Summer Arbour and a wooden Shed ; there are also useful **Car parking space** and Garden.

Part O.S. Map No. 210, Parish of Leek Wootton—area ·655 acre, or

2r. 24p. or thereabouts.

NOTE. The western boundary of this Lot is at the base of the stone wall as indicated by pegs on the ground.

Auction Particulars, 1946

Strikingly blonde, beautifully made-up and immaculately dressed, she presided over a superb pub with firmness and great good humour."

During the Gibbs' time, an equally well known couple worked at the pub. Tom Forrest had been a regular for at least sixty-five of his eighty-one years and "could well have been the model for his namesake in The Archers". Bertha Forrest (née Ecclestone) served as a barmaid for about fifty years and was affectionately known as "droopy drawers". If someone did or said something amiss, Bertha would claim to have spanked his backside when he was in short trousers and "wouldn't hesitate to do the same again." She was a bit of a Mrs Malaprop, speaking for instance of "asparrowgrass".

At this time, in the 1960s, mild was 1s 5d (12p) a pint and bitter 1s 9d (14p). No food was provided on a regular basis though there was bangers and mash for all-comers on Bonfire Night. More people drank mild than bitter and Mrs Gibbs always provided cheap, still, strong cider from a barrel in the bar. Later, in the late 1970s/early 1980s there was a revival of real ale appreciation and The Anchor appears in a number of editions of the CAMRA publication, The Good Beer Guide, as selling good real ale, and winning an award for the quality of its ale.

By the early 1980s the brewery was hoping to modernise the pub and increase its rental income from the site but was committed to honouring its agreement with Lily. She herself used to say, "I'll be carried out of here", but in the end she left very suddenly. Paul MacMahon, on a brewery visit, just prior to Christmas 1978, was surprised to hear her say "I want to leave on the 8th of January." The timing was appalling and potential replacements were few. Paul made the chance remark that he "wouldn't mind having it", and shortly thereafter he and his wife Mary took over.

The bulk of the day-to-day running fell to Mary, as Paul himself was still contracted to the brewery for the first twelve months.

Paul and Mary MacMahon, 1987
Kenilworth Weekly News

Five coal fires had to be cleaned out every day and the upstairs needed renovation, in addition to the running of the pub. Nevertheless things improved, lunches were started six days a week and the pub was twice nominated for Pub of the Month in the local press. Money was raised regularly for the Seniors' Christmas party, which was held every year between 1980 and 1993. A major refurbishment was completed in 1982, with the official pulling of the first pint being carried out by Bertha Forrest.

Mary MacMahon sadly died in 1988 but her legacy lived on. The Anchor had been involved with charity fund-raising for some time, which continued, and some seven thousand pounds was raised in her memory for the Walsgrave Cancer Appeal.

Happily, Paul later met and married Sheila, a local teacher, who settled into running the business with him for the last three years before they retired to Kenilworth in 1994.

Anchor Fundraisers, 1989
Kenilworth Weekly News

In the late seventies/early eighties regular events included Monday's Crib and Dominoes Night; Thursday's Darts Night (roast potatoes and black pudding provided); Shoot Lunches (with bottles of port, beer, whisky and sloe gin to wash down the meal) and; New Year's Eve celebrations, which went on until at least 3 o'clock in the morning.

Characters? Every pub has them and The Anchor is no exception. From the earlier times, Mick Ryan is remembered, playing his squeezebox; and Tom Dilworth, unofficial 'mayor' of Leek Wootton, who had used the pub since the 1920s, who knew everyone and worked as a carpenter in one of the big houses in the village. He would leave The Anchor at 9 pm to go visiting the sick of the village; Hamil Semple, head barman in his time; and Joyce Bates who, while Bertha Forrest presided over the Bar, worked in the Lounge with quiet, cheerful efficiency.

More recently, there was Joe Barnes the village handyman and specialist watch repairer, who used to bottle up each morning. Joe lived in one of the Anchor Cottages and would sit in the bar each evening with his King Edward cigar firmly between his lips, only occasionally removing it to drink his pint; The Reverend Charles Nettleship, Vicar and an ex-Army Brigadier, who was partial to pink gins; and Roger Cripps, a local solicitor and amateur auctioneer extraordinaire. He would try to get all and sundry involved in the pub auctions, held to raise money for charity, emphasising each item's uniqueness and potential investment value. And of course there were no doubt many, many others of which we have not heard.

Following the retirement of Paul and Sheila MacMahon, the licence was taken over by Patrick McCosker and colleagues, who run a local chain of pub/restaurants. They have changed the nature of most of the pub by extending the kitchens, adding more tables and offering an extensive menu throughout trading hours. The bar, however, still provides a watering hole for the locals.

This chapter began by asking why The Anchor is so named. We shall end it with Paul MacMahon's answer which is that it has no significance whatsoever. Paul's explanation, that it was just one on a list of names, regardless of its proximity to the coast, will have to satisfy our curiosity. There are, after all, some things that we will just never know.

Caroline Gath

18

Goodrest and Wedgnock Park

Until after the Second World War, the western border of our civil parish was drawn on an approximately north-south line along the western boundary of what is now The Warwickshire. Previously the land to the west had been a part of the estate of Warwick Castle, called Wedgnock Park. It served as a deer park for the Castle and, in order to keep the animals in, was bordered with a park 'pale' consisting of a fence or hedge on top of a bank with a ditch, evidence of which can still be seen on the southern side of Rouncil Lane and adjacent to Goodrest Farm.

Wedgnock Park was developed in the 13th Century and was owned by Warwick Castle from at least 1253 when Margery, Countess of Warwick, gave "the tithes of the assarts there and the pannage and venison to the Hospital of St Michael in Warwick". It encompassed land from Budbrooke to the south, west towards Hatton and Beausale, and north, beyond the present day Fernhill Farm, to the border with Honiley. The dimensions were set down in 1845 and the Park totalled nearly 3,000 acres. It contained in its north-east top corner a few fields that were within the old boundary of Leek Wootton, the access drive from Roundshill (Rouncil) Lane to Goodrest Farm, but not the farm buildings.

The western boundary of the civil parish was advanced in the 20th Century by taking in an area of the Parish of Beausale. This change brought into our parish a larger part of the Park's former land, including Goodrest Farm, Prospect Farm and Deer Park Farm.

Goodrest Farm is the site of the remains of the double-moated mediaeval manor house of Goodrest. It is not known when these moats were dug, but the peak period

Moat of Goodrest Lodge, 19th Century
Birmingham Library Service

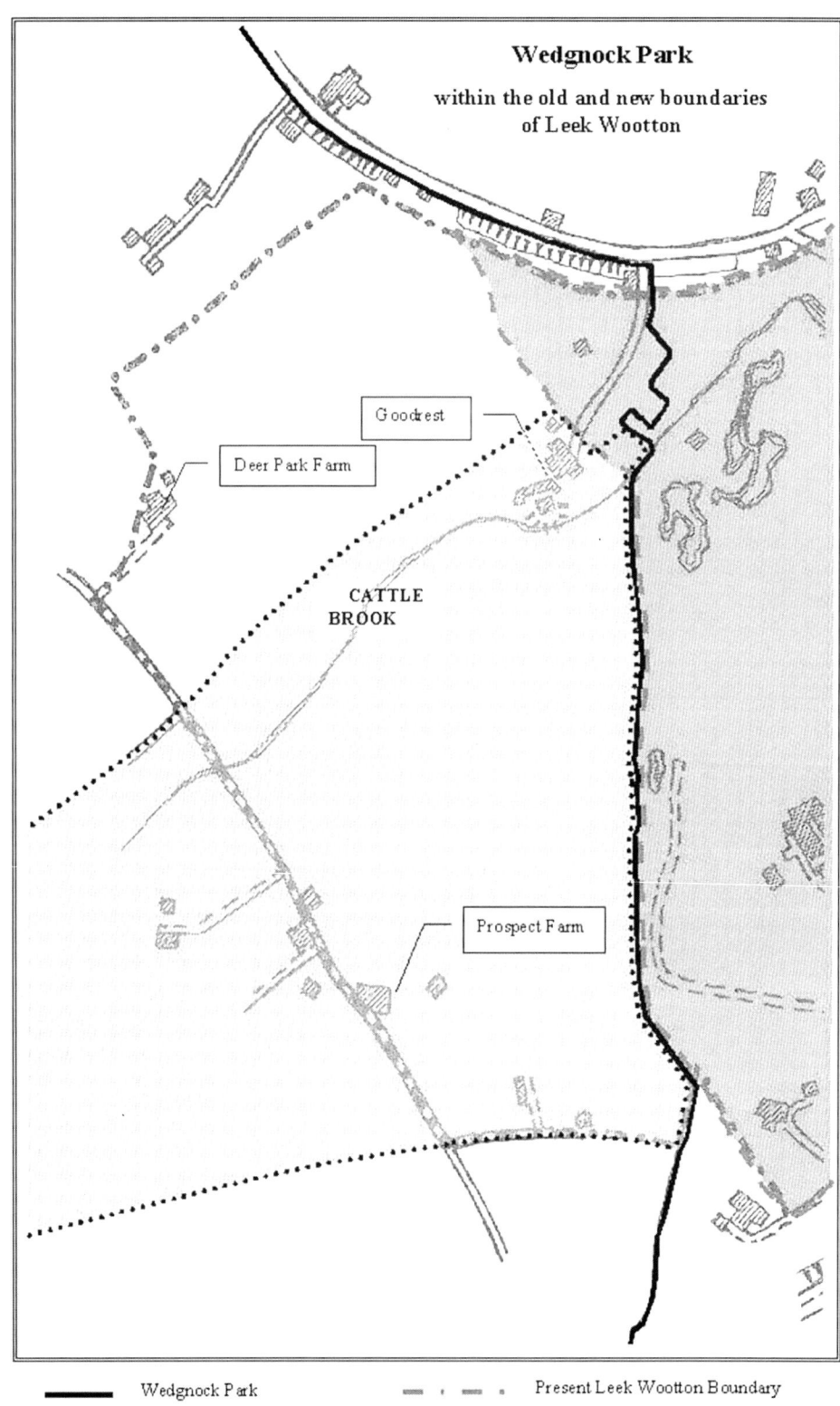

for construction of such moats was between 1250 and 1350. During that period they were built for reasons of status and anti-theft, rather than defence. The outer moat kept poachers away from the ponds in which fish were bred before they were turned out into a ten-acre lake. The lake was formed by a dam across the Cattle Brook, on either end of which probably stood watermills. The moated site, the area of the dam, watermills and a nearby section of the park pale are listed ancient monuments. The moats and the dam can be clearly seen today. There is a record of the dam being repaired in 1702 but the lake is likely to have ceased to exist not long after that date, from lack of water if the current flow through Cattle Brook is anything to go by.

Thomas Beauchamp, 12th Earl of Warwick, is believed to have built the original house some time between 1369, when he became the Earl, and 1374, when he obtained a licence to have divine offices celebrated in his oratory there. Subsequent records of repairs to the house indicate that it was a large three-storey timber framed building with wattle and daub in-fill. Excavations by the Birmingham Archaeological Society in 1922-3 revealed patterned glazed floor tiles similar to those found at Kenilworth Abbey. It was clearly a superior building and was probably used by the family to escape from the noise and bustle of the garrisoned Castle at Warwick. It is known that the Earl held a meeting of his Council at Goodrest in 1375. In 'The Antiquities of Warwickshire' Dugdale supposed that Goodrest "was so called, in respect that some of the Countesses of Warwick to avoid much concourse of people, retired hither when they were near the time of Childbirth; for 'tis plain, that many of their children were born here, as I have elsewhere observed". In 1404 Margaret was born there to Elizabeth, wife of Richard Beauchamp, Earl of Warwick, and in 1479 the Duke of Clarence was paying a gardener at Goodrest one penny per day. We do not know what was grown but it was most likely fruit and herbs as the aristocracy of the day would not have eaten vegetables, which they would have considered peasants' food.

In 1418 the Duke of Bedford, a brother of King Henry V, visited Goodrest. Six tons of oats were sold for £4 to pay for his hospitality. Later in 1426 he came to the Castle and this time 4,340 bundles of firewood were sold for £5 2s 0d to pay for his visit. The reason for these visits is not known; they may have been social occasions for deer hunting or perhaps high level political discussions took place between the Duke and Richard Beauchamp, arguably two of the most powerful men in the country at the time. The two were obviously close allies for in 1431, when Bedford was the Regent of France, he appointed Richard to supervise the trial of Joan of Arc in Rouen.

The house was no doubt used as a hunting lodge, but the Park was not just for sport. It was a thriving farm and in the early days Goodrest was the centre of the farming activities. Oats, barley, rye and hay were all grown and stored in a thatched barn at Goodrest. Oxen, cows, sheep, pigs and horses were all kept in the Park. In 1417 there was a dairy at Goodrest, which produced cheese from a herd of forty cows.

The area was more heavily wooded than today as quite a large part of the farm's income came from the sale of timber for firewood, and the lake would have provided fresh fish. Some of the output from the farm was used at the Castle for the Earl's household while a substantial amount was sold for revenue.

In 1590 Ambrose Dudley, the 21st Earl of Warwick, died without surviving issue and the estate passed to the Crown. In 1597, Sir Fulke Greville obtained the offices

Goodrest House, 20th Century

and fees relating to Wedgnock Park for life, "namely 2d a day as ranger, 2d as woodward, 4d as keeper of Goodrest Manor and 6d as keeper of Fernhill Woods". He promptly had repairs carried out to the house as the "timber frame had shrunk and needed to be forced back into place and secured with iron clamps", and the roof, windows and chimney were in want of repair. The estate was obviously a valuable one for in 1603 Robert Dudley, who claimed to be the rightful heir to Warwick Castle, challenged Fulke Greville's right to hold Wedgnock, but Dudley's claim was dismissed as he was considered to be illegitimate. In 1604 Sir Fulke Greville bought Warwick Castle which had been empty for fourteen years, and in 1609 he set up house at Goodrest while the Castle was being made habitable.

Between 1679 and 1682 the north-western parts of Wedgnock Park were inclosed, a number of new farmhouses were built, including Deer Park Farm, and leased to tenant farmers. Also in 1679 the Deer Park was reduced into what remained of the open parkland, with Goodrest at its north-eastern extremity. At this time the manor house fell back into disrepair and by 1696 it had ceased to appear on estate maps. In 1743 the process of inclosure of the park continued with most of the deer being removed to the new Temple Park. The remaining land was divided up and another new farmhouse was built at Prospect Farm.

After the manor house at Goodrest disappeared the farm remained and a barn was rethatched in 1750; in 1758 and 1760 a long hedge was planted between the Park and Mr Wise's estate, and in about 1784 the present farmhouse was built outside the moated area.

During the Second World Ward a Camp was set up at Goodrest and a Prisoner of War Camp in the area.

Goodrest and the other farms in this part of the parish continued to be part of the Warwick estate until 1959, when they were put up for sale in one lot, together with other local properties. The tenants clubbed together and were successful at the auction and purchased their own farms. Each then held his own farm, together with other peripheral parcels of land, such as the shooting range and Larch Covert, which they sold off at auction later in the same year. At the time of the sales the Lloyd family farmed Goodrest. The Merceron family then bought it and sold the farmhouse to Alan and Hilary Richardson in 1972, retaining the farm. Since 1973 the Collins family has worked Goodrest Farm.

Alan Richardson and Robin Lawrence

19

The Mothers' Union

In 1876 Mary Sumner, wife of the Rector of Old Alresford in Hampshire, started meetings in their parish to bring together the 'Lady Mothers' and the 'Cottage Mothers'. Mary's compassionate interest in all women and their families and her revolutionary vision of bringing the women of different classes together were the beginnings of a parochial fellowship that was eventually to become the Mothers' Union. It grew into a diocesan organisation and in 1896 a national society.

The social structure of the parish of Leek Wootton, no doubt like many other villages, was quite similar to Old Alresford and just one year later in his yearly Almanac of 1897, The Reverend Francis Grenville Cholmondeley wrote:

"We have started, since the beginning of last year, a branch of the Mothers' Union. Lady Waller kindly invited the mothers to tea in the grounds of Woodcote in the summer, when a very practical, helpful address was given by Mrs Hallet of Tachbrook, the wife of our Rural Dean. Since then we have had the pleasure of a visit from Mrs Phelps of Edgbaston, whose earnest words will not soon be forgotten by those who heard them. We should like all mothers to join, and yet we would have none to join without the full intention of proving themselves, as far as maybe, true members."

Again in 1899 he wrote:

"I hope members of the Mothers' Union are cherishing the helpful words addressed to them by Mrs Beechcroft and Mrs Hook at the meetings held in the course of the year."

There had been mothers' meetings held in the village for some years prior, often at the Reading Room, and possibly along the lines of Mary Sumner's meetings. In 1882 the meetings were directed by Mrs Trepplin of The Hayes (later Wootton Court), then by Mrs Goule, and later by Mrs Franklin of Cumnor Lodge. Miss Wright and Miss Waller took over for the last two years before the inauguration of the official Mothers' Union branch.

As The Reverend Cholmondeley was unmarried presumably direction of the branch was undertaken by one of the members, but in 1905 with the arrival of The

Reverend Edward Riley, Mrs Riley became Branch Leader or as it was known then, Enrolling Member. Meetings, with speakers, were held regularly mostly at the Vicarage but sometimes The Rock. The aim of the Mothers' Union was then, and still is, to help and support families, and particularly mothers, in the Christian upbringing of their children.

It became customary for the branch to have an annual service in church with an address by the Vicar. This was preceded by a drive, by horse drawn brake, into the countryside followed by a tea provided by Mrs Beresford Wright at Wootton Court and, after the First World War, by Lady Waller at Woodcote.

Meetings lapsed during the Second World War but the branch was re-opened in 1950 by Mrs Glover of Yew Tree Cottage. In Mrs Glover's absence meetings were taken by Mrs Bright.

In 1958 the new Vicar's wife, Mrs Cornes, took over responsibility for Mothers' Union in the village, followed by Mrs Nettleship until her death in 1978. In those days meetings were held mostly at the Vicarage.

Recently the leadership has once again been vested in one of the members, chosen by mutual agreement and restricted to six years' service (two terms of three years). Today members have a compassionate attitude towards "those whose marriage has met with adversity", and unmarried women and men can join. The MU branches in the Kenilworth Deanery meet together at annual festival services and there is an annual service for the whole diocese. A deanery prayer group meets monthly. At the start of the 21st Century the MU branch in Leek Wootton runs parenting courses and a monthly pram service, and supports projects working with families in the diocese, throughout the UK and worldwide.

Jean Chamberlain and Lesley Eldridge

Minutes of The Parish Council:

"Regarding the footpath on the Leek Wootton Warwick Road it was resolved that a further approach is made ... to have this footpath properly laid as a present, mothers with perambulators could not use the footpath in its present state."

Monday, 22nd March 1948

Minutes of The Parish Council:

"... the purpose of the (public) meeting, to ... learn about the proposed introduction of fluoride in the village water, Leek Wootton's isolated supply being easy to experiment on, we being more or less 'guinea pigs' for a future County Scheme ... a vote was taken on the subject, resulting in SIX votes 'FOR' and 32 'AGAINST'."

Tuesday 23rd January 1968

20

Leek Wootton War Memorial Recreation Ground

Eighteen men from the village gave their lives during the 1914-18 War and it was decided that a suitable memorial to them would be to create a recreation ground, as well as placing a memorial tablet in the church:

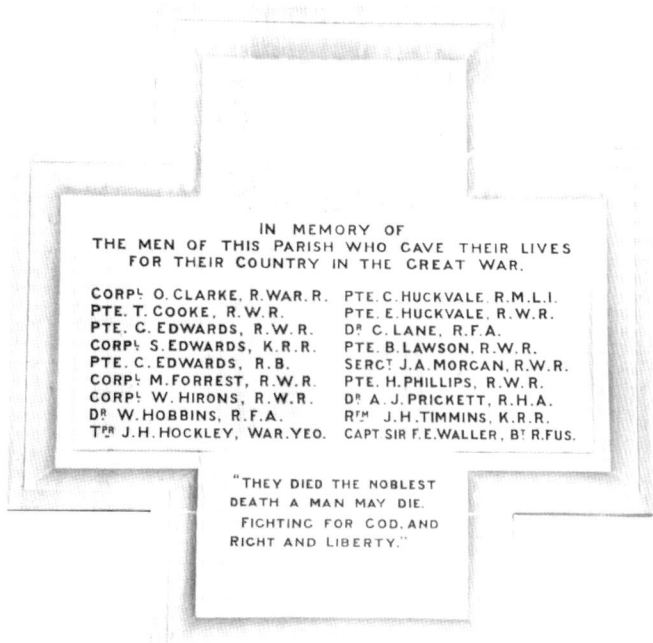

Previously the village football and cricket teams had played in the park at Woodcote, owned by the Waller family.

Leek Wootton AFC, circa 1890, outside The Rock

Cricket Team, circa 1890
Standing l-r: — Smith; C Goulé; G Goulé; — Barbary; — Hall; H Weston; — Reeves (Umpire)
Sitting l-r: L Hockley; The Reverend R Cholmondeley; G Gem; J Caves
Front: — Caves

Leek Wootton War Memorial Recreation Ground

The village raised the money to buy land from Sir Wathen Waller for a nominal sum and the Leek Wootton War Memorial Recreation Ground was opened in 1921. A Board of Trustees was set up to administer the new recreation ground, which originally comprised just over an acre of land, less than half of its size today. The Leek Wootton Sports Club was formed in 1920 to bring all sports into one organisation, and a small pavilion was built in the north-west corner of the ground near to where the maintenance shed now stands. Tennis courts were laid out in 1931 and a bowling green in 1933.

In 1939 it was decided that a larger pavilion was needed and Sir Wathen Waller gave extra land for this purpose. The new building was completed just prior to the outbreak of the Second World War and it was soon used as temporary accommodation for families bombed out of Coventry.

The old Pavilion

In the years following the Second World War various alterations were made to the timber building, including the closing in of a verandah to make more inside room. In 1961 Lady Waller gave yet more land and the pavilion was moved to a site on the eastern side of the ground adjacent to where the Village Hall car park is today. Further improvements were made in subsequent years including new toilets, showers and changing rooms in a building alongside the original pavilion.

By 1988 the pavilion and adjacent rooms were in a poor state of repair and permission was sought and granted for a new building. However, at this time the Working Men's Club, which had moved from the Reading Room, now part of Reading Room Cottage, to a purpose-built clubhouse on the south-west corner of the recreation ground in 1964, had to close down. The Sports Club decided to take over the Working Men's Club building and to reorganise and refurbish it for a new clubhouse/pavilion. The old sports pavilion and changing rooms were demolished and the site returned to grass.

The local branch of the Royal British Legion was re-formed in the 1980s and in 1987 members erected a memorial on the recreation ground in the form of a four-ton block of quartzite with a plaque which reads:

LEEK WOOTTON
WAR MEMORIAL GROUND.
IN MEMORY OF THOSE
WHO SERVED OUR COUNTRY
IN TIMES OF CONFLICT.

In 1926 the Leek Wootton Women's Institute erected an ex-First World War barrack hut on the recreation ground for their own use and that of the community, but by 1979 were unable to afford its upkeep and it was handed over to a committee of villagers and became the Village Hall. However, in 1996 the old timber building was condemned as being unsafe, and so after many discussions by the Parish Council and other interested bodies, both before and after its transfer from the Women's Institute, the opportunity was

Arthur Peat and Les Jones set the War Memorial Ground stone, 1987

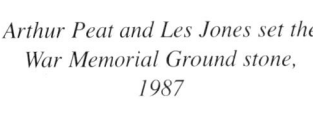

A Royal British Legion parade through the Village

The old Village Hall

<u>Minutes of The Parish Council:</u>

"<u>Children's Playground</u>. In view of a seat for use of parents being repeatedly moved from the playground, it was suggested Lord Leigh be approached as to providing a log for use in this respect, and to provide a waste paper basket."

Tuesday, 13th September 1966

finally taken to try and provide a purpose-built village hall for the benefit of the community. This proved to be fortuitous timing because, to celebrate the Millennium, the government of the day made available specific funds from the National Lottery for village hall developments. Following sterling efforts by a small committee of residents, significant grant funds were obtained from the National Lottery and District Council, money was raised within the community and on Saturday, 22nd May 1999 the Village Hall, costing a quarter of a million pounds, was officially opened. The ceremony was held in the presence of the local MP, County Council, District Council and Parish Council officials and officers, and a large number of parishioners. The ribbon was cut by Mrs Christina Jackson, as longest residing resident, together with Sophie Hall, aged 4, and Natalie Green, aged 2, representing the newest inhabitants. A reproduction 'tavern clock' was later generously donated for the hall by an amateur horologist living in the village, Reginald Chamberlain.

In 1965 the Parish Council leased a small part of the ground from the Trustees to set up a children's playground. The playground equipment was paid for by a donation from the Horticultural Society and the proceeds of a door-to-door collection. In 1988 the Parish Council purchased a piece of land adjacent to the recreation ground for the site of a dedicated children's playground. This site was the remaining part of a much larger area that had been acquired by Warwickshire County Council in the 1950s/60s for the development of local authority housing and a new school. Quarry Close was developed in the 1960s but the school was never built and in the 1980s the County Council sold the site for private housing, now Quarry Fields. The developers sold a fringe part of the site, adjacent to the recreation ground, to the Parish Council for £500. The equipment on the site and the ongoing maintenance has always been and is the responsibility of the Parish Council.

At the eastern end of the playground is a wooded area planted with trees in memory of The Reverend Charles Nettleship.

Cricket and football are now the only major sports played on the recreation ground. The tennis courts and bowling green no longer exist, and the school sports that used to be held on the ground are no longer, following the move to the new school when it was opened at the southern end of the village. The Sports Club organises various indoor activities such as whist drives, barbecues, quizzes and other events. The recreation ground is occasionally used when large open air events are planned and the Horticultural Society's Annual Show spills out of the Village Hall on to the adjacent land.

A Remembrance Day Service at the Memorial Stone is held every November. Leek Wootton War Memorial Recreation Ground is therefore still an important part of the village and provides a fitting living memorial to those who gave their lives for our freedom.

Robin Lawrence

21

Villagers Born and Bred

Christina Jackson and her late husband, Charles, were born and bred in Leek Wootton and contributed extensively to the community over the best part of the 20th Century. The following are Chris's reminiscences of her life in the village, and some of her memories and those of others of Charles Jackson.

Christina Golby, centre, on her grandmother's knee, with members of the Golby family

Christina Jackson (née Golby) was born in 1914 and brought up by her grandmother, Mary Ann, in a tied cottage on Woodcote Lane. After the death of her grandfather, Frederick, her grandmother was allowed to stay in her home provided she did all the laundry for the Waller family at Woodcote. Chris recalls that this job dominated the household for most of the week from the arrival of the large hamper full of dirty washing brought round by the handyman, for many years Frank Graley, on Monday mornings until all the ironing was finished on Friday. Washing was done in the cold outdoor washhouse behind the cottage using a brick-built copper and stone sink. With no mains, water had to be brought by bucket from a tap in the lane at the bottom of the garden. Whites were put in the first boil, followed by coloureds and finally the dirty clothes. Everything was put over the washboard and through the mangle and all the ironing done with flat irons, which were heated on the range.

Chris remembers Joseph William Golby playing a significant role in village life. Will Golby moved to Leek Wootton as a small boy and after leaving school worked in the gardens of Lord Algernon Percy at Guy's Cliffe where he received a useful training. After six years he moved on to a similar job in Newbold Revel where he learned all about growing fruit. When War broke out in 1914 he joined the King's Royal Rifle Corps and served until 1917 when he was wounded at the Battle of Arras and was invalided out. He returned to horticulture after the First World War, lived in Woodcote Lane and married Dorothy Strickland. One of his greatest loves was the church choir in which he sang for most of his long life. He was also a keen bell ringer, only retiring as Captain of the Tower when he was eighty. He was also a member of the church hand

bell team. During his lifetime he was Treasurer of the local branch of the British Legion and Secretary of the Horticultural Society, which he helped to resurrect after the War. He was also a talented artist and a press correspondent for the local paper. Will Golby died in 1973 and Dorothy in 1983.

Chris started school in 1919 and recalls that Jack London, who lived at the main lodge to Woodcote, where his father was Head Gardener, dragged her there. In those days the school was one big room divided by a sliding screen for the older children and one small room for infants. Many children came a long way, walking or cycling through the mud and the wet and some even went two miles home and back again in the dinner hour. 'Tortoise' stoves heated the classrooms and these were often hung with clothes and socks to dry. The toilets were a bucket in a shed at the bottom of the yard. The older boys all had a piece of ground to cultivate and grow vegetables on and they often sold the produce. If the pupils were only a few minutes late they were lined up and had a cane across the hand. The children were entered for singing and dancing competitions at the Leamington Festival. So much was achieved in the small space available at the school. Religious Education was very much an integral part of the school timetable. Miss Cordelia Leigh, Lord Leigh's sister, cycled to the school from Stoneleigh every week to teach the children and the Vicar was a regular visitor.

Chris's life also revolved around church attendance. The children went to Sunday school before the 11 o'clock service and learned the Collect every week. In those days there were gates across the entrance to the churchyard, opposite the Reading Room, and a squeaky old bier was used to carry coffins. A large coke boiler in the stoke hole heated the church, and lighting was by hanging oil lamps with mantles, which often flared up during services. Until 1938 the organ was pumped by hand and Chris remembers the ever smiling John Hobbins, Verger, Sexton and Clerk for fifty years, who usually operated the pump. When Chris played the organ herself later in her life John would sometimes fall asleep during the sermon and snore, so Chris had to get off the organ stool to wake him. John would toll the church bell at 8 am and 8 pm to mark the death of a villager, and the bell ringers would ring a muffled peal at a funeral.

The first Vicar Chris remembers was The Reverend Edward Riley and she recalls that he once got stuck while going up the church tower steps as he was very well built. Mrs Riley ran a weekly sewing class for the Girls' Friendly Society on the top floor of the Vicarage. The girls made dolls clothes and did many craft activities and Mrs Riley never minded how much mess they made. The Vicarage lawn was rarely mown and so by June, when it was very long and had to be cut, the school children were allowed a hay-making party with buns and lemonade. Chris recalls that her grandmother did Mr Riley's washing each week and would get embarrassed when, at the evening service, he would shout out to her "How much do I owe you?"

The Reverend Longland was apparently a different character; an intellectual, economical and well liked. The Reverend Ryecart was a colourful character who married an Austrian baroness and his son is the actor, Patrick Ryecart. The Reverend Charles Nettleship and his wife, Mireille, are perhaps best remembered for their time in the village. He had been a Brigadier and he called a spade a spade, but was much loved.

At home the Golby family kept chickens and a pig in the backyard and Chris also had bantams to look after. The highlight of the year was the killing of the pig, which Mr Fox, a Kenilworth butcher would do, and then cut it into joints. The kitchen was full of trotters, head, offal, etc and the children always had the bladder as a football after it was dried and blown up. The head was boiled and brawn made from it. Lard and dripping were made and also pork pies. All the neighbours received a joint and the big hams were salted and hung up in the kitchen and living room for months to provide bacon and meat for the year.

During her childhood Chris's home was always full of music as some of her uncles and others were always rehearsing with the hand bells or part-singing minstrel songs. They would then travel around the village, especially at Christmas time, performing with the hand bells and giving concerts. When she was about fifteen the Vicar introduced a hymn at the children's service and Chris was asked to play the accompaniment. She never had proper piano lessons but went on to play the church organ for many years.

When Chris left the village school she went to Kings High School in Warwick where she made some life-long friends from similar backgrounds. She left school at the age of sixteen and went to secretarial school, eventually to work for Mr Overell, a solicitor in Leamington.

Chris married Charles Jackson in 1940 just before Charles was called-up. For five years Chris continued her job and, amongst other activities, she helped organize entertainments in the WI Hut for patients from the convalescent home at Woodcote. She joined with other women mowing the tennis courts, and with the WI's industry of canning, and she also started a Girls' Club.

After the War Chris and Charles bought Hill Crest which was their home for many years. Hill Crest had previously been the wheelwright's premises where Charles Bright built carts and coffins. The house was later incorporated into the development of Wheelwright Mews.

They had two children and Chris continued to take a full part in village life. She ran the Girl Guides, played the organ at church, was Clerk to the Parish Council for forty years, served as a School Governor, was the school 'lollipop lady', and undertook anything else that was going. Chris is still the correspondent for the local newspaper.

In 1995 she was chosen to receive Maundy money from the Queen at Coventry Cathedral, an occasion which she remembers as being truly exciting and memorable. Chris continues to live in the village and when her health permits is always keen to attend church and village functions.

Charles Jackson was born very prematurely at the Lodge of Wootton Court in 1912 and was baptised in the kitchen, as he was not expected to survive. He was one of seven children and his father was Coachman to the Wright family of Wootton Court. He attended the village school and left at the age of fourteen to start work as Under Gardener at The Lodge in Hill Wootton Road. However, Charles soon discovered this did not suit him and he was subsequently apprenticed to the building firm of James Lawrence to work as a painter/decorator. At the age of seventeen Charles was very badly injured when a motorbike careered into the crowd at Coventry Carnival and hit him. He was told he would never walk again.

Charles and his future wife, Christina, were at school together but it was not until she became Entertainments Secretary of the Sports Club in the early 1930s that they first 'noticed' each other. Charles was particularly good at tennis and he and Chris played in many matches and tournaments together, and eventually became engaged in 1936. Charles gave Chris her ring at their 'rendezvous', the old Deer House in Woodcote Park.

Charles's first recollection of cricket at Leek Wootton was witnessing the laying of a cricket square on the new Leek Wootton War Memorial Recreation Ground in 1921. He started his playing career in 1925 and continued until 1969, and for many years was Captain or Vice Captain and wicket-keeper of the village team. He was also a keen footballer. In 1933 he was elected Secretary of the Cricket Section of the Sports Club and this meant he was also Fixtures Secretary. He remained Fixtures Secretary until 1971 and Cricket Secretary until 1976.

When War was declared in 1939 Charles joined the Local Defence Volunteers, later the Home Guard, which operated from Stone Edge under the direction of Mr W H Perkins. Eventually he was made the despatch rider as he could ride a motorbike, and was given a uniform. However, within a few weeks he received his call-up papers. In those days letters often went via Leek in Staffordshire, and this happened to Charles's call-up papers. He therefore had to make preparations to leave in only forty-eight hours. This was only about six months after he and Chris were married in the village church at Easter 1940, and Charles was one of the first young men in Leek Wootton to be called up. Gunner Jackson joined the 74th City of Glasgow Heavy Regiment of the Royal Artillery and served in the Middle East. He was later to be transferred to the Military Police Corps. Charles was on duty as an MP in Cairo when Winston Churchill met there with Franklin D Roosevelt in 1943.

During his time in the Middle East Charles passed through Cyprus whilst Robert Wright was Personal Secretary and ADC to the Governor of Cyprus. When Charles landed Robert sent an official car to meet him and take him to Government House for tea. The chauffeur driven car then returned him to his ship. When it was suggested to Robert that this was a rather unusual thing to do his comment in reply was "well he was my cricketing pal".

On Charles's return in early 1946 he received his £100 and 'de-mob' suit, like all returning service personnel. He also received £17 10s 0d from a village collection shared out to all serving forces members. He chose to use the latter to purchase a new bath rather than spend it "willy nilly", and settled down to married life with Chris. Their daughter Pauline and son Peter were born in the early post-war years but the beautiful navy-blue pinstriped 'de-mob' suit was never worn.

Apart from his family, Leek Wootton Sports Club was always Charles's main interest in life. He would tell Chris he was going to do a job in the garden and when she went to look for him he would have disappeared and was always to be found at the Club. He was elected Secretary of the Sports Club soon after the War and continued in that capacity until ill health forced him to retire in 1983. During those years he saw the small village club grow into one which provided cricket, football, tennis, darts, bowls, crib, dominoes and whist. In 1975 he was awarded the Leslie Jones Secretarial Trophy from the Midlands Club Cricket Conference for "a considerable contribution to the organisation and for holding office for so long". Charles was also a Class 1 Football referee but had to retire at the age of forty-eight due to sciatica.

During his lifetime Charles was involved at some time with the church choir, Parochial Church Council, British Legion, and Horticultural Society; was a School Governor, and a Parish Councillor and also found time to look after his garden, do all sorts of odd jobs for anybody, collect stamps and 12,600 matchboxes. No one could have spent more hours of their spare time working for the village and the Sports Club and it was often said that he almost ran the Club single-handed.

Charles died in 1986 and he is remembered with a roadside bench opposite to his last home, Sandbanks on Warwick Road, and by the Charles Jackson Memorial Lounge at the Sports Club.

Jane Pain

Minutes of The Parish Council:

"*Letters to wrong area*. In view of many letters during the past months having again been sent to "LEEK in STAFFS" in spite of their being correctly addressed, the Council felt the Post Office should again be asked to take urgent action on this matter."

Thursday, 26th November 1959

"A letter from the Postmaster General was read as to letters to LEEK, giving same excuses for this mis-direction, and promising to again look into matters. The ironic joke was the P.G's letter (though correctly addressed) went via LEEK!!"

Tuesday, 25th January 1966

"The letters to LEEK continued despite coding."

Friday, 24th May 1974

22

Reminiscences of the Wartime Years 1939-1945

Audrey Jones was born at Avon Cottage to Oliver Holmes and his wife Edith (née Gregory) and has lived in the village for most of her life.

At the outbreak of the Second World War Leek Wootton was a typical English village, where everyone knew each other and everything happened at an unhurried pace. Life centred on the church, the school, village shops, the Anchor Inn, the estates of Woodcote and Wootton Court and the local farms, which provided the livelihoods of the majority of the inhabitants.

When War was declared in September 1939 there was a great sense of uncertainty everywhere. The young men eligible for the armed services were called-up almost immediately. When different parts of the country began to suffer air raids, hundreds of children were evacuated to the countryside.

My family by this time lived at the Lodge to Wootton Court and my father worked for Mr Arthur Fitzherbert Wright. The Lodge was quite a large house and as it had spare rooms the family had to display a card in the window to show the availability of rooms. Consequently, in June 1940 when Leek Wootton received its first evacuees, my mother went to the WI Hut to be allocated two of the newly arrived children, Dick who was eleven and Grace who was seven. They had already been evacuated from Dagenham in Essex to the east coast, but when that came under attack they were re-evacuated to Leek Wootton. A few months later their four-year-old sister, Josie joined them, and they all stayed with our family until after the War.

l-r Dick Gunning (holding Rascal), Audrey Holmes, Grace and Josie Gunning

With their father in the RAF and their eldest sister in the WAAF, their sister Jean spent some time with the Forrest family in the village, and their mother, second eldest sister Joyce and the baby, Phyllis, some time at Wootton Court.

A boys' home was evacuated to Guys Cliffe House and, as many of these boys also attended the village school, there were suddenly many more pupils for the Headmistress, Mrs Davies, and the Infant Teacher, Mrs Cruikshank, to look after.

The Air Raid Warden system was first begun in the WI Hut in 1938. When War broke out the Warden Post was established at the Post Office, but in 1940 it was transferred to the small cottage now demolished but replaced by the front cottage of Stonehouse Mews. A rota was set up with usually two Wardens on duty every night, and as all residents had to have their windows blacked out at dusk, one of the Warden's

Members of the First Aid Team

jobs was to make sure that there were no chinks of light showing. The First Aid Post was set up in the garage of The Lodge, Hill Wootton Road.

The villagers were issued with ration books and sweet and clothing coupons, identity cards and gas masks, which had to be carried at all times. I remember that these were horrible, they smelt strongly of rubber and the visor soon became misted over. There were regular practices on how to use them, but fortunately they never had to be used for real. One person's ration for an average week in 1941 was 4 ounces of bacon and ham, 8 ounces of sugar, 2 ounces of butter, 8 ounces of cooking fats, 2 ounces of tea, 1 ounce of cheese and 2 ounces of jam (1 ounce = approx 25 grammes). Meat was rationed by price. There were an additional sixteen points allocated each month for other rationed foods, subject to availability. Liquid silk stockings were advertised. These were actually painted on to the legs and a seam was drawn up the back. Real silk stockings, when they were available, cost two coupons. Nylon had not yet been invented.

At this time Leek Wootton had two shops, both general stores, and the larger of the two, now The Old Post House, was also the Post Office and bakery. Mr and Mrs William Dee ran this. Mr Dee made the most wonderful bread, which he would deliver, sometimes as late as 10 pm. and it would still be warm. Large round cheeses were delivered into the hallway of the shop, and one day a farm labourer was seen with his cord trousers, tied with string under the knees, sitting on one of the cheeses while waiting his turn to be served.

The second and smaller shop was further along the main road, towards the Anchor Inn, and was run by Mrs Wood. She was a small lady with grey hair that was plaited and wound around her head. Her husband drove a pony and trap and had a milk round in Warwick, and Mrs Wood made and sold absolutely delicious ice cream.

During the War wireless or radio broadcasts were very important to us, as apart from newspapers it was the only way to keep abreast of the news. However, a large number of villagers did not have electricity, so their wirelesses were run by accumulators (batteries), which they would take to the village shop where Mr Dee would re-charge them. Apart from the news there were many programmes of entertainment designed to help keep up morale, such as 'Music While You Work', which were relayed through the factories to the workers as they turned out tanks and shells.

Mr W H Perkins, who was the County Education Officer and lived at Stone Edge, was in charge of the Local Defence Volunteers who became the Home Guard. In the early days of the War they made a large stock of 'Molotov Cocktails', bottles filled with a mixture of tar and petrol which were expected to destroy enemy tanks if the men could get them near enough to make contact. The Home Guard had regular exercises and on one occasion Sergeant Court's Sten gun jammed, and during the investigation of the cause it fired accidentally and he was shot through the leg, but luckily he wasn't seriously injured.

Reminiscences of the Wartime Years 1939–1945

The Scout Troup, 1940

The Girl Guide Company during the War

One of Mr Dee's sons, Dennis, became the Scout Master and his Troop collected scrap metal and paper which went towards the war effort. Chris Jackson was Captain of the Girl Guide Company, which comprised two patrols, The Robins and The Swallows. We also collected scrap paper etc, and during the summer months went fruit picking at Wootton Court. The members of the WI then canned the fruit, for which they must have had a special allocation of sugar.

The blacksmith's shop was opposite the Anchor Inn and adjoining Forge Cottage, and the blacksmith, Bernard Hart, used to repair a lot of tools as well as shoeing horses.

Sir Wathen and Lady Waller moved out of Woodcote to the Stone House in 1940 and Woodcote was taken over as a convalescent home for the 'boys in blue'. The soldiers who came to Woodcote to recuperate were all kitted out in blue suits, hence their name. The Red Cross was in charge at the home and Miss Powlett was Matron.

Canning at the WI Hut

Woodcote Auxiliary Hospital

Reminiscences of the Wartime Years 1939–1945

The garage to Leek Wootton House was used as a small factory and my mother, Dorothy Golby, Elizabeth Graley, Margaret Forrest and Winifred London worked there. A number of village residents were released from their regular jobs and went to work in factories in Coventry.

All cars were fitted with special slatted devices on their headlamps to keep what little light they produced shining downwards, but petrol was very scarce and could only be obtained with coupons, and not many people owned a car anyway.

Since it was difficult to travel very far, we had to make our own entertainment. There were weekly whist drives followed by a dance, the music being provided by a Mr Whitehouse from a Kenilworth radio shop, with his Victor Sylvester records. Chris Jackson wrote and choreographed concerts, which were put on in the WI Hut for three consecutive nights with a full capacity audience for every performance.

There were two grass tennis courts on the recreation ground situated where the Village Hall car park is now. The swings and a seesaw were alongside the WI Hut, and there was a bowling green in the corner behind the gardens of The Bungalow and Yew Tree Cottage.

Streams of people walked through Leek Wootton with their few possessions following the enormous air raid on Coventry on 14th November 1940. We had a family of three from Coventry to sleep every night, a Mr and Mrs Hyde and their daughter Jeanne. They would come out every evening and go back to Coventry during the day. Mrs Hyde was a very accomplished pianist and she spent many happy hours at our piano. Many other families in the village accommodated Coventrians overnight. The constant drone of aeroplanes and the frequent air raid warnings became so wearing that my mother, tired of waking us children every night, eventually put all the girls to sleep on a mattress in the cupboard under the stairs while the raids continued.

David Pope and his family were bombed out of Coventry and came to live with the Corson family at North Woodloes Farm, and David went to school in Warwick and joined the bell ringing team at All Saints.

As the War progressed the farmers had to rely on help from the Women's Land Army and older schoolchildren, who helped to hoe sugar beet, pick beans, peas, potatoes etc. German and Italian prisoners of war from the nearby POW camp were also used. At harvest time rabbits disturbed in the corn were shot for the pot as they tried to escape. As part of the 'Dig For Victory' campaign most villagers grew their own vegetables and fruit and kept hens. Some kept pigs and those with sufficient facilities could have two pigs. One pig was for the Ministry of Food and the other was for their own use and was deducted from their allowance. People never felt hungry although they did live on a very plain diet. There was dried egg powder, which was mixed with water and then fried; real eggs were put in a large earthenware pot in water for preservation, and beans were salted down. Everyone was very enterprising. My mother would boil and mash parsnips, and flavour them with banana flavouring as bananas disappeared almost as soon as the War began. There were various different advertisements put out by the Ministry of Food to advise the population on how to make the most of available foods, such as 'Shredded Cabbage Makes A Salad' and 'Six Stars From Your Winter Garden: Savoy the big-hearted tenor; Spinach the strongest man in the world; The Leeks - they know their onions; The Sprout sisters, very tasty, very sweet'. Recipes devised to use less of the rationed foods were passed around.

Girls' Club Concert at Home For Incurables, Leamington Spa, 1941

Mrs Graley Jean Graley Mrs Holmes Margaret Skelton Vera Jones Miss Davies
Hazel Graley Olive – Ciceley Marriott Jessie Barnett Mrs Mews Rita Bedding Thelma Tolley Chris Jackson
Brenda Jones Betty Green Jean Gunning
Edna Forrest Audrey Holmes Jean Stock Brenda Gregory Susan Smith
Leamington Spa Courier

Reminiscences of the Wartime Years 1939–1945

The Hammonds accommodated several different families at Hill Wootton Farm and one woman is well remembered because she emptied the contents of the chamber pot out of the bedroom window, on the quiet side of the house, and marked the wall.

American convoys would sometimes stop on their way through the village and we children were usually given Horlicks tablets and chewing gum. "Got any gum chum?" soon became a popular catchphrase.

The parish had its own 'roadman', Bill Watts who lived in Hill Wootton, who walked through the village regularly with his handcart which had a red flag stuck in the corner. He kept the roads, hedgerows and drains spotlessly clean. Mr Watts kept his cart in the old Pound which was on Hill Wootton Road.

There were, of course, sad times, when news came of loved ones either killed, missing or wounded, and the names of those who died are recorded on the memorial tablet in the church (see Chapter 23).

The one bomb that fell in the village landed on the stone wall between the church and The Stone House; it blew out all the windows on the north side of the church and many other windows in the village, but not a lot of structural damage was done. Bomb craters appeared in the fields between Hill Wootton and Blackdown, either as a result of unused bombs being dumped after raids on Coventry or the bombers attempting to destroy the railway line.

During the War the country was on double summer time so that farmers could make the most of daylight hours, working late into the evening to gather in the crops.

In 1942 a mixed heavy artillery gun battery was set up at Goodrest Farm on Rouncil Lane. The four gun emplacements and the foundations of the control room still remain in the fields, but were at that time part of a thriving Camp. Top-secret work went on with radar operators and height finders tracking enemy aircraft. Nearby some of the farmland was taken over and huts erected to form a Prisoner of War Camp for German and Italian prisoners.

There was great camaraderie among everyone during the war years, so when news came through in 1945 that the War was over there were great celebrations. The church bells rang out, which was a wonderful sound after six years of silence, and there was a big party in the WI Hut, for which Tom Edgar provided a barrel of beer. There was such an air of euphoria that people who were thought to be quite staid let themselves go with gay abandon and there were long lines of people of all ages dancing the Palais Glide in a marvellous atmosphere.

Gradually the evacuees started to return home, people in the forces were welcomed back and Leek Wootton began to return to its peacetime state.

Audrey Jones

<u>Minutes of The Parish Council:</u>

"The Vicar reported he had been appointed <u>Voluntary Food Officer</u> for the parishes of Leek Wootton and Ashow in case either or both of these parishes are isolated through invasion by the enemy."

Tuesday, 13th October 1942

23

Roll of Honour

In All Saints Church the Rolls of Honour record the names of local men killed in the First and Second World Wars. Some parishioners can still remember relatives, friends and neighbours who were lost in World War II and these are their memories and the stories of those who gave their lives:

Aircraftsman 1st Class Arthur E Bedding, Royal Air Force

Arthur Bedding was born in a cottage on Woodcote Lane in 1923. The Waller Estate owned the property and his father was employed by the estate as a gardener. He had one sister and they attended the village school and he was later educated at Kenilworth Secondary School in Priory Road. He was a member of the Scout Troop and a close friend of Bernard Dee.

Arthur, known as Archie, served in the Royal Air Force and when the war ended he was part of the Army of Occupation in Germany. He was stationed near to Belsen, the notorious concentration camp. Arthur sent his family some photographs of the released prisoners that the troops had been given, which so upset his mother that she ripped them up.

The winter of 1945-46 in Germany was exceptionally severe. Arthur wrote a letter to Bernard Dee stating that the cold weather would kill him but by the time Bernard received the letter, Arthur was already dead. He had developed a chest infection that turned into pneumonia. He was hospitalised and treated with penicillin, the new wonder drug, but unfortunately he was allergic to the drug and died in February 1946, aged 23 years..

Arthur's sister, Rita Martin, remembers him with affection as a jolly person who enjoyed a good social life.

Able Seaman Stephen E Dunn, Royal Navy

Stephen Dunn was one of seven children born into a farming family who lived at Banner Hill Farm on Rouncil Lane. This farm formed part of Wedgnock Park, which was owned by the Warwick Castle estate. He was educated in Kenilworth and he regularly worshipped in the village church. He joined the Royal Navy, eventually serving on the battlecruiser HMS Hood. This ship was the largest warship afloat at the time and was known to the British public as the "Mighty Hood". She had, however, been launched in 1918 and was relatively old in naval terms.

In 1941 the Norwegian Resistance and a reconnaissance 'plane notified London that two German battleships, the Bismark and the Prinz Eugen, were refuelling in the Kors Fjord in Norway. The British home fleet was put on full alert and moved to intercept. It was imperative that the German ships were prevented from breaking out into the Atlantic where they would attack vital merchant shipping. HMS Prince of Wales and six destroyers accompanied HMS Hood, and their instructions were to detain the German ships until a large support force could arrive to help them.

The German ships were sighted on 23rd May leaving the fjord and heading south. At 5.25 am on 24th May, the Hood and Prince of Wales opened fire. The noise was deafening, with shells raining down on both sides. The shells from the Bismark hurtling towards the British ships sounded like an underground train becoming louder and louder.

Shells landed on the boat deck of HMS Hood, igniting ammunition and starting a huge fire. One can never be sure what happened next, and two enquiries failed to find a definite reason, although one of several theories is that the ship's magazine took a direct hit, being inadequately protected by suitable deck armour due to her age. There was, however, a violent explosion and flames shot up over a thousand feet into the air. When the black smoke cleared, witnesses saw that she had broken her back; the stern and bow were fifty yards apart. Within ninety seconds the ship had disappeared into the sea taking 1,416 crew with her, leaving only three survivors in the water. The battle had lasted eight minutes from the start of action until the Hood sank.

HMS Prince of Wales managed to damage the Bismark before suffering a direct hit on her bridge and withdrawing. The Bismark headed towards occupied France for repairs, but was destroyed three days later by the support force that had now arrived.

Bernard Dee recalls that a dance was taking place in the WI Hut in the village when news came through of the loss of HMS Hood. Someone came in and announced that the Hood had been lost with all her crew. There was silence and the dance fizzled out as everyone just drifted home. Stephen Dunn was 18 years old when he died off the coast of Norway.

Lieutenant F Graham Mitchell, Royal Berkshire Regiment

Francis Graham Mitchell was the younger son of William and Mabel Mitchell who had purchased The Lodge on Hill Wootton Road in 1913. He was born in 1918 and educated at public school. He later gained a BA at Cambridge University.

Although he was in the Royal Berkshire Regiment, he was attached to The Loyal Regiment (The North Lancashires). He died taking part in the Anglo-American amphibious assault on the Italian mainland at Anzio.

German-held Monte Cassino dominated the route to Rome and posed a major obstacle to the advancing Allied armies. Allied bombs reduced the monastery to ruins but the crack German troops remained dug in, and it was well nigh impregnable. With the Allies held up at Cassino, Churchill saw a 'quick' way to break the deadlock. The idea was to land troops to the north of the Gustav Line at Anzio and to then make a swift dash to Rome, but it became a four-month nightmare.

When 40,000 Allied troops landed on the beach on 22nd January 1944 they initially met no opposition because the civilians had been evacuated and the German troops had abandoned it. However the American General in command decided to wait for reinforcements, a delay that proved disastrous. The Germans sent 40,000 troops to the beachhead and the Allies were trapped under heavy bombardment by 'planes and artillery. On 25th January 1944 British patrols were sent to test the German defences at Campoleone but came up against Panzer Grenadiers and fierce fighting ensued. Lieutenant Mitchell died taking part in this action. He was 26 years old.

Monte Cassino was finally taken on 13th May; the Allied forces were reinforced and eventually broke out from the beach head on 23rd May, but the number of casualties was huge. The list of dead, missing and injured on all sides at Anzio numbered over 30,000.

Acting Leading Seaman (TY) George W Tolley, Royal Navy

George Tolley was born in 1920, one of five children in a village family which lived in one of four cottages that were part of an old court known as Birches Cottages or Birch's Yard. These cottages were built of the village sandstone, part beamed and situated to the south of the Anchor Inn and Anchor Cottages, and behind other cottages fronting the main road. They were humble properties, that were sold in the early 1960s, and demolished in 1963. Most of the residents moved to the new council houses in Quarry Close.

George attended the village school, and since he was very keen on motorbikes he trained as a mechanic at Chapman's garage on Clinton Lane, Kenilworth. He was a very tough young man and neighbours remember him washing under the pump in the garden all year round, even in the coldest weather. His father thought it a good idea if George and his brother Ted learned to box in case they ever needed to defend themselves so they joined the Leamington Boys Boxing Club and were trained and coached by George Middleton. George Tolley won several club trophies and once defeated Dick Turpin, one of the three famous Turpin brothers, and Gordon Skelton recalls seeing George compete in an open air boxing ring in a field in Kenilworth.

George joined the Royal Navy, trained as a Telegraphist, and served on HMS Manchester. He saw plenty of action, including the attack on the Italian Fleet at Spartivento in November 1940. Much to his father's annoyance, George then volunteered for the Submarine Service, but when HMS Manchester was torpedoed by the Italian Navy in August 1942, and then scuttled by its crew, his father was relieved that George was not on the ship.

George had joined the submarine HMS Talisman, which was active in the Mediterranean. The boat left Gibraltar on 10th September 1942 with stores for Malta, which was under siege, where it was due eight days later. On 15th September it reported sighting a U-Boat off Philippeville in Algeria and, as a Telegraphist, George would probably have transmitted the message. HMS Talisman was never heard from again and was presumed mined in the Straits of Sicily. The Italians claimed to have sunk a submarine on 17th September to the north west of Malta and this was probably HMS Talisman. All fifty-six men on board were lost.

George's sister, Thelma Jones, who still lives in the village, remembers him as a carefree and handsome young man and a wonderful brother. He had a great sense of humour, he liked the girls and enjoyed his beer. George Tolley was 22 years old when he died.

Flying Officer Gilbert F M Wright, Royal Air Force

Gilbert Wright was one of the nine children of Arthur Fitzherbert Wright and his wife Daisy who lived at Wootton Court. He was born in 1905 at Aldercar, Derbyshire, and moved to Leek Wootton with his family in 1927. He was a member of The Royal Air Force Volunteer Reserve, so when war was declared he joined up immediately.

Gilbert was trained as a fighter pilot; he held the rank of Flying Officer and was stationed at Tangemere, near Chichester. His dry sense of humour was illustrated when he first flew a Hurricane after previously flying Tiger Moths. He commented that it had sixty-seven switches and only two worked.

He was reported missing in France in May 1940. He was last seen coming down by parachute, under control, near Arras, some sixty miles south east of Calais.

This was a desperate and chaotic time in the area. The German army was rapidly advancing and the British and French troops were retreating towards the beaches. The Allied Forces made a surprise counter-attack at Arras with two battalions of the Durham Light Infantry and two tank battalions on 21st May.

The German opposition included Rommels 7th Panzer Division and the SS Totenkopf Tank Division. The Germans were taken by surprise and there was a fierce battle that lasted for nine hours. It was only after Rommel called in the Stuka dive-bombers that the allied troops were forced to withdraw. The British fighters were sent in to attack the German 'planes, Gilbert's 'plane was damaged and he parachuted down onto the battlefield below, near the village of Berneville.

He was reported missing and his wife did not receive any more news of him. Gilbert was 34 years old when he died. His widow, Doreen, remembers him as a typical engineer, a very determined character, with a quiet temperament and a sense of humour.

After the battle the French villagers buried him with the soldiers of the Durham Light Infantry. When the Allies liberated the area in 1944 he was reburied by the War Graves Commission as an unknown soldier of the Durham Light Infantry, but later he was correctly identified as the missing RAF Pilot Gilbert Wright.

The battle at Arras was very important because it gave a valuable breathing space to allow many more of the retreating Allied troops to reach the coast. It inflicted substantial damage on Rommel's Panzers who suffered 700 casualties and lost 20 tanks. Hitler also took the momentous decision not to risk his Panzers in an all-out attack on Dunkirk and halted his troops outside the Dunkirk Canal basin. This allowed the British and French troops to escape and between 23rd May and 4th June, despite heavy bombing, 338,226 men were evacuated from the beaches at Dunkirk in 848 ships, ranging from warships to sailing boats. It was a miracle of deliverance.

When we wear our poppies on 11th November, let us remember with pride these five young men of the parish, who died in the Second World War, giving their lives in different parts of the world so that we should be free.

Rest In Peace

Catherine Sandwell

24

The Women's Institute

On 20th February 1920 a Miss Warner came to Leek Wootton and gave a talk in the Garden Room at Leek Wootton House on how to form a branch of the Women's Institute. As a result of that meeting the Leek Wootton branch of the WI was formed.

The first President was Lady Waller of Woodcote and the two Vice Presidents were Mrs Mitchell and Miss Peyton. Mrs Leigh was the Secretary and Miss Peyton the Treasurer. The committee consisted of Mesdames Barbary, Cattel, Hegham, Hodgetts, Legge, Lucas, Mead, Riley and the Misses Lynes, Peyton, Wright and Edwards, a total of twelve. There were fifty-eight members altogether and for the first six years they met in the Working Men's Club at the Reading Room.

By 1926 the branch had raised enough money to buy an ex-government hut for £202, which, with the permission of the Trustees of Leek Wootton War Memorial Recreation Ground, was erected in the south-east corner of the ground and became known as the WI Hut. It was officially opened by Lady Ilkeston on 16th February 1926.

In the early days the Institute concentrated on handicrafts and domestic issues. Quilting, plain sewing, linen embroidery, cross-stitch, glove making and raffia work were among the crafts practised by members. The craft was of a very high standard for in 1930 Mrs Farley passed the Guild of Learners Examination and passed a test for linen embroidery gaining the highest marks in the country, and Mrs Douch passed with the third highest marks. A 1930 lecture entitled 'Minor Accidents in the Home and How To Treat Them' given by Dr Orton of Allesley Hall was typical of the talks being given to members at the time. Cookery was also a popular activity, especially the preservation of fruit and vegetables, and at the outbreak of the Second World War a Preservation Centre was set up in the WI Hut for canning fruit and vegetables.

The skills acquired by members were no doubt very useful during the War years with rationing and the need to 'make do and mend'. Some members also played their part in helping the war effort by working part time in the factory unit set up in the garage of Leek Wootton House by the Rotherhams, inspecting and packing small munitions components.

In 1947 WI members canned nearly 2,500 cans during the year, mainly fruit, but by 1955 they canned only 700 cans.

After the end of the War the WI carried on the tradition of handicrafts and other domestic activities, but began to extend its range of activities. In 1951 they produced an outdoor pageant relating the history of the village. They began to hold 'Garden Meetings' in members' gardens, weather permitting, during the summer months, and once a year the members would invite residents from a local old people's home or care home, such as the hospital at Weston-under-Wetherley, to one of these garden meetings for an afternoon out. Entertainments would be laid on for them, games of tennis or perhaps a show by the village school children, and they were always guaranteed a cracking tea at the end of the afternoon.

During the 1960s the WI pantomimes were very much a feature of village life.

These were presented at the WI Hut and included titles such as Cinderella, Aladdin, Robinson Crusoe, Snow White and the Seven Dwarfs and other traditional pantos, but also the not so traditional 'Leek Wootton Up The Totem Pole'.

Outings were popular and included trips to Shugborough Hall, a boat trip on the Grand Union canal and a visit to the Birmingham Hippodrome to see the musical 'My Fair Lady'.

For several years members assisted in the WI Pavilion during the Royal Show at Stoneleigh, giving cookery and craft demonstrations.

Members made a survey of all the trees in the parish, and in 1973 a survey of village footpaths was highly commended in a Warwickshire Federation competition.

In April 1978 members created a garden on a piece of waste ground in the centre of the village as a WI Silver Jubilee Project. This was planted with flowers and shrubs and Warwickshire County Council installed a seat, presented by Miss Wright.

The WI was beginning to shed its 'Jam and Jerusalem' image, becoming a significant pressure group in national affairs, and the Leek Wootton branch played its part by sending delegates to the national conference to vote on issues of concern to members. For instance, in 1988 the branch voted in favour of a resolution to urge the government to control excessive sale on credit, and also to ban the irradiation of food in Great Britain.

During its lifetime Leek Wootton WI produced four scrapbooks, one in 1956 for the Warwickshire Federation's Village History Scrapbook competition for which it received a Highly Commended Award; the second in 1965 for the National Federation's Golden Jubilee for which it again received a Highly Commended Award; the third in 1988 was for the Warwickshire Federation's Village Scrapbook Competition for which it was judged a Joint Winner. The fourth book was an informal collection of cuttings and photographs dating from 1930 to 1968. All these books are beautifully bound and lavishly illustrated with photographs, articles, newspaper cuttings, and drawings and paintings by WI members and children from the village school.

The WI Hut was not only used by members but by other organisations in the village, such as the Horticultural Society for its annual show, and was effectively used as the village hall. So when by 1979 the branch was finding the cost of upkeep and maintenance of the hut too great the members reluctantly decided to hand it over to a committee made up of representatives of the various organisations that used it, to operate it as the Village Hall.

By 1993 membership of the branch had fallen so low that the remaining members agreed to wind it up and it was officially closed in December of that year. However, a number of ex-members formed a group to continue the upkeep the WI Garden as a village amenity. They continue to meet and the garden is regularly maintained and replanted.

Comparing the WI membership roll with the village population gives some indication of social change in the village. In 1920, when the branch was formed, there were fifty-eight members out of a village which comprised a population that was over 50% women. By 1951 the population of the village had hardly changed but the membership had risen to over seventy. However, by 1991, whilst the population had risen to over a thousand, the membership had fallen to less than thirty, and the closure of the branch followed just two years later.

Robin Lawrence

The Women's Institute

21st Anniversary of Leek Wootton WI

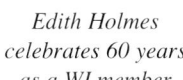

Edith Holmes celebrates 60 years as a WI member

70th Anniversary of Leek Wootton WI

The WI Scrapbooks

The WI scrapbooks are wonderful snapshots of life in the community when they were produced. It was felt that we should give the reader some idea of their content and the pictures of life that they depict:

Scrapbook for 1930-1968
This is an informal collection of photographs and newspaper cuttings relating to the WI. It includes pictures of their handicraft activities, garden parties and the pantomimes that were produced.

Scrapbook for 1956
In 1956 the Warwickshire Federation of Women's Institutes held a competition for a Village History Scrapbook. Leek Wootton WI entered the competition and received a Highly Commended award. This book begins with the history of the village from Domesday onwards, contains a short history of the Church and has a map of field names. There are several photographs of the village in 1956.

The various sporting activities of the village are covered and illustrated with old photographs, including, for example, a photograph of the football team of 1891.

Other organisations are also mentioned, such as the Horticultural Society, Boy Scouts and Girl Guides and The British Legion.

The school is mentioned with photographs ranging from 1893 to 1955. There is a section devoted to the Second World War.

At the end of the book is a list of all the wild flowers found in the village in 1955.

Scrapbook for 1965
In 1965 the National Federation of Women's Institutes held a scrapbook competition to celebrate the Golden Jubilee of the Federation. The Leek Wootton entry was again Highly Commended.

This scrapbook records village, national and international events during the year, illustrated with photographs, newspaper cuttings and drawings. At the end of the book is a list of all the villagers of the year.

We list some entries from each month of the year:

January:
Pheasant shoots take place every fortnight, five new houses were built and alterations to the Hamlet cottages were made, including installation of bathrooms. The price of beer in the Anchor Inn increased by 1d a pint. The Vicar resigned because of ill health. There were seven road accidents in the area.

February:
The WI Hut needed vital repairs. A bring-and-buy sale at Stone Edge raised £50 towards the building fund. The WI members went to see 'My Fair Lady' at the Birmingham Hippodrome. The North Warwickshire Hunt met at the Kennels in Rouncil Lane. The Horticultural Society donated £75 towards the cost of a children's playground on the recreation ground.

March:
The Queen of Sweden died. She apparently used to visit the Misses Wheatley at Little Woodcote and had complimented Mr Dee on his bread. The WI held a 45th Anniversary party. An application to extract gravel from land at Elms Farm was refused.

April:
Mr and Mrs Golby celebrated their Silver Wedding Anniversary. The WI held a rummage sale and painted the inside of the Hut. The County Council plans to close seventy schools including that in Leek Wootton. Two heifers died at North Woodloes farm after eating yew leaves from a tree blown over in gales on Easter Monday.

May:
Several WI members entered the National WI Golden Jubilee Exhibition at Solihull and were awarded a certificate. The WI entertained forty-four patients from the Central Hospital, Hatton. Developers were asked to submit plans for a scheme for twenty-eight houses on Hill Wootton Road.

June:
The Reverend C Nettleship was appointed Vicar. The Mothers' Union met at Mrs Dodridge's home. A Cancer Campaign coffee morning was held at the home of Mrs Wilkins.

July:
WI members helped at the Royal Show as cashiers and stewards in the flower and refreshment tents. The school sports were abandoned because of wet ground. Gillian Selwyn was crowned 'School Queen'.

August:
The price of milk has gone up by 1d. Mr Dee has closed the bakery after thirty-three years. The WI Hut is to get a new roof costing £240. A man from Coventry was fined £7 10s for depositing litter in Hill Wootton Road.

September:
The Horticultural Show had three hundred exhibits and made a profit of £23 4s 0d. The cricket team beat a Warwick 2nd Xl and a team from the Loft Theatre. The Esso Petroleum Company failed in a bid to build a service station near to Gaveston's Cross. The Mothers' Union toured the Cadbury factory at Bournville.

October:
The WI held a Harvest Supper and also presented the pantomime 'Sleeping Beauty'. Work started on the Kenilworth Bypass. Houses were still being built at the Police Headquarters. 0.68 inches of rain fell and there were two nights of frost.

November:
PC Wager, the village policeman for sixteen years, and his wife Molly celebrated their Silver Wedding anniversary. The local footpaths were inspected and various obstructions noted. Damage was caused to the WI Hut hired for a young people's party.

December:
A club for 'Senior Parishioners' is to be launched by the Mothers' Union and the Working Men's Club. The school held a Concert of Songs and Carols. The church

choir collected £27 14s 0d for St. Anne's Church of England Home when they went carol singing round the village.

Scrapbook for 1987-1988

This was entered into the Warwickshire Federation's Village Scrapbook competition 1988 and was adjudged a Joint Winner.

It covers the period from 1st April 1987 to 31st March 1988. It is similar to the 1965 scrapbook although it only deals with the village.

Again we list some entries from each month of the year:

April:
Forge Cottage was being renovated. The school held an Easter Fair. Mr Mike Smith sold Leek Wootton Country Club.

May:
Mrs J Compton was elected to the District Council. WI members produced a map showing the agricultural uses in the parish.

June:
The Anchor Inn was named Pub of the Month by CAMRA. The 1st Leek Wootton Guides camped in the grounds of the Police Headquarters at Woodcote. The church fête was held in the grounds of Leek Wootton House. A seat was placed in the WI garden in memory of Charles Jackson.

July:
The village was second in the Best Kept Village competition in the Warwick area. The priest-in-charge, The Reverend Clive Raybould was appointed Chaplain for the Warwickshire British Legion. The school held its sports day.

August:
The WI held a garden party at the home of Mrs D Rogers in Wheelwright Mews. British Legion members placed a 4 ton piece of quartzite from a Nuneaton quarry on the recreation ground as a memorial to those who gave their lives. Entries and attendance at the Horticultural Show were well down because of wet weather.

September:
Six hippies arrived in Hill Wootton apparently looking for 'Magic Mushrooms'; the police were informed but could take no action. The Parish Council expressed concern about the speed of traffic through the village, and also applied to have the red telephone box listed.

October:
The Home Secretary, Mr Douglas Hurd, visited Police Headquarters at Woodcote. It was the wettest October for 20 years. Liz Edgar won two major events at the Horse of the Year Show.

November:
A Remembrance Day Service was held in the church attended by the local branch of the Royal British Legion and the Guides and Brownies. A founder member of the WI, Mrs Edith Annie Holmes, died aged 87. Holly Ann Watson was born.

December:
The elderly people of the village were treated to a Christmas lunch at the Anchor Inn. The Guides and the Youth Club had Christmas parties.

January:
The District Council refused the Parish Council's request to include Hill Wootton in the Conservation Area. The Leek Wootton School of Dance held a show that raised £273 for the Church Fabric Appeal Fund. Snow fell on the 22nd and there was flooding at Blackdown and the Saxon Mill on the 24th.

February:
Workmen carrying out repairs to the church found three skeletons under the vestry floor. The Village Hall Committee were continuing with their refurbishment of the Village Hall.

March:
A new leader was found for the Youth Club. The school celebrated St. David's Day.

Minutes of The Parish Council:

"Royal Record Tree Planting – Trees planted in clumps on the Village Recreation Ground – Oaks & beeches – Presented by Sir Wathen Waller & Lady Bird."

Monday, 31st January 1938

Minutes of The Parish Council:

"Circular letter … re 'Dig for Victory' … Mrs Rotherham stated the Women's Institute had taken up this matter & everything that can be done is being done."

Tuesday, 16th April 1940

Minutes of The Parish Council:

"Mrs Yarker, President of the WI attended the meeting for the purpose of enlisting the help of the Parish Council in the planting of trees the WI had won in the recent Tree Survey Competition, including a specimen oak as the chief prize."

Friday, 27th November 1970

25

Post War Developments

The Forge and Forge Cottage
Birmingham Library Service

Massive oak beams from the by now derelict village forge were used as the basis of the bonfire lit in the village to celebrate the end of World War II, and that act in itself perhaps marked the start of a very different time for Leek Wootton and its surrounding community. As will be clear from previous chapters, much of Leek Wootton had been an 'estate' village, made up of cottages for employees on the farms and in the large houses, or for the families of rural traders, and into the early 1950s many of the roads we know today were still country lanes. Even where there were roadside paths for pedestrians they were simply laid with ash and cinders and flooding was a common occurrence, making them unusable. The cottages were not up to the standard that 'post-war' people were starting to expect of their homes, with little or no sanitation, no indoor facilities and limited running water.

The Town & Country Planning Act was passed in 1947 and brought in control of development, although house building at the time was severely restricted, partly due to a lack of skilled labour, partly due to a shortage of materials and partly due to the pressures on available resources for repair of war damage priorities in places like Coventry. Licences were required to build private housing and the materials that could be used, particularly timber, were severely restricted, hence the advent of concrete, plastic-tiled flooring, hardboard doors and the like.

The pre-war parish had been dogged by inadequate water, power and sewerage services, and any early post-war development was severely hampered by the same lack of amenities. Some street lighting was introduced in 1950, and the Parish Council negotiated for other better services through the Rural District Council, County Council and the Ministry of Housing. Eventually a bore hole on the east side of the main road (only named Warwick Road in the 1970s) was established, with a reservoir as the principle source of water for the village. An electricity substation was installed in 1957, and a ministerial decision in the late 1950s heralded the laying of a new sewage system through the village, and the building of a disposal plant off Hill Wootton Road (the road sometimes commonly referred to then as The Hamlet, perhaps taken from the name of the old cottages on that part of the lane). The bore hole remained in use at times of peak demand, until 1989 when questions were raised regarding high iron content. Severn Trent had by now laid a new pipeline between Coventry and Leamington and the borehole was shut down.

Although the Police Authority commenced building homes for employees in the early 1950s (Waller Close and Woodcote Drive) to accompany its new HQ in the village, and some private moderate sized housing developments were begun during the 1950s (on Warwick Road opposite the church, north from Gypsy Cottage and on either side of Hill Wootton Road) it was the early 1960s before the Council provided local authority housing (Quarry Close).

The private developments involved the demolition of many period properties including a row of cottages opposite the church and the earth-floored cottages on Hill Wootton Road, which stood in the shadow of the eastern wall of The Lodge (on the site now occupied by Romary (No 19) and Rest Harrow (No 21)). The building work also called for the destruction of the extensive gardens of The Lodge, and use of the by then redundant quarry off Warwick Road.

In 1960, as the properties on the south side of Hill Wootton Road now known as Long Reach (No 18) and The Pound (No 16) neared completion, the prospective owners sought the permission of the Parish Council and Lord Leigh to have the village pound demolished. It still stood, in a poor state of repair, on what was to become their front gardens.

Hamlet Cottage

In 1962 two cottages bordering the main road, and directly to the north of Forge Cottage, were demolished. Cracks had developed in the gable end of one cottage, and the heavy sandstone foundations had shifted. Around this time the owner of Forge Cottage, Billy Nicholls, sold half of his front

The Pound

Cottages on Warwick Road
Helen Scott Collection

The same cottages just before demolition in 1962

garden to the Council, and the combined land was used for road widening. The WI garden now occupies part of what was left of the site of the old sandstone cottages.

Apart from the Quarry Close development, which comprised seven 2-bed homes, twelve 3-bed homes, and four bungalows for older people, and unlike urban post war redevelopment, there was no replacement of the humble cottages with properties appropriate for the families who had previously lived and worked in the community. The demise of the large privately-owned estates and major changes in farming practices meant that many of the new generation of the workforce looked for work and a home outside the rural community, reducing the demand for such housing in the village.

Whilst the smaller-scale developments referred to above seem to have been accepted by the community without significant objection when, in 1964, application was made for development of fourteen acres of land adjacent to the school, the Parish Council raised objections to such large-scale development, clearly and understandably not wanting the character of the village destroyed. The residents probably were not fully aware of the changes occurring in society at the time.

The developments that had already taken place were of what are now called 'executive homes' designed for the senior and middle management employees in the many industries in nearby towns. The large estate houses were also being purchased by the most senior executives in manufacturing and industry, converted for business uses such as hotels and country clubs, or were being split up. The large farmhouses were being bought up in a similar way, and redundant farm buildings were being demolished or re-modelled for residential use, as the nature of farming changed. Various old properties in the village continued to be vacated, as they were condemned as being unhealthy or unsuitable for habitation and the fashion for restoration of quaint period properties was only in its infancy.

A further application for thirty-three houses off Hill Wootton Road was refused but the application was taken to appeal and eventually the southern end of The Hamlet and some of Tidmarsh Road was developed together with four houses and a bungalow at the eastern end of Hill Wootton Road. Subsequent to this initial development a further ninety houses were proposed, eventually approved and built, despite some objection from the Parish Council, although this was more muted. Perhaps such changes in the village were beginning to be appreciated as enabling community facilities such as shops, school and public house to be sustained.

With the benefit of hindsight it can be seen that this development, and the subsequent developments of Home Farm (early 1980s), The Elms (early 1980s), Quarry Fields (mid 1980s), Wheelwright Mews (1985) and Stonehouse Mews (1987), did indeed help to sustain the village community and, in fact, bred new life into the society by bringing children to the area enabling the school to survive and eventually to grow, and the village organisations and clubs to continue. During a similar period there had also been some development in Hill Wootton (as described in Chapter 5), and conversions were being started at some of the more remote sites such as Middle Woodloes.

In 1969 the Conservation Area was drawn up and various remaining historic buildings were listed and the passing away of the character buildings of the village was at last stopped. It is, of course, conjecture what might have happened to the community had these developments not been undertaken, but clearly the society that had existed before was no longer there and the village was changing to become the 'commuter village' of today.

Despite the regeneration that was beginning in the late 1960s the last remaining village shop (there having been two post-war) closed in 1970. However, with much concern amongst the residents, the community continued without any shop facility until the development on Home Farm in the early 1980s. A shop and Post Office was re-established in 1982 and continued to exist until finally closing again in 2000.

The original Elms Farmhouse, situated close to the side of the main road, had long since disappeared, but post-war the Edgar family farming activities continued to be run from the Warwick Road site. However, in 1980/1981 Ted and Liz Edgar (international show jumpers) sought and received approval to build a replacement ranch-style home, together with barns and equestrian facilities, off Hill Wootton Road, between the new bridge of the A46 and the 'skew' bridge that carries the railway over the crossroads with the B4115. This development, and in particular the laying out of paddock areas, resulted in the removal of a very basic 'farm' complex in the shadow of the A46, Woottonwood Farm, after the death of Fred West, who had lived in a caravan on the site and supplied fresh eggs to the community for many years.

Woottonwood Farm

The site that Mr and Mrs Edgar vacated off the Warwick Road was developed with detached homes in a period cottage style which completed a cycle in building styles, albeit a modern concept thereof.

As a result of changes in the policies of both government and the police, many of the houses built in Quarry Close, Waller Close and on Woodcote Drive have now been acquired privately, although some local authority tenants and police officers remain.

Whilst the village was developing and changing from the rural community of the pre-war and immediate post-war years, other events were happening and developments occurring.

The infamous winter of 1947 led to the village being snowbound for seven weeks and cut off for three, but the village shop was well stocked and the villagers managed until the roads were reopened. Arthur Fitzherbert Wright wrote to his son, Robert, on 17th March 1947: "We have had another devastating 'cyclone' similar to the 1896 one. I have just been round with Mother and Judy assessing damage. I don't know where to begin. Going East from front door. Fir down across junction of drives taking another with it. Fir near Holmes' house, which always gives anxiety, stood the blast but drove Holmes to the laundry for the night. … When lighting up began, no switch acted, so candles had to be hunted up; … Burning bush blown up by the roots, the big white rhods in the row blown down but not uprooted. … The mistletoe thorn in the kitchen garden was broken off near the ground and pitched off the wall, knocking off 3 heavy coping stones. … A poplar near the rubbish tip was blown across the road, but we soon dealt with that and traffic is running again. … I believe a few other trees were across the road but traffic was held up much longer in 1896 when we turned out needlessly on the Sunday to clear our bit..."

In April 1951, nearly four hundred years after Elizabeth I's progress through the great park of Warwick, King George VI and Queen Elizabeth passed through the parish and local residents lined the street to cheer them on their way.

Whereas in the past the owners of the village estates had usually organised celebrations of national events, with their general demise it was necessary, in order to celebrate the Coronation of Queen Elizabeth II, for a collection to be made between December 1952 and June 1953 to fund the festivities. On the day there were sports, square dancing, teas for children and the elderly and Coronation mugs filled with sweets for the children. A new bus shelter was eventually erected at the foot of the wall of The Rock to commemorate the Coronation, but this has long since disappeared.

Post War Developments

The Prime Minister, Sir Anthony Eden, outside the Committee Rooms at Yew Tree Cottage on Election Day 1955
Birmingham Gazette and Despatch Limited

In April 1955, The Right Honourable Sir Anthony Eden MP, having been the local Member of Parliament and Prime Minister in waiting for some years became Prime Minister upon the retirement of Sir Winston Churchill. He was already in poor health, and presided only until January 1957 when he resigned as a result of his government's handling of the Suez Crisis.

With the growth of the community the number of Parish Councillors representing the residents was increased in 1962 to eight, yet there was still very much a rural slant to the community. At about the same time it is recorded that the Council "…wants a health man to take a look and a sniff at a local piggery at weekly intervals", and there were invasions of flies into the Post Office and other properties "…according to the proximity of the premises to a manure heap which has become a flytopia".

1967 saw the retirement of the last truly 'local bobby' when PC Wager retired after seventeen years' service. Charlie and his wife Molly retired to live in Kenilworth but they continued to support village organisations and activities until the end of their lives. The Police House, 85 Warwick Road, passed into private ownership and has been extensively modernised.

Discussions took place in the early 1970s with a view to the civil Parish of Leek Wootton being combined with the separate parishes of Old Milverton, Blackdown and Guy's Cliffe. This proposal was abandoned when Old Milverton and Blackdown decided to amalgamate but stay separate from Leek Wootton, and the residents of the sole property in the Parish of Guy's Cliffe chose to remain 'independent'. It was not until 1986 that an amalgamation was decided upon and Leek Wootton & Guy's Cliffe Parish Council was formed.

The speed and care with which traffic travelled through Leek Wootton caused grave and consistent concern from the advent of the first motor vehicle, and by the 1960s the volume of traffic through the village was enormous. The main road was classified as the A46, and it is recalled that a pedestrian could stand for a very long time on one side of the road before being able to cross to the opposite pavement. There are numerous Parish Council reports of the necessity to repair or rebuild the bus shelters, giving a further indication of the problems being experienced. In 1967 plans were unveiled for the construction of a dual-carriage road designed to extend the Warwick Bypass past Leek Wootton and Kenilworth, and onwards to the outskirts of Coventry. Initial response to the plans was muted, but once the enormity of the changes that would be wrought on the countryside and in the community were realised, a resident's association was formed and, along with the Parish Council, the members became active in securing the best possible consideration for the users of local roads, those living nearest to the road, and others affected in any way by the development.

Minutes of The Parish Council:

"*Speed of Motors Proposed ... that the Clerk be instructed to request the County Council to restrict the pace of motor traffic through the village of Leek Wootton to ten miles an hour.*" *(this followed the example of Hill Morton)*

Thursday, 9th February 1905

"*It was mentioned that Petitions were in existence to regulate the furious driving of Motor cars through villages.*"

Tuesday, 16th October 1906

"*A cutting from a newspaper re Motor traffic, damages & nuisance was read at the meeting.*"

Monday, 20th July 1908

"*Owing to complaints of furious driving of motors &c through the village the Clerk was requested to write to Captain Brinkley Chief Constable, Warwick.*"

Wednesday, 11th February 1920

The new A46 was opened in 1974, and the main road through the village was declassified. A certain amount of traffic continued to use the road as a direct route between Kenilworth and Warwick, but the opening of the Bypass served to calm and re-unify the village and in the 1970s and 1980s the enlarged but rejuvenated village allowed young families to enjoy the community and its amenities in relative safety.

> *Minutes of The Parish Council:*
>
> "*Pedestrian Crossing … if no crossing was possible would they get in touch with the Police with a view to reducing the speed limit to 20 m.p.h. at least. At the moment there is complete disregard of any speed limit by most motorists.*"
>
> Tuesday, 29th May 1956
>
> *(Newspaper Cutting) "Indignation of residents reached a new height when at the beginning of this year the school headmistress was badly smashed up, while on the pavement, by a van which bounced its way from side to side through the village. The headmistress is still very much a casualty."*
>
> *(Newspaper Cutting) "A slight bend near the Anchor Inn is said to be the cause of most of the trouble, as vehicles heading for Kenilworth mount the kerb and others going in the opposite direction frequently cross the white line in the middle of the road."*
>
> Thursday, 25th May 1961

Queen Elizabeth's Silver Jubilee in 1977 was celebrated with a Jubilee Fête and children's sports and every child was presented with a specially minted Jubilee crown. The evening barn dance held in a barn at Elms Farm must clearly have been a very good party since The Reverend Charles Nettleship was wheeled home in a wheelbarrow.

Members of families new to the community began to form a significant part of the committee set up to take on responsibility for the Village Hall when it was handed over by the WI in 1979, and they worked very hard to modernise and maintain the Hall, and to lay out a car parking area with landscaping.

A youth club was established at the newly acquired Hall, and the Parish Council purchased an inaugural gift of a tape recorder. The club went on to produce an annual pantomime and to hold discos for young people. The Brownie Pack and Guide Company had been re-established after the War, and both prospered. The Brownie Pack is temporarily suspended for want of leaders, but the Guides are fully active. Regrettably, it was not possible to re-establish a Scout Troop, and many of the boys from the community travelled to Kenilworth or Warwick to join Cubs and Scouts. Well-attended classes for young people were also organised at the church, and for a long time these took place in a portable cabin-style building erected in the churchyard.

Natalie Cripps, a young mother from one of the new families on The Hamlet, opened Wootton Dancing at the Village Hall, which provided young girls with the opportunity to learn ballet, tap and modern dance. Her pupils took exams, competed very successfully in the Kenilworth Carnival on a number of occasions, and performed at many village events, including the church fêtes. In 1984 the girls took part in a one-off 'Leek Wootton Palace Of Varieties' alongside many adults from the community. It was a hugely successful occasion, played to a 'costumed' audience, and was perhaps reminiscent of some of the entertainment that had taken place in the parish during earlier times.

Despite there being times when there was an apparent reluctance on the part of new people to take office, The Leek Wootton & District Horticultural Society is, after some 132 years, still very much in existence. No longer are the entrants the gardeners from the big houses and the majority do not have an allotment, but the classes reflect today's amateur skills with blooms, fruit and vegetables grown mostly on domestic garden plots. There are also classes for flower arranging, cookery and for children, and many new names have appeared on the cups and prize lists over recent years.

An additional annual event within the village in recent years has been the Police Gala Day at Woodcote, with displays of police dog agility and skydivers, as well as many side-shows. The Police have been active members of the community, including allowing the Leek Wootton Guide Company to camp in the grounds at Woodcote, and providing a venue for some social events.

Members of Wootton Dancing in the 1982 Kenilworth Carnival entry 'The Queen of Hearts'
Kenilworth Weekly News

On 29th July 1981, after everyone had watched the wedding of Prince Charles and Lady Diana Spencer on television, another committee of gallant volunteers organised a wonderful afternoon of sports and activities for the children, with tea served in the Village Hall. Whole families gathered in the evening to attend a party held in a marquee erected on one of Ted Edgar's fields, with electricity supplied courtesy of the Pain family at Chauncey on Hill Wootton Road (No 28).

Having entered the competition for a number of years, in 1985 residents 'pulled out all the stops' and were finally successful in the Best Kept Village Competition. A plaque can still be seen at the foot of a tree that was the competition prize, close by the entrance to the footpath from Warwick Road to Tidmarsh Road, which reads:

"EDYVEAN-WALKER" TREE
AWARDED TO
LEEK WOOTTON
BEST KEPT
LARGE VILLAGE
IN THE WARWICKSHIRE
RURAL COMMUNITY COUNCIL'S
1985
COMPETITION

Leek Wootton & District Horticultural Society Show, late 1950s
l-r   Oliver Holmes   Will Golby   Les Jones   Bill Harris   Show Judge

The Leek Wootton Cancer Research Committee was formed in the late 1960s, and whilst they are one of many charities to fund raise within the community, it has been that hard working and evolving team of people that has, through its fundraising activities, contributed significantly to the life of residents. The annual summer 'garden evening', coffee mornings, talks and other social events are all part of the fabric of the parish.

The 8th of May 1995 was declared a national public holiday to mark the 50th Anniversary of VE Day. The Sports Club entertained to lunch those from the community who had given service during the War, and in the afternoon there were sports, activities and stalls for all on the recreation ground. The Reverend Guy Cornwall-Jones led a short act of remembrance, and an original Tiger Moth aeroplane belonging to and piloted by Kathy Silk overflew the celebrations. In the evening a pig roast, again organised by The Sports Club, preceded a much-enjoyed barn dance held in a large marquee on the ground.

Throughout the years the annual church fête has been held come rain or shine. As previously recorded it was for some years held at Wootton Court, and post-war it has been held there in the arboretum, in the garden of The Stone House (courtesy of Audrey and Barry Gillitt), in the garden of Leek Wootton House (courtesy of Ann and Ian McAllester), on the recreation ground and in the Village Hall when it became impossible to proceed out of doors. Stalls, activities and teas are organised by members of the church and village organisations, and they have always been very enjoyable and successful occasions.

The parish is, therefore, a thriving living community today, albeit different from the past. This is illustrated by the many active groups and societies that continue to run today: the school's Parent Teacher & Friends Association, Children's Playgroup, After School Club (Rascals), Pre-School, Mother & Toddler Group, Babysitting Circle, 1st Leek Wootton (All Saints) Guides and a fledgling youth club for younger members of the community; church choir, bell ringers, handbell ringers and Mothers' Union related to All Saints; Leek Wootton Sports Club (with its wide variety of activities and bar), a sewing group and the Young At Heart Club for those with other interests and for senior members.

As referred to in earlier chapters, businesses in the community continue to thrive with The Chesford Grange Hotel continuing to expand as we write, and the Saxon Mill housing a 'Harvester' restaurant and public house. The Anchor Inn is now owned and run as part of a small local chain of public houses/restaurants, and The Warwickshire, now part of Clubhaus plc, continues to grow and is reported to be one of the flagship properties within the group. Broad Lane Caravans continues with a vibrant business from its site on Warwick Road, and Adventure Sports at Wedgnock Rifle Range has a reputation for providing the opportunity to engage in all manner of exciting activities. The presence of the Warwickshire Constabulary Headquarters at Woodcote also continues to bring residents and employment opportunities to the community.

Traditional rural life is still alive with a number of farms in the community and some contract farming by outside operators, Ted and Liz Edgar's equestrian centre and farm, and livery stabling at more than one establishment. There are also plans, currently at the exploratory stage, to use some of the existing woodland in the parish to found a conservation scheme that will study ancient woodland and demonstrate traditional woodland management techniques and related crafts together with an associated educational centre. There are also, no doubt, many businesses operating from behind the front doors of homes in the community, in the modern fashion of home working.

Development continues at the village school to cope with further demand for places requiring expansion of capacity. Residential development continues but at a low level by infilling within the village envelope which is established in statutory law and has been drawn tightly around the village to maintain the separateness of the community to try and avoid continued development pressure that could lead to the parish merging with the conurbations of Kenilworth, Warwick or Leamington.

To mark the advent of the Third Millennium three projects were undertaken in the parish: the creation of the impressive Millennium Room and facilities within the tower of the church (see Chapter 2), the building of the magnificent Village Hall on the War Memorial Recreation Ground (see Chapter 20), and the writing of this book. The writers hope that all three will endure.

Mrs Christina Jackson wrote a poem to mark the Millennium and it was read at the Inaugural Dinner held on the evening of the opening of the Village Hall. Mrs Jackson has been a significant source of anecdotal content for this book, and to publish her words seems a fitting way to conclude.

Peter Butler, Lesley and Paul Eldridge

MILLENNIUM

Millennium, Millennium
Is all we hear folks say
Is it so important
Or simply another day?

What of that Millennium bug
Is it large or small
Has anybody seen it
Is it really there at all?

Think of the first century
Did they celebrate like us
Did they build a golden dome
Costing millions - what a fuss.

Think back a thousand years
What wonders have been achieved
Such wonderful inventions
Around our lives have weaved.

Whoever would have believed
A man would walk on the moon
Rockets would explore the skies
Travel would be by balloon.

What next will a new year bring
Day trips to the Moon or Mars
Perhaps to Jupiter as well
And a galaxy of stars?

Computers control our lives
Violence and drugs are rife
Nations bomb and kill each other
Destroying the gift of life.

Despite world problems today
It's such a beautiful place
And there for all to enjoy
Any colour, creed or race.

So let's walk to the unknown
With trust and hope and no fear
Greet the 21st century
With "A very happy new year".

Christina Jackson

*Christina Jackson and Natalie Green at the opening of the
Village Hall, May 1999*
Kenilworth Weekly News

Millennium Residents

The eight hundred and thirteen adults registered as resident in the Parish at the time of compiling this book are:

Allen, Julian
Allen, Julie
Allen, Lesley
Anderson, Ewen
Anderson, Jane
Appleby, John
Appleby, Pamela
Asghar, Paula
Asghar, Zagham
Atkins, Diane
Atkins, Russell
Bailey, Gillian
Bailey, Joanne
Bailey, John
Bailey, Stephen
Baker, Alan
Baker, Carol
Baker, Denis
Ball, Jean
Ballard, Mark
Bancroft, Jeannette
Bancroft, Roy
Barnes, Beverley
Barnes, Nicholas
Barr, Andrew
Barr, James
Barr, Rosemary
Barr, Sarah
Bassett, Margaret
Baxter, Gwendoline
Baxter, John
Baxter, Timothy
Baylis, Julianne
Bayliss, Christopher
Bayliss, Helen
Bayliss, Lesley
Bayliss, Leslie
Bayliss, Robert
Baylis-Stranks, Suzanne
Baylis-Stranks, Wayne
Beards, Dorian
Beards, Fiona
Bell, Hazel
Bell, Simon
Bevan, Sheila
Bevis, Christopher
Bevis, Selina
Biddle, Debra
Biddle, William
Biggerstaff, Maureen
Biggerstaff, Michael
Billington, Margaret
Birch, Alice
Birch, Geoffrey
Birch, Phyllis
Bishop, Adam
Bishop, Sarah
Bjorkman, Emelie
Bjorkman, Eva
Bostock, Andrew
Bostock, Diana
Bostock, Jennifer
Boucher, Ian
Boucher, Margaret
Bound, Kenneth
Bound, Lynda
Bound, Nicholas
Bound, Timothy
Bowles, Howard
Bowyer, Greta
Bowyer, Ian
Bowyer, Russell
Boyden, Daryl
Boyden, Robert
Boyden, Sarah
Boyden, Zoe
Brain, James
Brain, Jill
Bridges, Lee
Bridges, Linda
Brockbank, Michael
Brockbank, Sarah
Brooks, Barbara
Brooks, John
Brooks, Sarah
Brown, Peter
Burbury, Jackie
Burbury, Paul
Burden, Violet
Butler, Esme
Butler, Kenneth
Butler, Peter
Cadman, George
Cadman, James
Cadman, Janet
Calvert, Sheila
Calvert, Shirley
Calvert, William
Campbell, Keith
Campbell, Valerie
Cannings, Alison
Cannings, Christopher
Carter, Paul
Carter, Sarah
Casadei, Augusto
Casadei, Ruth
Castelino, Brian
Castelino, Teresa
Catherall, Christine
Catherall, Peter
Chalkley, Adrian
Chalkley, Dorothy
Chalkley, Richard
Chalmers, John
Chalmers, Julie
Chamberlain, Mavis
Chamberlain, Reginald
Champion, Barbara
Champion, Peter
Chapman, James
Chapman, Sheila
Clark, Michelle
Clark, Thomas

Clarke, Anne
Clarke, Peter
Clayton, Eileen
Clayton, Norman
Clements, David
Clements, Gail
Clifford, Brigitte
Clifford, Martin
Clive-Smith, Martin
Clive-Smith, Rosemary
Clothier, Michael
Clothier, Pamela
Coates, Jill
Coates, Richard
Cockrell, Neil
Coldwell-Horsfall, John
Coldwell-Horsfall, Mary
Coleman, Beverly
Coleman, Michael
Coleman, Nicholas
Coles, Doris
Collins, Norman
Collins, Peter
Collins, Rosalind
Coltman, Judith
Commander, Edward
Commander, Roselyn
Compton, Robert
Connolly, Gordon
Cooke, Catherine
Cooke, Robert
Cooknell, Derek
Cooknell, Rachel
Cotterell, Marjorie
Couchman, Graeme
Couchman, Lorraine
Courtney, Irmgard
Covington, Lilian
Cox, Percy
Crookes, Diane
Crookes, John
Crookes, Lisa
Crosby, Audrey
Crosby, Keith
Cunningham, Louise
Dale, Andrew
Dale, Claire

Darby, Marian
Darby, Martyn
Darling, Julie
Dash, Augusta
Dash, Philip
David, Hilary
David, Peter
Davies, Anthony
Davies, Claire
Davies, Daphne
Davies, Debora
Davies, George
Davies, Gilbert
Davies, Helene
Davies, Maureen
Davies, Michelle
Davies, Richard
Davies, Stephen
Davies, Susan
Davies, Sylvia
Davies, William
Davis, David
Davis, Susan
Dayman, John
Dayman, Linda
Dee, Anne
Dee, Bernard
Deeley, Janet
Dewar, Andrew
Dickinson, David
Dickinson, Lynda
Dickinson, Matthew
Digby, Sandra
Digby, Stephen
Dineley, Emma
Dineley, Malcolm
Dineley, Pauline
Dineley, William
Dixon, Patricia
Donnelly, Andrew
Donnelly, Elena
Dore, Jean
Dore, Nicholas
Draper, Kathryn
Eassom, Dennis
Eassom, Iris
Edgar, Elizabeth

Edgar, Frederick
Edgar, Marie
Edwards, Lesley
Elder, Judith
Elder, Nigel
Eldridge, Lesley
Eldridge, Paul
Elliott, Jennifer
Elliott, Richard
Elliott, Sarah
Ellis, June
Ellwood, Belinda
Ellwood, Donald
Ellwood, Edward
Ellwood, Elizabeth
Ellwood, William
Ensall, Derek
Ensall, Lilah
Farndon, Anthony
Farr, Glyn
Farr, Jean
Farr, Richard
Fellowes, Craig
Fellowes, Jane
Ferguson, William
Fewtrill, Amelia
Fewtrill, Deborah
Fewtrill, Lancelot
Fewtrill, Oliver
Fewtrill, Sigrun
Fisher, Joanne
Fleming, Evelyn
Fleming, Patrick
Fletcher, Andrew
Fletcher, Deborah
Fletcher, Michael
Fletcher, Sylvia
Forrester, Ann
Forrester, Jayne
Forrester, Joseph
Forrester, Joseph D
Fox, Owen
Fox, Susan
Frampton, Anita
Frampton, Michael
Frampton, Steven
Fuller, Bryan

Fuller, Christine
Gates, Ivy
Gath, Anne
Gee, Joanne
German, Michael
Gibson, Guy
Gibson, Susan
Giles, Phyllis
Gillitt, Audrey
Gillitt, Barry
Gittings, Barbara
Gittings, Clive
Goode, Audrey
Goode, Joan
Goulding, Paul
Goulding, Susan
Green, Helen
Green, Julia
Green, Peter
Green, Richard R.
Green, Richard W.
Greenbank, Alistair
Greenbank, Kay
Greenfield, Eileen
Greenfield, Peter
Gregory, Clifford
Gregory, Denise
Gregory, Mark
Gregory, Sarah
Griffin, Derek
Griffin, Wendy
Griffiths, Clive
Griffiths, Sarah
Guest, Brian
Guest, Carl
Guest, Emma
Guest, Rose
Gwilliam, Gloria
Gwilliam, Jeffery
Hall, Alison
Hall, Andrew
Hall, Charlotte
Hall, David
Hall, Dene
Hall, Janet
Hall, Judith
Hall, Linda

Hall, Ronald
Hall, Sally
Hall, Simon
Hall, Thomas
Hall, Timothy
Hamilton, Robert
Handy, Anthony
Handy, Kay
Handy, Timothy
Hanlon, Duncan
Hanlon, Judith
Harlow, Benjamin
Harlow, Jenifer
Harlow, John
Harmer, Mary
Harrhy, Margaret
Harriman, Constance
Harriman, Malcolm
Harrison, Margery
Harrison, Peter
Hatton, Beatrice
Hayes, Barbara
Hayter, Ann
Hayter, Richard
Hegan, Kathleen
Hermolle, Kathleen
Higginson, David
Hill Derek
Hill, Caroline
Hill, Elizabeth
Hill, George
Hill, Gloria
Hill, Kathleen
Hill, Linda
Hill, Mathew
Hill, Michael
Hill, Murray
Hill, Rowland
Hill, Ruth
Hill, Sarah
Hill, Susan
Hines, Barbara
Hines, Christopher
Hogg, Simon
Holt, Brian
Holt, Clare
Holt, Jennifer

Holt, Nicholas
Holt, Peter
Holt, Sally
Holt, Sarah
Hood, Gwyneth
Horgan, Anthony
Horgan, Christine
Horgan, Kaye
Horgan, Timothy
Hotchin, Clare
Hotchin, John
Hough, Audrey
Hough, Ronald
Hudson, Helen
Hughes, Alexander
Hughes, David
Hughes, Elizabeth
Hughes, Ruth
Hynes, Jacqueline
Hynes, Jonathan
Jackson, Christina
Jackson, Janet
Jackson, Peter
James, Reginald
James, Rosemary
Jarvis, Dinah
Jeanes, Timothy
Jeffries, Jill
Jeffries, Michael
Jenkins, Clodagh
Jenkins, John
Johnstone, Jane
Johnstone, Mark
Joiner, Merilyn
Joiner, Roy
Jones, Andrew
Jones, Barbara
Jones, Bernard
Jones, Brian
Jones, Gordon
Jones, Helen E.
Jones, Helen P.
Jones, Jayne
Jones, Jennifer
Jones, Margaret
Jones, Marjorie
Jones, Pamela

Jones, Robert I.
Jones, Robert L.
Jones, Rosemary
Jones, Simon
Jones, Stephanie
Jones, Thelma
Kearsey, Frederick
Kearsey, Georgina
Kearsey, Paul
Kelly, John
Kelly, Veronica
Kempton, Douglas
Kempton, Elizabeth
Kersley, Elsie
Kiernan, Michael
Kimberley, Barry
Kimberley, Jennifer
King, George
King, Karin
King, Margaret
King, Martin
King, Robert
Kirkwood, James
Kirkwood, Lesley
Knott, Keith
Kruze, Joan
Kruze, Roy
Kruze, Susan
Kruze, Zoe
Lambert, Kenneth
Lambert, Susan
Lane, Jacqueline
Lane, Janet
Lane, Philip
Lane, Robert
Lane, Roger
Lane, Sarah
Langhorn, Brenda
Lashley, Gillian
Lashley, Terence
Lawrence, Jill
Lawrence, Robin
Lawton, Glyn
Lawton, Vivienne
Leitch, Lynda
Leitch, William
Lennox, John

Lennox, Patricia
Levisohn, Vera
Lewis, David
Lewis, Jill
Lickfold, Lorraine
Lickfold, Roger
Lloyd, Jacqueline
Lloyd, Katy
Lloyd, Richard
Lloyd, Sophie
Lloyd, Thomas
Lock, Susan
Lockley, Jean
Long, Kathleen
Lowe, Joan
Lowe, Michael
Mackenzie, Ian
Mackenzie, Lynda
MacLaurin, James
Magee, Brenda
Magee, Peter
Maisey, Joy
Maisey, Simon
Markgraf, Joanna
Markgraf, Paul
Marlow, Amanda
Marlow, Keith
Marsh, Audrey
Marsh, Joanne
Marsh, William
Marshall, Carolyn
Marshall, Howard
Marshall, Michael
Marston, Gary
Marston, Pamela
Marston, Philippa
Mash, Betty
Massey, Kathleen
Massey, Roy
May, Alan
May, Alwyn
McAllester, Andrew
McAllester, Ann
McAllester, Ian
McCann, Bernard
McCann, Christina
McGrath, Anna

McGrath, Anthony
McGrath, Mary
McGrath, Simon
Meakins, Jennifer
Melling, Brian
Melling, Sandra
Middleton, Paul
Mitchell, Charles
Mitchell, John
Mitchell, Josephine
Mitchell, Ryan
Mitchell, Vera
Moddy, Adam
Montgomery, Constance
Moody, Pamela
Moody, Peter
Moore, Alan
Moore, Hilary
Moore, Roger
Morris, Adrian
Morris, Joyce
Morris, Martin
Moules, Ada
Murdoch, James
Murdoch, Mary
Murdoch, William
Murray, Diane
Murray, John
Newsome, Alan
Newsome, Mary
Nicholls, Michael
Nicholls, Suzanne
Nicol, Alan
Nicol, Yvette
Olds, Eric
Olds, Nancy
Ord, Jean
Ord, John
Owen-Evans, Elizabeth
Owen-Evans, Peter
Owen-Evans, Susan
Page, Ronald
Pardo, Antonio
Pardo, Clair
Partridge, Margaret
Partridge, Michael
Patel, Janneke

Patel, Piyush
Patterson, Alexander
Patterson, Mary
Peat, Arthur
Peat, Doris
Pennington, Angela
Pennington, Horace
Perkins, Irene
Perkins, John
Perkins, Sandra
Perry, Robert
Perry, Rosemarie
Peters, Cyril
Peters, Meryl
Phillips, Susan
Pollard, Louise
Pollard, Timothy
Pollock, Catherine
Pollock, Thomas
Ponting, Gerald
Ponting, Pamela
Poole, Diana
Poole, Michael
Poole, Sarah
Pounder, Desmond
Pounder, Sheila
Powell, Charles
Powell, Margaret
Prince, Deborah
Prince, John
Pritchard, Gillian
Pritchard, Olwyn
Pritchard, Ronald
Pritchard, Rosemary
Pruthi, Arvinder
Quirke, Dawn
Quirke, Colin
Quirke, Helen
Quirke, Michael
Quirke, Paul
Rand, John
Ray, Betty
Reeve, Patricia
Reeve, Simon
Rennolds, Jamie
Rennolds, Martin
Rennolds, Matthew

Rennolds, Sheila
Renshaw, Martin
Renshaw, Sharon
Reynolds, Anthony
Reynolds, Marie
Reynolds, Raymond
Reynolds, Rita
Rice, Anthony
Rice, Francesca
Rice, Sandra
Richardson, Alan
Richardson, Diana
Rixon, Beverley
Rixon, Caroline
Rixon, Simon
Robbins, Stephen
Robbins, Susan
Roberts, Caroline
Roberts, Euan
Roberts, John
Roberts, Jonathon
Roberts, William
Robins, Mary
Robins, Peter
Rodgers, Kathleen
Rodgers, Stanley
Rogers, David
Rogers, Dorothy
Rogers, Stuart
Rollins, Anthony
Rollins, Myra
Rollins, Peter
Roots, David
Rose, Bryan
Rose, Jayne
Rowberry, Audrey
Rowberry, Philip
Rudge, Betty
Rudge, Reginald
Russell, Jane
Russell, Julian
Ryan, Anne
Ryan, Bridget
Ryan, Michael
Ryan, Michael A
Sandwell, Catherine
Sandwell, Ronald

Savage, Jane
Savage, Peter
Sayers, Avril
Sayers, Jonathon
Sayers, Mark
Scrimshire, David
Scrimshire, Sonia
Semple, Brenda
Semple, John
Semple, Lesley
Shenton, Andrew
Shenton, Emma
Shenton, Geoffrey
Shenton, Hazel
Shields, Francis
Simpson, George
Simpson, Ronald
Singleton, Jean
Singleton, William
Skelton, Anthony
Skelton, Audrey
Skelton, Gordon
Skinner, Debbie
Skinner, Michael
Sledge, Pamela
Smillie, Rebecca
Smith, Adam
Smith, Alison
Smith, Anthony
Smith, Colin
Smith, Dean
Smith, Emiko
Smith, Geoffrey
Smith, Godfrey
Smith, Jill
Smith, Leo
Smith, Linda
Smith, Lorraine
Smith, Nanami
Smith, Saori
Smolin, Ethel
Snelson, Iris
Snelson, Rachel
Snelson, Richard A
Snelson, Richard D
Springett, Joe
Springett, Katherine

Springett, Sarah
Stanforth, Richard
Stanley, Andrew
Stanley, Matthew
Stanley, Philip
Stanley, Shirley
Sternagel, Wolf
Stevens, Daniel
Stevens, Graham
Stevens, Joan
Stevens, Margaret
Stock, Donald
Stock, Malcolm
Stock, Violet
Stockton, Susan
Stuart-Finch, Judith
Stuart-Finch, Timothy
Sturt, Mary
Sturt, Trevor
Suckling, Gillian
Suckling, William
Sullivan, Arthur
Sullivan, Shirley
Sullivan, William
Sutcliffe, Douglas
Sutton, Leslie
Sylvester, Philip
Tandy, Vera
Taylor, Leith
Taylor, Maureen
Taylor, Richard
Taylor, Roger
Terry, Eva
Thomas, Catherine
Thomas, James
Thompson, Erika
Thompson, Frederick
Thursby, John
Tomlinson, Clare
Tomlinson, David
Tomlinson, Glyn
Tomlinson, Helen
Took, Michael
Trundle, Lesley
Trundle, Richard
Tudway, David
Tudway, Kathleen
Tunkle, Peter
Upwood, Mary
Upwood, Robert
Upwood, Susan
Varney, Andrew
Varney, Beverly
Vaughan, Gloria
Vaughan, Roy
Vetter, Dagmar
Wakeman, David
Wakeman, Kay
Walden, Herbert
Walsh, David
Walsh, Patricia
Ward, Jill
Ward, Judith
Ward, Nina
Ward, Peter
Ward, Robert
Warner, Bernard
Warner, Tina
Wartnaby, Patricia
Wartnaby, Peter
Wartnaby, Suzanne
Wassell, Jill
Wassell, Roderick
Watson, Carole
Watson, Ian
Watts, Martin
Watts, Wendy
Weatherall, Peter
Weatherall, Rachel
Weatherall, Ruth
Webb, Annette
Webb, Joanne
Webb, John
West, Brian
West, Verena
Wheeler, Roslyn
Whimpenny, Florence
Whimpenny, Martin
Whittall, Roger
Whittingham, Andrew
Whittingham, Kjurste
Wiglesworth, Gillian
Wiglesworth, Roger
Wilkins, Andrew
Wilkins, Louise
Williams, Anthony
Williams, Christopher
Williams, Clare
Williams, David
Williams, Gillian
Williams, Gordon
Williams, John
Williams, Margaret
Williams, Nigel
Williams, Sarah
Williams, Sheila
Williamson, Ian
Williamson, Jayne
Wilson, Craig
Wilson, Edna
Wilson, Frederick
Wilson, Glenys
Wilson, Roger
Wimperis, Carl
Wimperis, Joan
Wood, Jacqueline
Worrall, Glynis
Worrall, James
Wosket, Kirsty
Wosket, Margaret
Wosket, Simon
Wright, Elizabeth
Wright, Joseph
Wright, Joyce
Yeomanson, Charles
Yeomanson, Mary

*(The above information is taken from the **REGISTER OF ELECTORS – 2000**)*

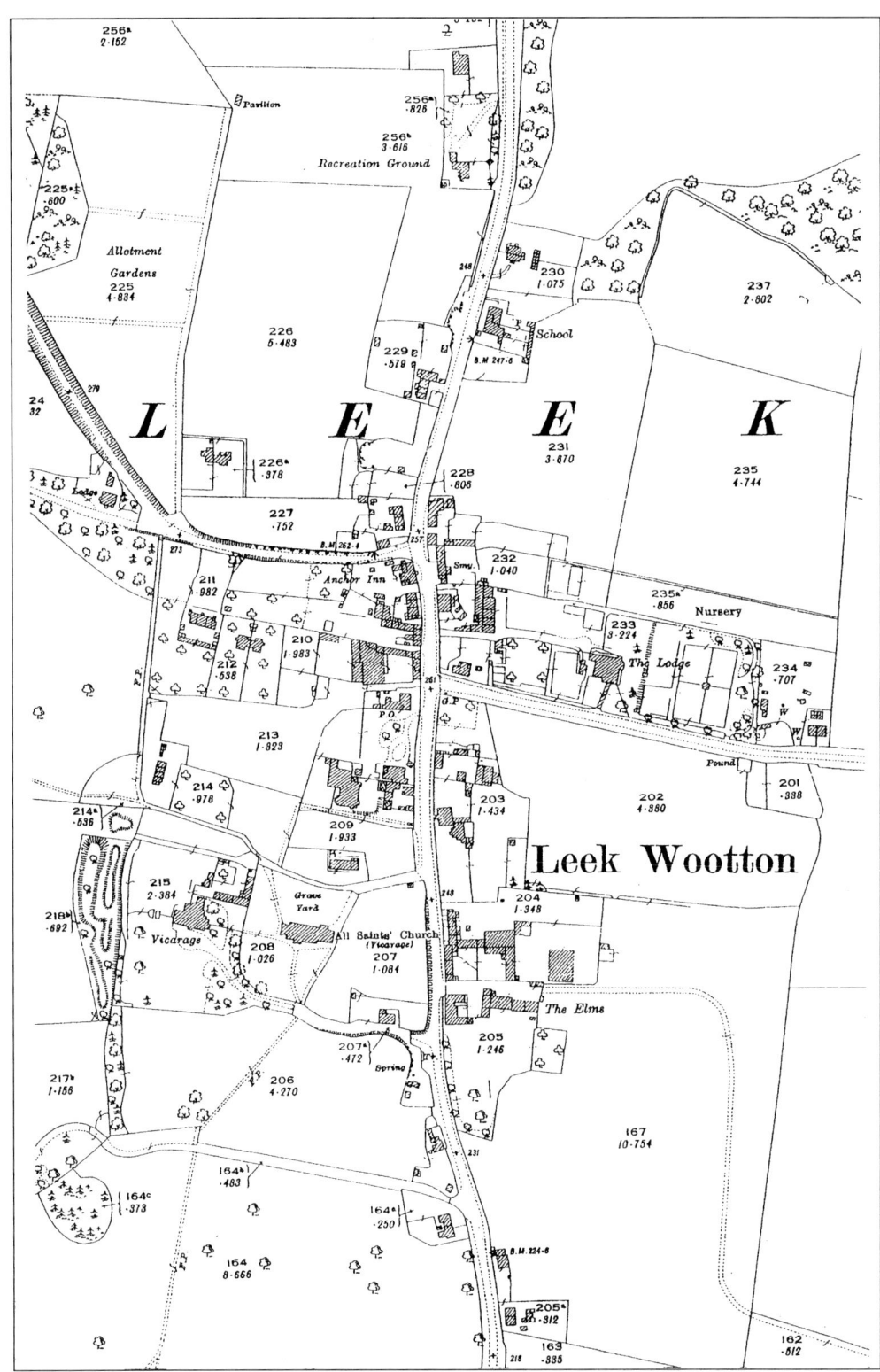

The Village, 1925
Warwickshire County Record Office, OS Sheet 33.6 dated 1925

Village Maps

The Village, 2001

Home Farm, Warwick Road viewed from the top of Hill Wootton Road
Helen Scott Collection

A cottage in Leek Wootton damaged by a storm on Monday, 27th December 1915, in a gale reported to have been the worst since the 'cyclone' of 1896
Helen Scott Collection

Acknowledgements

The Team would like to thank all those kind people, libraries and institutions listed below who have assisted us in our pursuit of the stories that make up this history of our parish by providing documents, maps, letters, newspaper articles, photographs and personal reminiscences:

Mrs Margaret Angless (née Jackson)	Mrs Rita Martin (née Bedding)
Mrs Gil Baylis	Mr Kevin Meredith
Mrs Muriel Bostock	Mr Jonathan Miller-Mead
Mr Colin Brown	Mr and Mrs Piyush Patel
Mr Brian Chester	Mrs Pam Ponting
Mr and Mrs Martin Clive-Smith	Mrs Diana Richardson (née Jones)
Mr P Dennis Cole	Mrs Helen Scott
Mr Norman Collins	Mr Derek Siddle
Mrs Judith Coltman	Mr Oswald Silk
Mrs Liz Edgar	Mr Ronald Simpson
Mrs Audrey Gillitt	Mr Gordon Skelton
Mrs Elizabeth Goodson	Mr Bob Snelson
Mrs Ann Hill	Mr Phil Sylvester
Mr Cyril Hobbins	Mrs Vera Tandy
Colonel and Mrs John Horsfall	Mrs Hazel Truslove (née Graley)
Mr Les Jones	Mr Andrew Varney
Mrs Thelma Jones (née Tolley)	Mr Gordon Williams
Mrs Lesley Kirkwood	Mr Fred Wilson
Mrs Irene Levett-Prinsep	Mr Bill Wright
Ms Sue Lock	Mrs Doreen Wright
Mr and Mrs Paul MacMahon	Mr Robert Wright

Coventry City Record Office
Shakespeare Birthplace Trust Record Office
Warwickshire County Record Office
Warwickshire Museum
Warwick District Council Art Gallery & Museum

Birmingham Central Library
Warwickshire County Libraries

Broad Lane Caravans
Clubhaus plc
Harvester Restaurants

Kenilworth Weekly News & Leamington Spa Courier
The Observer, Warwick
Coventry Evening Telegraph

Pen and ink sketches by Helen Eldridge

Editors: Lesley Eldridge, Paul Eldridge, Jane Pain

The Village Stores and Post Office prior to closure in 2000

The School, 2000

Bibliography

Leek Wootton & Guy's Cliffe
Parish Records
Parish Council Minute Books 1894-2000
Leek Wootton School Logs and Registers
Leek Wootton Women's Institute Scrapbooks
Enclosure Award Leek Wootton 1822
The History of Leek Wootton and its hamlets, The Reverend F L Colvile,
    1843 and later
Almanac of the Reverend Francis G Cholmondeley (1880-1905)
Notes on the History of Leek Wootton, The Reverend S E Longland (1935)
Notes on the History of Leek Wootton, The Reverend Charles Nettleship
    (SuDak, 1977)
Warwickshire Sites and Monuments Records (various)
Wedgnock Park: a dissertation by Ms C A Jones (1981)
Account Rendered (Kenilworth History & Archaeology Society, 1983)
Archaeological Evaluation (for The Warwickshire) (1991)
Leek Wootton Cricket Club Centenary Handbook (1989)
A Short History of St Mary Magdalen Chapel, Guy's Cliffe, Warwick,
    A F Porter (Guy's Cliffe Masonic Rooms, 1993)

Private Papers
The Wise and Waller Family Archives
The Wright Family Archive

Kenilworth
Kenilworth: A Manor of the King, John H Drew (Malcolm Peters, 1971)
Yesterday's Town: Kenilworth, John H Drew (Barracuda Books Limited, 1980)
Kenilworth's Railway Age, Robin D Leach (Odibourne Press, 1985)
A Kenilworth Chronology, Harry Sunley (Odibourne Press, 1989)
Tea At The Castle – Kenilworth in the 1930s, Philip Hames (Odibourne Press, 1992)
Kenilworth's Ancient Tracks, Robert J Steward (Odibourne Press, 1997)

Leamington Spa
Lillington Parish Magazine (1914)
Royal Leamington Spa, Lyndon F Cave (Phillimore & Co Ltd, 1988)

Warwick and Warwickshire
1813 Victuallers Recognizances for Knightlow Hundred
The Antiquities of Warwickshire Illustrated, Sir William Dugdale (1656)
Dugdale's Topography of Warwickshire, Sir William Dugdale and later
    authorities (1817)
Pamphlet and Sermon, The Reverend Vaughan Thomas, Vicar of Stoneleigh (1854)
The Worthies of Warwickshire: who lived between 1500 and 1800,
    Frederick Leigh Colvile (Henry T Cooke & Son, 1869)

Victoria History of the County of Warwick, L F Salzman (ed), R B Pugh (ed)
The Stoneleigh Leger Book (Oxford University Press, 1960)
Land Agents to William Henry Second Baron Leigh of Stoneleigh by Norma Hampson
   (The Journal of the Warwickshire Local History Society, Winter 2000/2001)
Historic and New Inns of Interest: Wining & Dining in Warwickshire
   (Weardale Press Ltd, 1969)
Kelly's Directory, Warwickshire (1956)
Ripples from Warwickshire's Past, Paul Bolitho (Warwickshire Press/Wheaton, 1992)
More Ripples from Warwickshire's Past, Paul Bolitho (The Author, 1997)
Warwick in Times Past, P J E Gates (Countryside Publications, 1986)
Warwick in Old Picture Postcards, Rosemary Booth (European Library, 1983)
Warwickshire Real Ale Guide (CAMRA, 1976)

General
Caravans 1919-1959, Andrew Jenkinson (Veloce Publishing plc, 1998)
Encyclopedia of World War II, John Keegan (Hamlyn Publishing Group, 1977)
Kelly's Directory, Birmingham (1900)
Kelly's Directory, Berkshire (1911)
The Battle of the Atlantic, World War II (Time Life Books, 1977)
The Garden (Magazine of the Royal Horticultural Society, 1902)
The Kings and Queens of Britain (Harper Collins, 1991)
The Concise Encyclopedia of World History, Rodney Castleden (Parragon, 1994)
The World at Arms (Readers Digest, 1989)

Leek Wootton Women's Institute Charabanc Outing, circa 1920